Ira David Sankey, James McGranahan, George C. (George Coles) Stebbins, P. P. (Philip Paul) Bliss

Gospel hymns consolidated

embracing volumes no. 1, 2, 3 and 4, without duplicates, for use in gospel

meetings and other religious services

Ira David Sankey, James McGranahan, George C. (George Coles) Stebbins, P. P. (Philip Paul) Bliss

Gospel hymns consolidated
 embracing volumes no. 1, 2, 3 and 4, without duplicates, for use in gospel meetings and other religious services

ISBN/EAN: 9783744737715

Printed in Europe, USA, Canada, Australia, Japan

Cover: Foto ©Lupo / pixelio.de

More available books at **www.hansebooks.com**

GOSPEL HYMNS

CONSOLIDATED,

EMBRACING VOLUMES

No. 1, 2, 3 and 4,

WITHOUT DUPLICATES,

FOR USE IN

GOSPEL MEETINGS

AND

OTHER RELIGIOUS SERVICES.

PUBLISHED BY

Biglow & Main,	John Church & Co.
76 East Ninth Street, New York,	74 West Fourth Street, Cincinnati
81 Randolph Street, Chicago.	19 East 16th St., New York.

May be ordered of Booksellers and Music Dealers.

PREFACE.

THIS collection embraces in one volume all the hymns and tunes, as used by D. L. MOODY, and others, found in "Gospel Hymns and Sacred Songs," (vol. 1,) "Gospel Hymns No. 2," compiled by P. P. BLISS and IRA D. SANKEY, "Gospel Hymns No. 3," and "Gospel Hymns No. 4," by IRA D. SANKEY, JAMES McGRANAHAN and GEORGE C. STEBBINS.

The hymns from No. 2, No. 3 and No. 4, have been *renumbered* in consecutive order; all duplicates omitted.

We are sure that "Gospel Hymns Consolidated," will prove acceptable and helpful to all who desire a large collection of favorite Gospel Songs.

THE PUBLISHERS

Gospel Hymns Consolidated.

No. 1.   Old Hundred. L. M.

"Come before His presence with singing.—Psa. 100: 2.

Rev. Wm. Kethe, 1561.   G. Franc, 1545.

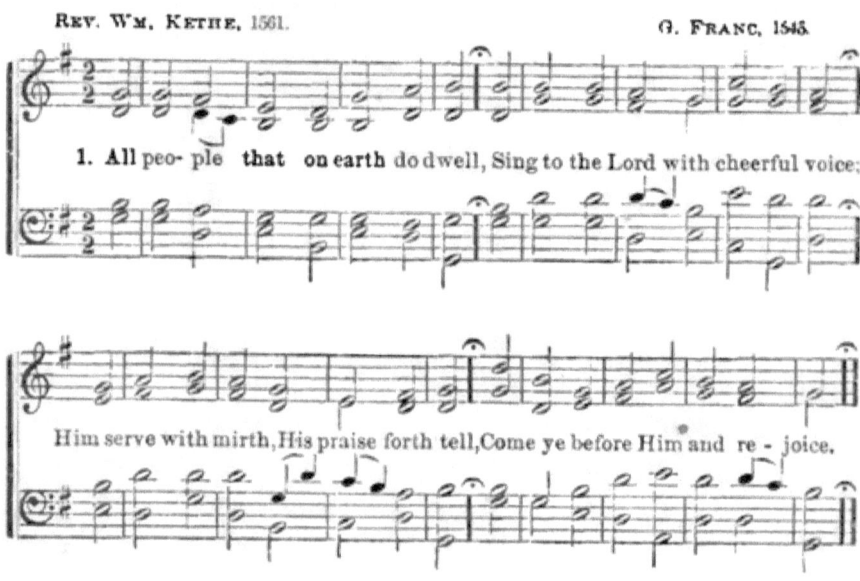

1. All peo-ple that on earth do dwell, Sing to the Lord with cheerful voice; Him serve with mirth, His praise forth tell, Come ye before Him and re-joice.

2
Know that the Lord is God indeed;
  Without our aid He did us make:
We are His flock, He doth us feed,
  And for His sheep He doth us take.

3
O enter then His gates with **praise**,
  Approach with joy His courts unto:
Praise, laud, and bless His name always,
  For it is seemly so to do.

4
For why? the Lord our God is good,
  His mercy is for ever sure;
His truth at all times firmly stood.
  And shall from age to age endure.

DOXOLOGY. L. M.
Praise God, from whom all blessings flow;
Praise Him, all creatures here below;
Praise Him above, ye heavenly host;
Praise Father, Son, and Holy Ghost.
         Bp. Thos. Ken, 1697.

No. 2. Hallelujah, 'tis Done!

"For God so loved the world, that He gave His only begotten Son, that whosoever believeth in Him, should not perish, but have everlasting life."—JOHN 3: 16.

P. P. BLISS.   P. P. BLISS, by per.

1. 'Tis the promise of God, full salvation to give
Unto him who on Jesus, his Son, will believe.
2. Tho' the pathway be lonely, and dangerous too,
Surely Jesus is able to carry me through.

Chorus:
Hallelujah, 'tis done! I believe on the Son;
I am saved by the blood of the crucified One.

3 Many loved ones have I in yon heavenly throng,
They are safe now in glory, and this is their song:
Hallelujah, 'tis done! etc.

4 Little children I see standing close by their King,
And He smiles as their song of salvation they sing:
Hallelujah, 'tis done! etc.

5 There are prophets and kings in that throng I behold,
And they sing as they march through the streets of pure gold:
Hallelujah, 'tis done! etc.

6 There's a part in that chorus for you and for me,
And the theme of our praises forever will be
Hallelujah, 'tis done! etc.

No. 3. I Need Thee Every Hour.

"Without Me ye can do nothing."—JOHN 15: 5.

Mrs. ANNIE S. HAWKS.   Rev. ROBERT LOWRY, by per.

1. I need Thee ev'-ry hour, Most gra-cious Lord; No ten-der voice like

Thine Can peace af-ford.   REFRAIN. I need Thee, oh! I need Thee; Ev'ry hour I

need Thee; O bless me now, my Sav-iour! I come to Thee.

2 I need Thee every hour;
  Stay Thou near by;
Temptations lose their power
  When Thou art nigh.—*Ref.*

3 I need Thee every hour,
  In joy or pain;
Come quickly and abide,
  Or life is vain.—*Ref.*

4 I need Thee every hour;
  Teach me Thy will,
And Thy rich promises
  In me fulfil.—*Ref.*

5 I need Thee every hour,
  Most Holy One;
Oh, make me Thine indeed,
  Thou blessed Son.—*Ref.*

No. 4. Safe in the Arms of Jesus.

"Underneath are the everlasting arms."—DEUT. 33: 27.

FANNY J. CROSBY.   W. H. DOANE, by per.

1. Safe in the arms of Jesus, Safe on His gentle breast,
CHO.—Safe in the arms of Jesus, Safe on His gentle breast,
There by His love o'er-shaded, Sweetly my soul shall rest.
There by His love o'er-shaded, Sweetly my soul shall rest.

Hark! 'tis the voice of angels, Borne in a song to me,
O-ver the fields of glo-ry, O-ver the Jas-per sea......

2 Safe in the arms of Jesus,
  Safe from corroding care,
Safe from the world's temptations,
  Sin cannot harm me there.
Free from the blight of sorrow,
  Free from my doubts and fears:
Only a few more trials,
  Only a few more tears!—Cho.

3 Jesus, my heart's dear refuge,
  Jesus has died for me;
Firm on the Rock of Ages
  Ever my trust shall be.
Here let me wait with patience,
  Wait till the night is o'er;
Wait till I see the morning
  Break on the golden shore.—Cho.

No. 6. **The Ninety and Nine.**

"Rejoice with me, for I have found my sheep that was lost."—LUKE XV.

ELIZABETH C. CLEPHANE, 1868.   IRA. D. SANKEY, by per.

To be sung only as a Solo.

1. There were ninety and nine that safe-ly lay In the shel-ter of the fold, But one was out on the hills away, Far off from the gates of gold— A - way on the mountains wild and bare, Away from the tender Shepherd's care, A-way from the ten-der Shepherd's care.

2. "Lord, Thou hast here Thy nine-ty and nine; Are they not e-nough for Thee?" But the Shepherd made answer: "This of mine Has wan-dered away from me. And although the road be rough and steep I go to the desert to find my sheep, I go to the desert to find my sheep."

3
But none of the ransomed ever knew
  How deep were the waters crossed;
Nor how dark was the night that the Lord
    passed through
  Ere He found His sheep that was lost.
Out in the desert He heard its cry—
Sick and helpless, and ready to die.

4
"Lord, whence are those blood-drops all
    the way
  That mark out the mountain's track?"
"They were shed for one who had gone
    astray

Ere the Shepherd could bring him back."
"Lord whence are Thy hands so rent and
    torn?"
"They are pierced to-night by many a
    thorn."

5
But all thro' the mountains, thunder-riven,
  And up from the rocky steep,
There arose a glad cry to the gate of heaven,
  "Rejoice! I have found my sheep!"
And the angels echoed around the throne
"Rejoice, for the Lord brings back own!"

Jesus of Nazareth.—Concluded.

Jesus! 'tis He who once below
Man's pathway trod, 'mid pain and woe;
And burdened ones, where'er He came,
Brought out their sick, and deaf, and lame,
The blind rejoiced to hear the cry:
"Jesus of Nazareth passeth by."

Again He comes! From place to place
His holy footprints we can trace.
He pauseth at our threshold—nay,
He enters—condescends to stay.
Shall we not gladly raise the cry—
"Jesus of Nazareth passeth by?"

5 Ho! all ye heavy-laden, come!
Here's pardon, comfort, rest, and home.
Ye wanderers from a Father's face,
Return, accept His proffered grace.
Ye tempted ones, there's refuge nigh,
"Jesus of Nazareth passeth by."

6 But if you still this call refuse,
And all His wondrous love abuse,
Soon will He sadly from you turn,
Your bitter prayer for pardon spurn.
"Too late! too late!" will be the cry—
"Jesus of Nazareth *has passed by*."

No. 9. ## Calling Now.

"To-day if ye will hear His voice, harden not your hearts."—HEB. 3: 15.

P. P. BLISS.   P. P. BLISS, by per.

1. This loving Sav-iour Stands pa-tient-ly; Tho' oft re-ject-ed,
2. Oh, boundless mer-cy, Free, free to all! Stay, child of er-ror,
3. Tho' all un-wor-thy, Come, now, come home—Say, while he's waiting,

Calls a-gain for thee. Calling now for thee, prod-i-gal, Calling now for
Heed the ten-der call. Calling, etc.
"Je-sus, dear, I come." Calling, etc.

thee; Thou hast wandered far a-way, But He's calling now for thee.

No. 10.   "Whosoever Will."

"Whosoever will, let him take the water of life freely."—Rev. 22:1.

P. P. Bliss.   P. P. Bliss, by per.
Joyfully.

1. "Who-so-ev-er hear-eth," shout, shout the sound! Send the blessed tidings all the world a-round; Spread the joyful news wher-ev-er man is found:
2. Who-so-ev-er com-eth, need not de-lay, Now the door is o-pen, en-ter while you may; Je-sus is the true, the on-ly Liv-ing Way:
3. "Who-so-ev-er will," the prom-ise se-cure; "Whoso-ev-er will," for ev-er must en-dure; "Who-so-ev-er will," 'tis life for ev-er-more:

CHORUS.

"Who-so-ev-er will, may come." "Who-so-ev-er will, who-so-ev-er will," Send the proc-la-ma-tion o-ver vale and hill; 'Tis a lov-ing Fa-ther calls the wand'rer home: "Who-so-ev-er will, may come."

No. 11. I Am Praying for You.

"Evening, and morning, and at noon, will I pray."—PSA. 55. 17.

S. O'MALEY CLUFF. IRA D. SANKEY, by per.

1. I have a Saviour, He's pleading in glo-ry, A dear, loving Saviour tho' earth-friends be few; And now He is watching in ten-derness o'er me, And oh that my Saviour were your Saviour too!

CHORUS.
For you I am pray-ing, For you I am praying, For you I am pray-ing, I'm pray-ing for you.

2.
I have a Father: to me He has given
  A hope for eternity, blessed and true:
And soon will He call me to meet Him in heaven,
  But oh that He'd let me bring you with me too!

3.
I have a robe: 'tis resplendent in whiteness,
  Awaiting in glory my wondering view;
Oh, when I receive it all shining in brightness,
  Dear friend, could I see you receiving one too!

4.
I have a peace: it is calm as a river—
  A peace that the friends of this world never knew:
My Saviour alone is its Author and Giver,
  And oh, could I know it was given to you!

5.
When Jesus has found you, tell others the story,
  That my loving Saviour is your Saviour too;
Then pray that your Saviour may bring them to glory,
  And prayer will be answered—'twas answered for you!

No. 12. **Where Are the Nine?**

Read LUKE 17. 12-19.

P. P. Bliss. Moderato.   P. P. Bliss, by per.

1. Wand'ring a-far from the dwellings of men, Hear the sad cry of the lep-ers—the ten; "Je-sus, have mer-cy!" brings healing di-vine;
2. Loud-ly the stranger sang praise to the Lord, Knowing the cure had been wrought by His word, Grate-ful-ly own-ing the Heal-er Di-vine;

CHORUS.
One came to wor-ship, but where are the nine? Where are the nine?
Je-sus says ten-der-ly, "Where are the nine?"
Where are the nine? Were there not ten cleansed? Where are the nine?

3 "Who is this Nazarene?" Pharisees say;
"Is He the Christ? tell us plainly, we pray."
Multitudes follow Him seeking a sign,
Show them His mighty works—Where are the nine?—Cho.

4 Jesus on trial to-day we can see,
Thousands deridingly ask, "Who is He?"
How they're rejecting Him, your Lord and mine!
Bring in the witnesses—Where are the nine?—Cho.

No 14. Hold the Fort.

"That which ye have, hold fast till I come."—Rev. 3:2.

P. P. Bliss.   P. P. Bliss, by per.

1. Ho! my comrades, see the signal Waving in the sky!
Reinforcements now appearing, Victory is nigh!

CHORUS.
"Hold the fort, for I am coming," Jesus signals still,
Wave the answer back to Heaven,—"By Thy grace we will."

2 See the mighty host advancing,
   Satan leading on:
Mighty men around us falling,
   Courage almost gone.—*Cho.*

3 See the glorious banner waving,
   Hear the bugle blow;
In our Leader's name we'll triumph
   Over every foe.—*Cho.*

4 Fierce and long the battle rages,
   But our Help is near;
Onward comes our Great Commander,
   Cheer, my comrades, cheer!—*Cho.*

2 That gate ajar stands free for all
  Who seek through it salvation;
  The rich and poor, the great and small,
  Of every tribe and nation.—*Ref.*

3 Press onward then, though foes may frown,
  While mercy's gate is open:
  Accept the cross, and win the crown,
  Love's everlasting token.—*Ref.*

4 Beyond the river's brink we'll lay
  The cross that here is given,
  And bear the crown of life away,
  And love Him more in heaven.—*Ref.*

Once for all.—Concluded.

2 Now are we free—there's no condemnation,
   Jesus provides a perfect salvation;
   "Come unto *Me.*" oh, hear His sweet call,
   Come, and He saves us once for all.—*Cho.*

3 "Children of God," oh, glorious calling,
   Surely His grace will keep us from falling;
   Passing from death to life at His call,
   Blessed salvation once for all.—*Cho.*

No. 17. Knocking, Knocking, Who is There?

"Behold, I stand at the door and knock; if any man hear My voice and open the door, I will come in to him and will sup with him, and he with Me."—REV. 3:20.

Mrs. H. B. STOWE, arr.   GEO. F. ROOT, by per.

With feeling.

1. Knocking, knocking, who is there? Waiting, waiting, oh, how fair!
'Tis a Pilgrim, strange and kingly, Never such was seen before.
Ah! my soul, for such a wonder, Wilt thou not undo the door.

2
Knocking, knocking, still He's there,
Waiting, waiting, wondrous fair;
But the door is hard to open,
For the weeds and ivy-vine,
With their dark and clinging tendrils,
Ever round the hinges twine.

3
Knocking, knocking,—what still there?
Waiting, waiting, grand and fair;
Yes, the pierced hand still knocketh,
And beneath the crowned hair
Beam the patient eyes, so tender,
Of thy Saviour, waiting there.

Home of the soul.—Concluded.

2 Oh, that home of the soul in my visions and dreams,
　Its bright, jasper walls I can see;
　Till I fancy but thinly the vail intervenes
　　‖: Between the fair **city and me**. :‖ Till I fancy, etc.

3 That unchangable home is for you **and** for me,
　Where Jesus of Nazareth stands,
　The King of all kingdoms forever, is He,
　　‖: And He holdeth our crowns in His hands. :‖ **The King of**, etc

4 Oh, how sweet it will be in that beautiful land,
　So free from all sorrow and pain;
　With songs on our lips and with harps in our hands,
　　‖: To meet one another again. :‖ With songs on, etc.

No. 21. What Hast Thou Done for Me?

"So Christ was once offered to bear the sins of many."—HEB. 9: 28.

Miss FRANCES R. HAVERGAL.　　　　　　　　　　P. P. BLISS, by per.

3 I suffered much for thee,
　More than thy tongue can tell,
　Of bitterest agony,
　To rescue thee from hell;
　I've borne, I've borne it all for thee,
　What hast thou borne for Me?

4 And I have brought to thee,
　Down from My home above,
　Salvation full and free,
　My pardon and My love;
　I bring, I bring rich gifts to thee,
　What hast thou brought to Me?

No. 22. We're Going Home To-morrow.

"Willing rather to be absent from the body, and to be present with the Lord."—2 Cor. 5: 8.

Mrs. E. W. Griswold. P. P. Bliss, by per.

1. We're go-ing home, No more to roam, No more to sin and sor-row;
   No more to wear The brow of care, We're go-ing home to mor-row.
2. For wea-ry feet A-waits a street Of wondrous pave and gold-en;
   For hearts that ache, The an-gels wake The sto-ry, sweet and old-en.

CHORUS.
We're go - - - ing home, we're go-ing home to mor-row;
We're go-ing home, we're go-ing home, we're go-ing home to mor-row;
We're go - - - ing home, we're go-ing home to - mor-row.
We're go-ing home, we're go-ing home, we're go-ing home to - mor-row.

3. For those who sleep,
   And those who weep,
     Above the portals narrow,
   The mansions rise
   Beyond the skies—
     We're going home to-morrow.

4. Oh, joyful song!
   Oh, ransomed throng!
     Where sin no more shall sever
   Our King to see,
   And, oh, to be
     With Him at home forever.

No. 23. **Jesus Loves Even Me.**

"God is love."—1 JOHN 4:8.

P. P. BLISS.   P. P. BLISS, by per

1. { I am so glad that our Father in heav'n Tells of His love in the
   { Wonderful things in the Bible I see; This is the dearest, that

Book He has giv'n, Jesus loves me.

CHORUS.

I am so glad that Jesus loves me, Jesus loves me, Jesus loves me, I am so glad that Jesus loves me, Jesus loves even me..........

2 Though I forget Him and wander away,
  Still He doth love me wherever I stray;
  Back to His dear loving arms would I flee,
  When I remember that Jesus loves me.
    I am so glad, etc.

3 Oh, if there's only one song I can sing,
  When in His beauty I see the Great King,
  This shall my song in eternity be
  "Oh, what a wonder that Jesus loves me."
    I am so glad, etc.

1 Jesus loves me, and I know I love Him,
  Love brought Him down my poor soul to
      redeem;
  Yes, it was love made Him die on the tree,
  Oh, I am certain that Jesus loves me.
    I am so glad, etc.

2 If one should ask of me, how could I
      tell?
  Glory to Jesus, I know very well
  God's Holy Spirit with mine doth agree,
  Constantly witnessing—Jesus loves me.
    I am so glad, etc.

3 In this assurance I find sweetest rest,
  Trusting in Jesus, I know I am blest;
  Satan dismayed, from my soul now doth flee,
  When I just tell him that Jesus loves me.   I am so glad, etc

No. 24. Rejoice and be Glad.

"The poor among men shall rejoice in the Holy One of Israel."—Isa. 29: 14

Rev. HORATIUS BONAR. 1874.　　　　　　　　　　　　　　　JOHN J. HUSBAND.

1. Re-joice and be glad! The Redeem-er has come! Go look on His
2. Re-joice and be glad! It is sun-shine at last! The clouds have de-
3. Re-joice and be glad! For the blood hath been shed; Re-demp-tion is
4. Re-joice and be glad! Now the par-don is free! The Just for the
5. Re-joice and be glad! For the Lamb that was slain O'er death is tri-
6. Re-joice and be glad! For our King is on high, He plead-eth for
7. Re-joice and be glad! For He com-eth a-gain; He com-eth in

CHORUS.

cra-dle, His cross, and His tomb. Sound His prais-es, tell the
- part-ed, the shad-ows are past.
fin-ished, the price hath been paid.
un-just has died on the tree.
- umph-ant, and liv-eth a-gain.
us on His throne in the sky. *(Cho. for 7th verse.)*
glo-ry, the Lamb that was slain. Sound His prais-es, tell the

Sto-ry, Of...... Him who was slain; Sound His
Sto-ry, Of...... Him who was slain; Sound His

prais-es tell with glad-ness, He liv-eth a-gain.
prais-es tell with glad-ness, He com-eth a-gain.

No. 25. ## Revive us Again.

(Tune on Page 26.)

"O Lord, revive Thy work."—HAB. 3: 2.

1 We praise Thee O God! for the Son of Thy love,
For Jesus who died, and is now gone above.

CHO.—Hallelujah! Thine the glory, Hallelujah! amen.
Hallelujah! Thine the glory, revive us again.

2 We praise Thee, O God! for Thy Spirit of light,
Who has shown us our Saviour, and scattered our night.—*Cho*

3 All glory and praise to the Lamb that was slain,
Who has borne all our sins, and cleansed every stain.—*Cho.*

4 All glory and praise to the God of all grace,
Who has bought us; and sought us, and guided our ways.—*Cho.*

5 Revive us again; fill each heart with Thy love;
May each soul be rekindled with fire from above.—*Cho.*

Rev. WM. PATON MACKAY, 1866.

No. 26. ## Something for Jesus.

"Lord, what wilt thou have me to do?"—ACTS 9: 6.

Rev. S. D. PHELPS, D.D.   Rev. R. LOWRY, by per.

1. Sav-iour! Thy dy-ing love Thou gav-est me, Nor should I
2. At the blest mer-cy-seat, Plead-ing for me, My fee-ble
3. Give me a faith-ful heart—Like-ness to Thee— That each de-
4. All that I am and have—Thy gifts so free— In joy, in

aught with-hold, Dear Lord, from Thee; In love my soul would bow,
faith looks up, Je-sus, to Thee: Help me the cross to bear,
-part-ing day Henceforth may see Some work of love be-gun,
grief, through life, Dear Lord, for Thee! And when Thy face I see,

My heart ful-fill its vow, Some offering bring Thee now, Something for Thee.
Thy wondrous love declare, Some song to raise, or pray'r, Something for Thee.
Some deed of kindness done, Some wand'rer sought and won, Something for Thee.
My ransomed soul shall be, Through all e-ter-ni-ty, Something for Thee.

No. 27.

Pass Me Not.

"Whosoever shall call upon the name of the Lord shall be saved."—Acts 2: 21.

FANNY J. CROSBY, 1868.   W. H. DOANE, by per.

1. Pass me not, O gentle Saviour, Hear my humble cry;
   While on others Thou art smiling, Do not pass me by.
2. Let me at a throne of mercy Find a sweet relief.
   Kneeling there in deep contrition, Help my unbelief:

CHORUS.

Saviour, Saviour, hear my humble cry,
While on others Thou art calling, Do not pass me by.

3.
Trusting only in Thy merit,
  Would I seek Thy face;
Heal my wounded, broken spirit,
  Save me by Thy grace.—*Cho.*

4.
Thou the Spring of all my comfort
  More than life to me,
Whom have I on earth beside Thee?
  Whom in Heaven but Thee?—*Cho.*

No. 28. One more Day's Work for Jesus.

"I must work the works of HIM that sent Me, while it is day."—JOHN 9: 4.

Miss ANNA WARNER. Rev. ROBERT LOWRY, by per

1. One more day's work for Je-sus; One less of life for me! But heav'n is
2. One more day's work for Je-sus; How glo-rious is my King! 'Tis joy, not
3. One more day's work for Je-sus; How sweet the work has been, To tell the
4. One more day's work for Je-sus—Oh, yes, a weary day; But heav'n shines

near-er, And Christ is dear-er, Than yes-ter-day to me; His love and
du-ty, To speak His beau-ty; My soul mounts on the wing At the mere
sto-ry, To show the glo-ry, When Christ's flock enter in! How it did
clear-er, And rest comes nearer, At each step of the way; And Christ in

CHORUS.

light Fill all my soul to-night. One more day's work for Je-sus, One
tho't How Christ my life has bought.
shine In this poor heart of mine!
all— Be-fore His face I fall.

more day's work for Je-sus, One more day's work for Je-sus,

One less of life for me.

5 Oh, blessed work for Jesus!
   Oh, rest at Jesus' feet!
      There toil seems pleasure.
      My wants are treasure.
   And pain for Him is sweet,
      Lord, if I may,
      I'll serve another day.—*Cho.*

No. 29. What a Friend We have in Jesus.

"There is a Friend that sticketh closer than a brother."—PROV. 18: 24

"JUBILEE HARP." CHARLES C. CONVERSE, 1868, by per.

1. What a friend we have in Jesus, All our sins and griefs to bear
What a priv-i-lege to car-ry Ev'-ry thing to God in prayer.
Oh, what peace we oft-en for-feit, Oh, what needless pain we bear—

All because we do not car-ry Ev'-ry thing to God in prayer.

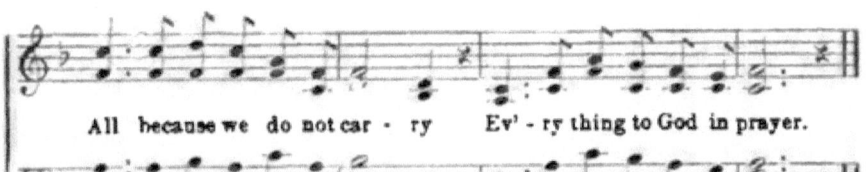

2 Have we trials and temptations?
  Is there trouble anywhere?
We should never be discouraged,
  Take it to the Lord in prayer.
Can we find a Friend so faithful,
  Who will all our sorrows share?
Jesus knows our every weakness,
  Take it to the Lord in prayer.

3 Are we weak and heavy laden,
  Cumbered with a load of care?
Precious Saviour, still our refuge,—
  Take it to the Lord in prayer.
Do thy friends despise, forsake thee?
  Take it to the Lord in prayer;
In His arms He'll take and shield thee,
  Thou wilt find a solace there.

No. 30. Wondrous Love.

"God so loved the world."—JOHN 3: 16.

Mrs. M. Stockton.   Wm. G. Fischer, by per.

1. God loved the world of sinners lost And ruined by the fall; Salvation full, at highest cost, He offers free to all.

CHORUS.

Oh, 'twas love, 'twas wondrous love! The love of God to me; It brought my Saviour from above, To die on Calvary.

2 E'en now by faith I claim Him mine,
   The risen Son of God;
Redemption by His death I find,
   And cleansing through the blood.

3 Love brings the glorious fulness in,
   And to His saints makes known
The blessed rest from inbred sin,
   Through faith in Christ alone.

4 Believing souls, rejoicing go,
   There shall to you be given
A glorious foretaste, here below,
   Of endless life in heaven.

5 Of victory now o'er Satan's power
   Let all the ransomed sing,
And triumph in the dying hour
   Through Christ the Lord our King.

"More to Follow."—Concluded.

Oh, His matchless, boundless love! Still there's more to fol-low.

No. 32. ## Bless Me Now.

"Behold, now is the accepted time; behold, now's the day of salvation."—2 COR. 6: 2.

Rev. ALEXANDER CLARK.   Rev. ROBERT LOWRY, by per.

1. Heaven-ly Fa-ther, bless me now; At the cross of Christ I bow;
Take my guilt and grief a-way; Hear and heal me now, I pray.

REFRAIN.
Bless me now, bless me now, Heaven-ly Fa-ther, bless me now.

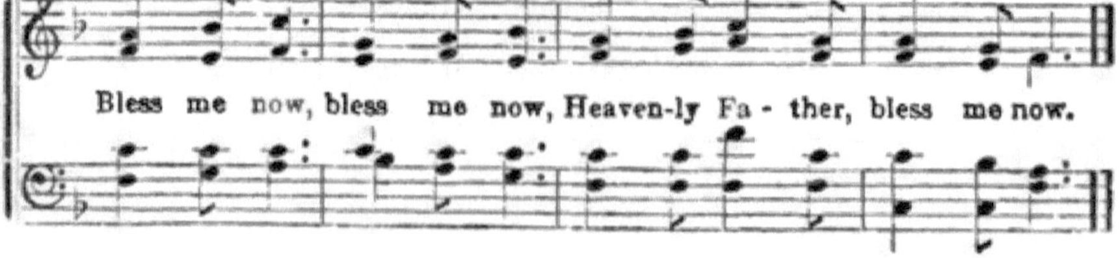

2 Now, O Lord! this very hour,
  Send Thy grace and show Thy power;
  While I rest upon Thy word,
  Come and bless me now, O Lord! *Ref.*

3 Now, just now, for Jesus' sake,
  Lift the clouds, the fetters break;

While I look, and as I cry,
  Touch and cleanse me ere I die. *Ref.*

4 Never did I so adore
  Jesus Christ, thy Son, before;
  Now the time! and this the place!
  Gracious Father, show Thy grace. *Ref.*

Where Hast Thou Gleaned?—Concluded.

All day long in the field a-bide, Gleaning close by the reap-ers' side.

No. 34. Ah, My Heart.

"Come unto Me, all ye that labor and are heavy laden."—MATT. 11: 28.

Tr. JOHN M. NEALE.   P. P. BLISS, by per.

1st SOLO.

1. Ah, my heart is heav-y la-den, Wea-ry and oppressed!

2d SOLO.

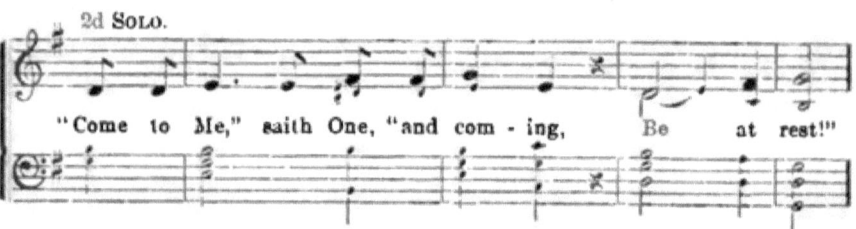

"Come to Me," saith One, "and com-ing, Be at rest!"

CHORUS. *Repeat last two lines of each verse.*   rit.   p

"Come to Me," saith One, "and com-ing, Be at rest!"

2 Hath He marks to lead me to Him,
    If He be my Guide? [prints,
"In His feet and hands are wound-
    And His side."—*Cho.*

3 Is there diadem, as monarch,
    That His brow adorns?
"Yes, a crown in very surety,
    But of thorns!"—*Cho.*

4 If I find Him, if I follow,
    What's my portion here?
"Many a sorrow, many a conflict,
    Many a tear."—*Cho.*

5 If I still hold closely to Him,
    What have I at last?
"Sorrow vanquished, labor ended,
    Jordan past!"—*Cho.*

6 If I ask Him to receive me,
    Will He say me nay?
"Not till earth and not till heaven
    Pass away!"—*Cho.*

No. 35. All to Christ I Owe.

"Who His own self bare our sins."—1 PETER 2. 24.

Mrs. ELVINA M. HALL.   JOHN T. GRAPE, by per.

1. I hear the Saviour say, Thy strength indeed is small;

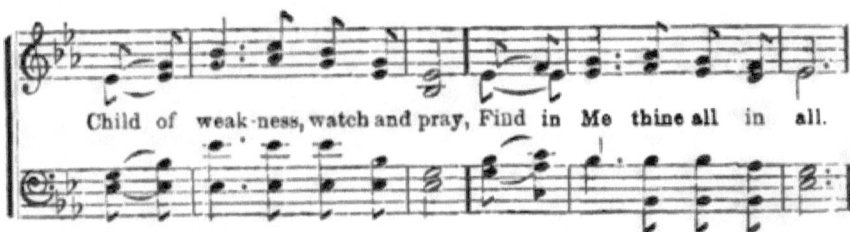

Child of weakness, watch and pray, Find in Me thine all in all.

CHORUS.

Jesus paid it all, All to Him I owe;

Sin had left a crimson stain: He washed it white as snow.

2 Lord, now indeed I find
   Thy power, and Thine alone,
Can change the leper's spots,
   And melt the heart of stone.—*Cho.*

3 For nothing good have I
   Whereby Thy grace to claim—
I'll wash my garment white
   In the blood of Calvary's Lamb.—*Cho.*

4 When from my dying bed
   My ransomed soul shall rise,
Then "Jesus paid it all"
   Shall rend the vaulted skies.

5 And when before the throne
   I stand in Him complete,
I'll lay my trophies down,
   All down at Jesus' feet.—*Cho.*

No. 36. Oh, how He Loves.

"A Friend that sticketh closer than a brother."—PROV. 18: 24.

Adp. by Miss MARIANNE NUNN.   HUBERT P. MAIN, by per.

1. One there is a-bove all oth-ers, Oh, how He loves! His is love be-
yond a broth-er's, Oh, how He loves! Earth-ly friends may
fail or leave us, One day soothe, the next day grieve us;
But this Friend will ne'er de-ceive us, Oh, how He loves!

2. 'Tis e-ter-nal life to know Him, Oh, how He loves! Think, oh, think how
much we owe Him, Oh, how He loves! With His pre-cious
blood He bought us, In the wil-der-ness He sought us,
To His fold He safe-ly brought us, Oh, how He loves!

3
Blessed Jesus! would you know him,
  Oh, how He loves!
Give yourselves entirely to Him,
  Oh, how He loves!
Think no longer of the morrow,
From the past new courage borrow,
Jesus carries all your sorrow,
  Oh, how He loves!

4
All your sins shall be forgiven,
  Oh, how He loves!
Backward shall your foes be driven,
  Oh, how He loves!
Best of blessings He'll provide you,
Nought but good shall e'er betide you,
Safe to glory He will guide you,
  Oh, how He loves!

Tell Me the Old, Old Story.—Concluded.

3 Tell me the story softly,
   With earnest tones, and grave;
Remember! I'm the sinner
   Whom Jesus came to save;
Tell me that story always,
   If you would really be,
In any time of trouble,
   A comforter to me.

4 Tell me the same old story,
   When you have cause to fear
That this world's empty glory
   Is costing me too dear.
Yes, and when that world's glory
   Is dawning on my soul,
Tell me the old, old story:
   "Christ Jesus makes thee whole.

No 38. **The Prodigal Child.**

"I will arise, and go to my father."—LUKE 15: 18.

Mrs. ELLEN H. GATES.   W. H. DOANE, by per.

1. Come home! come home! You are wea-ry at heart, For the way has been dark, And so lone-ly and wild. O prod-i-gal child! Come
2. Come home! come home! For we watch and we wait, And we stand at the gate, While the shad-ows are piled. O prod-i-gal child! Come

CHORUS.

home! oh come home! Come home! Come, oh come home!
home! oh come home! Come home! Come, oh come home, come home!
Come home, come home!

3 Come home! come home!
   From the sorrow and blame,
   From the sin and the shame,
And the tempter that smiled,
   O prodigal child!
Come home, oh come home!

4 Come home! come home!
   There is bread and to spare,
   And a warm welcome there,
Then, to friends reconciled,
   O prodigal child!
Come home, oh come home!

No. 39. I Love to Tell the Story.

"I will speak of Thy wondrous work." — PSAL. 145: 5.

Miss KATE HANKEY, 1867.　　　　　　　　　　　　W. G. FISCHER, by per.

1. I love to tell the Story Of unseen things above, Of Jesus and His Glory, Of Jesus and His Love! I love to tell the Story! Because I know it's true; It satisfies my longings, As nothing else would do.

2. I love to tell the Story! More wonderful it seems, Than all the golden fancies Of all our golden dreams. I love to tell the Story! It did so much for me! And that is just the reason, I tell it now to thee.

CHORUS.

I love to tell the Story! 'Twill be my theme in glory, To tell the Old, Old Story Of Jesus and His love.

I Love to Tell the Story.—Concluded.

3 I love to tell the Story!
 'Tis pleasant to repeat
What seems, each time I tell it,
 More wonderfully sweet.
I love to tell the Story;
 For some have never heard
The message of salvation
 From God's own Holy Word.

4 I love to tell the Story!
 For those who know it best
Seem hungering and thirsting
 To hear it, like the rest.
And when, in scenes of glory,
 I sing the NEW, NEW SONG,
'Twill be—the OLD, OLD STORY
 That I have loved so long.

No. 40. Holy Spirit, Faithful Guide.

"I will guide thee with mine eye."—PSALM 32: 8.

M. M. WELLS, 1858.   M. M. WELLS, by per.

1. Ho-ly Spir-it, faith-ful guide, Ev-er near the Christian's side;
Gent-ly lead us by the hand, Pil-grims in a des-ert land;
Wea-ry souls for e'er re-joice, While they hear that sweet-est voice
D.S. Whisp'ring soft-ly, wander-er, come! Fol-low me, I'll guide thee home.

2 Ever present, truest Friend,
Ever near Thine aid to lend,
Leave us not to doubt and fear,
Groping on in darkness drear,
When the storms are raging sore,
Hearts grow faint, and hopes give o'er,
Whispering softly, wanderer, come !
Follow me, I'll guide thee home.

3 When our days of toil shall cease,
Waiting still for sweet release,
Nothing left but heaven and prayer,
Wond'ring if our names were there;
Wading deep the dismal flood,
Pleading nought but Jesus' blood ;
Whispering softly, wanderer, come !
Follow me, I'll guide thee home !

The Light of the World.—Concluded.

Once I was blind, but now I can see; The Light of the world is Jesus.

No. 42. ## The Holy Spirit.

Three warnings: Resist not, Grieve not, Quench not.

P. P. BLISS. P. P. BLISS, by per.

1. The Spirit, oh, sinner, In mercy doth move, Thy heart, so long hardened, Of sin to reprove; *Resist* not the Spirit, Nor longer delay; God's gracious entreaties, May end with to-day.

2. Oh, child of the kingdom, From sin service cease: Be filled with the Spirit, With comfort and peace. Oh, *grieve* not the Spirit, Thy Teacher is He, That Jesus, thy Saviour, May glorified be.

3. Defiled is the temple, Its beauty laid low, On God's holy altar The embers faint glow. By love yet rekindled, A flame may be fanned; Oh, *quench* not the Spirit, The Lord is at hand.

No. 43. **The Cross of Jesus.**

"His children shall have a place of refuge."—Prov. 14: 26.

Miss E. C. Clephane.   Ira D. Sankey, by per.

1. Beneath the Cross of Jesus I fain would take my stand—The shadow of a mighty Rock, Within a weary land. A home within the wilderness, A rest upon the way, From the burning of the noontide heat, And the burden of the day.

2 O safe and happy shelter,
  O refuge tried and sweet,
O trysting-place where Heaven's love,
  And Heaven's justice meet!
As to the Holy Patriarch
  That wondrous dream was given,
So seems my Saviour's Cross to me,
  A ladder up to heaven.

3 There lies beneath its shadow,
  But on the further side,
The darkness of an awful grave
  That gapes both deep and wide;
And there between us stands the Cross,
  Two arms outstretch to save,
Like a watchman set to guard the way
  From that eternal grave.

4 Upon that Cross of Jesus,
  Mine eye at times can see
The very dying form of One,
  Who suffered there for me;
And from my smitten heart with tears
  Two wonders I confess,—
The wonders of His glorious 〃 〃
  And my own worthlessness

5 I take, O Cross, Thy shadow,
  For my abiding place;
I ask no other sunshine
  Than the sunshine of His face
Content to let the world go by,
  To know no gain nor loss,—
My sinful self, my only shame,—
  My glory all the Cross.

No. 44. **The New Song.**

"And they sung as it were a new song before the throne."—Rev.

Rev A. T. Pierson.   P. P. Bliss, by per.
Allegretto.

1. With harps and with vi-ols, there stands a great throng
In the presence of Jesus, and sing this new song:—

CHORUS.
Unto Him who hath loved us and washed us from sin, Unto Him be the glory forever. A-men.

2 All these once were sinners, defiled in His sight,
Now arrayed in pure garments in praise they unite.—*Cho.*

3 He maketh the rebel a priest and a king,
He hath bought us and taught us this new song to sing.—*Cho.*

4 How helpless and hopeless we sinners had been,
If He never had loved us till cleansed from our sin.—*Cho.*

5 Aloud in His praises our voices shall ring,
So that others believing, this new song shall sing.—*Cho.*

No. 45. **Near the Cross.**

"Peace through the blood of His cross."—Col. 1: 20.

FANNY J. CROSBY. W. H. DOANE, by per.

1. Je-sus, keep me near the cross, There a pre-cious fount-ain
   Free to all— a heal-ing stream, Flows from Calvary's mountain.
2. Near the cross, a trembling soul, Love and mer-cy found me;
   There the bright and morn-ing star Sheds its beams a-round me.

CHORUS.
In the Cross, in the Cross, Be my glo-ry ev-er;
Till my rap-tured soul shall find Rest beyond the riv-er.

3 Near the Cross! O Lamb of God,
Bring its scenes before me;
Help me walk from day to day,
With its shadows o'er me.—*Cho.*

4 Near the Cross I'll watch and wait,
Hoping, trusting ever,
Till I reach the golden strand,
Just beyond the river.—*Cho.*

No. 46. Oh, Sing of His Mighty Love.

"Mighty to save."—ISAIAH 63: 1.

Rev. FRANK BOTTOME, D.D. 1869.   Wm. B. BRADBURY, by per.

1. Oh, bliss of the pu-ri-fied, bliss of the free, I plunge in the crimson tide o-pen'd for me; O'er sin and un-cleanness ex-ult-ing I stand, And point to the print of the nails in His hand. Oh, sing of His mighty love, Sing of His mighty love, sing of His mighty love, Mighty to save.

2. Oh, bliss of the pu-ri-fied, Je-sus is mine, No longer in dread-condem-na-tion I pine; In conscious sal-va-tion I sing of His grace, Who lift-eth up-on me the light of His face.

3 Oh, bliss of the purified! bliss of the pure!
No wound hath the soul that His blood cannot cure;
No sorrow-bowed head but may sweetly find rest,
No tears but may dry them on Jesus' breast.—*Cho.*

4 O Jesus the crucified! Thee will I sing,
My blessed Redeemer, my God and my King;
My soul, filled with rapture, shall shout o'er the grave,
And triumph in death in the "Mighty to save."—*Cho.*

No. 47. ## Not Now, My Child.

"Oh, that I had wings like a dove, for then would I fly away, and be at rest."—PSALM 4:6.

Mrs. CATHERINE PENNEFATHER. 1863.   IRA D. SANKEY, by per.

Slow, and with expression.

1. Not now, my child,— a lit-tle more rough toss-ing, A lit-tle lon-ger on the bil-lows' foam; A few more journeyings in the des-ert darkness, And then, the sun-shine of thy Fa-ther's Home!
2. Not now; for I have wanderers in the dis-tance, And thou must call them in with pa-tient love; Not now, for I have sheep up-on the mountains, And thou must follow them where'er they rove.

3 Not now; for I have loved ones sad and weary;
　　Wilt thou not cheer them with a kindly smile?
Sick ones, who need thee in their lonely sorrow;
　　Wilt thou not tend them yet a little while?

4 Not now; for wounded hearts are sorely bleeding,
　　And thou must teach those widowed hearts to sing:
Not now; for orphans' tears are quickly falling,
　　They must be gathered 'neath some sheltering wing.

5 Go, with the name of Jesus, to the dying,
　　And speak that Name in all its living power;
Why should thy fainting heart grow chill and weary?
　　Canst thou not watch with Me one little hour?

6 One little hour! and then the glorious crowning,
　　The golden harp-strings, and the victor's palm;
One little hour! and then the hallelujah!
　　Eternity's long, deep, thanksgiving psalm!

No. 49. ## The Wondrous Gift.

"By grace are ye saved."—EPH. 2:8.

Dr. PHILIP DODDRIDGE.   IRA D. SANKEY, by per.

1. Grace! 'tis a charming sound, Har-mo-nious to the ear; Heaven with the ech-o shall resound, And all the earth shall hear.

REFRAIN.

Saved by grace a-lone, This is all my plea; Je-sus died for all mankind, And Je-sus died for me.

2 Grace first contrived a way
    To save rebellious man;
And all the steps that grace display,
    Which drew the wondrous plan. *Ref.*

3 Grace taught my roving feet
    To tread the heavenly road;

And new supplies each hour I meet,
    While pressing on to God. *Ref.*

4 Grace all the work shall crown,
    Through everlasting days;
It lays in heaven the topmost stone,
    And well deserves our praise. *Ref.*

No. 50. Precious Promise.

"Whereby are given unto us exceeding great and precious promises."—2 PET. 1:4.

NATHANIEL NILES.   P. P. BLISS, by per.

1. Pre-cious promise God hath giv-en To the wea-ry pass-er by,
2. When tempta-tions al-most win thee, And thy trust-ed watch-ers fly,

On the way from earth to heaven, "I will guide thee with Mine eye."
Let this promise ring with-in thee, "I will guide thee with Mine eye."

REFRAIN.

I will guide thee, I will guide thee, I will guide thee with Mine eye;
On the way from earth to heaven, I will guide thee with Mine eye.

3 When thy secret hopes have perished,
   In the grave of years gone by,
Let this promise still be cherished,
   "I will guide thee with Mine eye."

4 When the shades of life are falling,
   And the hour has come to die,
Hear thy trusty Pilot calling,
   "I will guide thee with Mine eye."

No. 51. He Leadeth Me.

"He leadeth me by the still waters."—PSALM 23:2.

Rev. JOS. H. GILMORE. 1861.   WM. B. BRADBURY, by per.

1. He leadeth me! oh! blessed thought, Oh! words with heav'nly comfort fraught;
2. Sometimes 'mid scenes of deepest gloom, Sometimes where Eden's bowers bloom,

Whate'er I do, where'er I be, Still 'tis God's hand that lead-eth me.
By waters still, o'er troubled sea,—Still 'tis His hand that lead-eth me.

REFRAIN.

He lead-eth me! He lead-eth me! By His own hand He leadeth me;
His faithful follower I would be, For by His hand He lead-eth me.

3. Lord, I would clasp Thy hand in mine,
Nor ever murmur nor repine—
Content, whatever lot I see,
Since 'tis my God that leadeth me.—*Ref.*

4. And when my task on earth is done,
When, by Thy grace, the victory's won,
E'en death's cold wave I will not flee,
Since God through Jordan leadeth me.—*Ref.*

No. 52. When Jesus Comes.

"Unto them that look for Him shall He appear the second time, without sin, unto salvation."—Heb. 9:28.

P. P. Bliss.   P. P. Bliss, by per.

1. Down life's dark vale we wander, Till Jesus comes; We watch and wait and wonder,
2. Oh, let my lamp be burning When Jesus comes; For Him my soul be yearning,

CHORUS.

Till Jesus comes. All joy His loved ones bringing, When Jesus comes:
When Jesus comes.

All praise thro' heaven ringing, When Jesus comes. All beauty bright and vernal,

When Jesus comes; All glory, grand, eternal, When Jesus comes.

3 No more heart-pangs nor sadness,
   When Jesus comes;
 All peace and joy and gladness,
   When Jesus comes.—*Cho.*

4 All doubts and fears will vanish,
   When Jesus comes;
 All gloom His face will banish,
   When Jesus comes.—*Cho.*

5 He'll know the way was dreary,
   When Jesus comes;
 He'll know the feet grew weary,
   When Jesus comes.—*Cho.*

6 He'll know what griefs oppressed me,
   When Jesus comes;
 Oh, how His arms will rest me!
   When Jesus comes.—*Cho.*

No. 53. **White as Snow.**

"Come now, and let us reason together, saith the Lord: though your sins be as scarlet, they shall be as white as snow."—ISA. 1: 18.

Words by L. N. P. P. BLISS, by per.

1. What! "lay my sins on Je - sus?" God's well - be - lov - ed Son!
No! 'tis a truth most pre - cious, That God e'en *that* has done.

CHORUS.
Hal - le - lu - jah, Je - sus saves me, He makes me "white as snow."
Hal - le - lu - jah, Je - sus saves me, He makes me "white as snow."

2.
Yes, 'tis a truth most **precious**,
 To all who do **believe**,
God laid our sins on **Jesus**,
 Who did the load receive.—*Cho.*

3.
What? "bring our guilt to **Jesus?**"
 To **wash** away our **stains**;
The act is passed that freed **us**,
 And nought to do remains.—*Cho.*

No. 54. Just as I Am. L. M.

"Him that cometh to Me, I will in no wise cast out."—JOHN 6: 37.

Miss CHARLOTTE ELLIOTT, 1834.   WM. B. BRADBURY, by per.

1. Just as I am, with-out one plea, But that Thy blood was shed for me,
And that Thou bidd'st me come to Thee, O Lamb of God! I come, I come!

2 Just as I am, and waiting not
To rid my soul of one dark blot, [spot,
To Thee, whose blood can cleanse each
O Lamb of God! I come, I come!

3 Just as I am, though tossed about,
With many a conflict, many a doubt,
Fightings and fears within, without,
O Lamb of God! I come, I come!

4 Just as I am, poor, wretched, blind,
Sight, riches, healing of the mind,
Yea, all I need, in Thee to find,
O Lamb of God! I come, I come!

5 Just as I am; Thou wilt receive,
Wilt welcome, pardon, cleanse, relieve;
Because Thy promise I believe,
O Lamb of God! I come, I come!

No. 55. To-Day. 6s & 4s.

"To-day if ye will hear His voice."—PSA. 95: 7.

Rev. S. F. SMITH.   Dr. L. MASON, 1831.

1. To-day the Saviour calls: Ye wand'rers come; O, ye benight-ed souls,

Why longer roam?

2 To-day the Saviour calls:
Oh, listen now:
Within these sacred walls
To Jesus bow.

3 To-day the Saviour calls:
For refuge fly;

The storms of justice falls,
And death is nigh.

4 The Spirit calls to-day:
Yield to His power;
Oh, grieve Him not away
'Tis mercy's hour.

No. 56. The Great Physician.

"Is there no balm in Gilead; is there no physician there?"—JER. 8: 22.

Rev. WM. HUNTER, 1842.   Arr. by Rev. J. H. STOCKTON.

1. The great Phy-si-cian now is near, The sym-pa-thiz-ing Je-sus: He speaks the drooping heart to cheer, Oh, hear the voice of Je-sus.

CHORUS.
"Sweetest note in ser-aph song, Sweetest name on mor-tal tongue, Sweetest car-ol ev-er sung, Je-sus, bless-ed Je-sus."

2 Your many sins are all forgiven,
  Oh, hear the voice of Jesus;
Go on your way in peace to heaven,
  And wear a crown with Jesus.

3 All glory to the dying Lamb!
  I now believe in Jesus;
I love the blessed Saviour's name,
  I love the name of Jesus.

4 "The children too, both great and small,
  Who love the name of Jesus,
May now accept the gracious call
  To work and live for Jesus."

5 Come, brethren, help me sing His praise,
  Oh, praise the name of Jesus;
Come, sisters, all your voices raise,
  Oh, bless the name of Jesus.

6 His name dispels my guilt and fear,
  No other name but Jesus:
Oh, how my soul delights to hear
  The precious name of Jesus.

7 And when to that bright world above,
  We rise to see our Jesus,
We'll sing around the throne of love
  His name, the name of Jesus.

No. 57. Substitution.

*"He was wounded for our transgressions."—*Isaiah 53: 5.

Mrs. A. R. Cousin.   Ira D. Sankey, by per.

1. O Christ, what burdens bowed Thy head! Our load was laid on Thee; Thou
2. Death and the curse were in our cup— O Christ, 'twas full for Thee; But

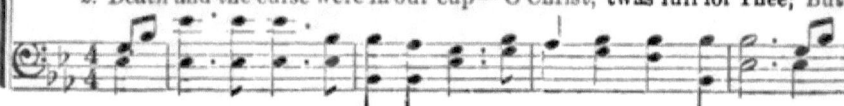

stood-est in the sin-ner's stead, Didst bear all ill for me. A
Thou hast drained the last dark drop—'Tis emp-ty now for me. That

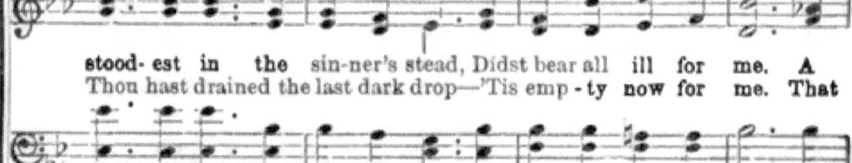

Vic-tim led, Thy blood was shed; Now there's no load for me.
bit-ter cup—love drank it up; Now bless-ings' draught for me.

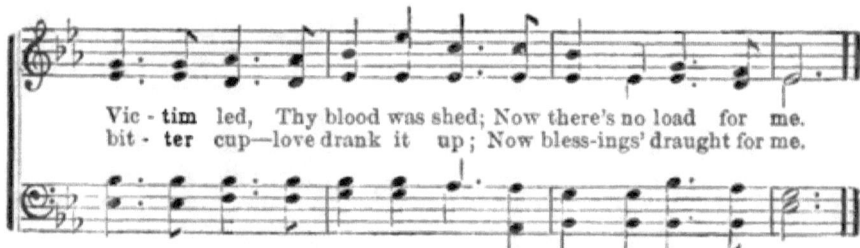

3.
Jehovah lifted up His rod—
  O Christ, it fell on Thee!
Thou wast sore stricken of Thy God;
  There's not one stroke for me.
Thy tears, Thy blood, beneath it flowed;
  Thy bruising healeth me.

4.
The tempest's awful voice was heard—
  O Christ, it broke on Thee!
Thy open bosom was my ward,
  It braved the storm for me.
Thy form was scarred, Thy visage marred;
  Now cloudless peace for me.

5.
Jehovah bade His sword awake—
  O Christ, it woke 'gainst Thee!
Thy blood the flaming blade must slake;
  Thy heart its sheath must be—
All for my sake, my peace to make;
  Now sleeps that sword for me.

6.
For me, Lord Jesus, Thou hast died,
  And I have died in Thee;
Thou'rt risen: my bands are all untied,
  And now Thou liv'st in me.
When purified, made white, and tried,
  Thy GLORY then for me!

No. 58. **In the Presence of the King.**

"In Thy presence is fulness of joy, at Thy right hand there are pleasures for evermore."—PSALM 16: 11.

Miss FLORENCE C. ARMSTRONG, 1864. English.

1. Oh, to be o-ver yon-der! In that land of won-der, Where the an-gel voi-ces min-gle, And the an-gel harpers ring; To be free from pain and sor-row, And the anxious, dread to-mor-row, To rest in light and sunshine In the pres-ence of the King.

2. Oh, to be o-ver yon-der! My yearning heart grows fonder Of look-ing to the east, to see the bless-ed day-star bring Some tid-ings of the wak-ing, The cloud-less, pure day breaking; My heart is yearn-ing—yearn-ing for the com-ing of the King.

3 Oh, to be over yonder!
　Alas! I sigh and wonder
Why clings my poor, weak, sinful heart
　to any earthly thing;
　Each tie of earth must sever,
　And pass away for ever;
But there's no more separation in the
　presence of the King.

4 Oh, when shall I be dwelling
　Where angel voices, swelling
In triumphant hallelujahs, make the
　vaulted heavens ring?
　Where the pearly gates are gleaming,
　And the morning star is beaming?
Oh, when shall I be yonder in the presence of the King?

In the Presence of the King.—Concluded.

5 Oh, when shall I be yonder?
　　The longing groweth stronger
To join in all the praises the redeemed
　ones do sing
　　Within those heavenly places,
　　Where the angels vail their faces,
In awe and adoration in the presence of
　the King.

6 Oh I shall soon be yonder,
　　And lonely as I wander,
Yearning for the welcome summer—longing for the bird's fleet wing,
　　The midnight may be dreary,
　　And the heart be worn and weary,
But there's no more shadow yonder, in
　the presence of the King.

No. 59.　I am Coming to the Cross.

"Him that cometh to Me I will in no wise cast out."—JOHN 6:37.

Rev. WM. MCDONALD.　　　　　　　　　WM. G. FISCHER, by per.

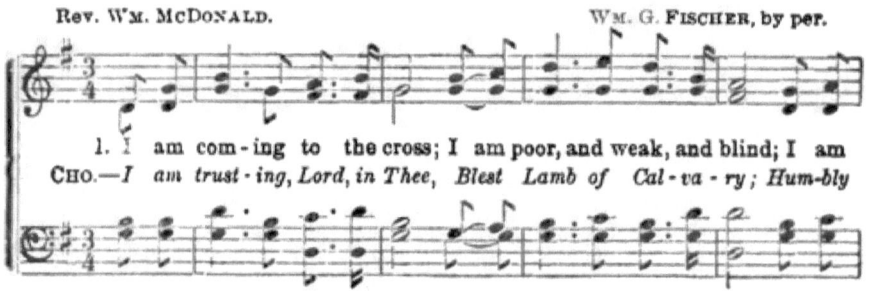

1. I am com-ing to the cross; I am poor, and weak, and blind; I am
CHO.—I am trust-ing, Lord, in Thee, Blest Lamb of Cal-va-ry; Hum-bly

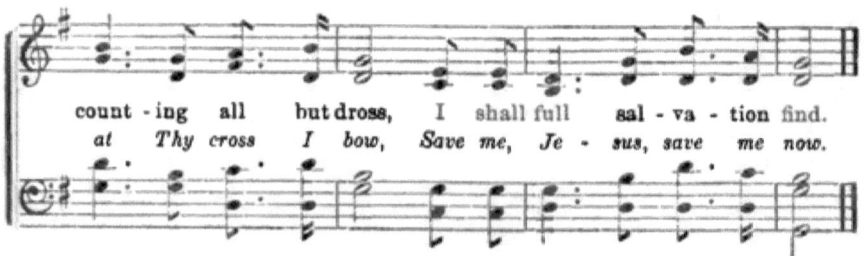

count-ing all but dross, I shall full sal-va-tion find.
at Thy cross I bow, Save me, Je-sus, save me now.

2 Long my heart has sighed for Thee,
　　Long has evil reigned within;
　Jesus sweetly speaks to me,—
　　"I will cleanse you from all sin. *Cho.*

3 Here I give my all to Thee,
　　Friends, and time, and earthly store;
　Soul and body Thine to be,—
　　Wholly Thine for evermore. *Cho.*

4 In thy promises I trust,
　　Now I feel the blood applied;
　I am prostrate in the dust,
　　I with Christ am crucified. *Cho.*

5 Jesus comes! He fills my soul!
　　Perfected in Him I am;
　I am every whit made whole:
　　Glory, glory to the Lamb. *Cho.*

All the Way.—Concluded.

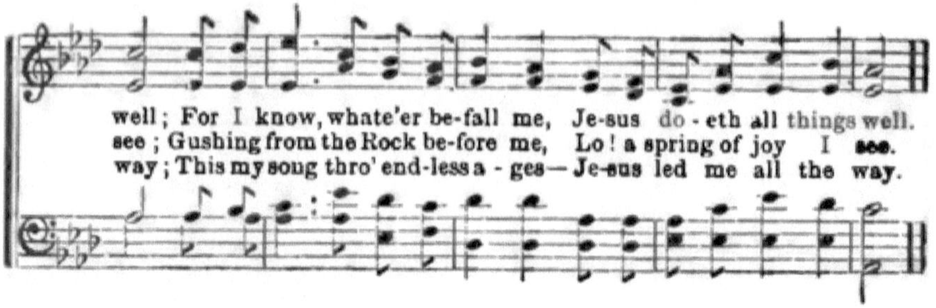

well; For I know, whate'er be-fall me, Je-sus do-eth all things well.
see; Gushing from the Rock be-fore me, Lo! a spring of joy I see.
way; This my song thro' end-less a - ges— Je-sus led me all the way.

No. 61. **Go Bury thy Sorrow.**

"They shall obtain joy and gladness, and sorrow and sighing shall flee away."—ISAIAH 35: 10.

ANON. P. P. BLISS, by per.

1. Go bu-ry thy sor-row, The world hath its share;
2. Go tell it to Je-sus, He know-eth thy grief;

Go bu-ry it deep-ly, Go hide it with care, Go think of it calm-ly,
Go tell it to Je-sus, He'll send thee re-lief, Go gath-er the sunshine

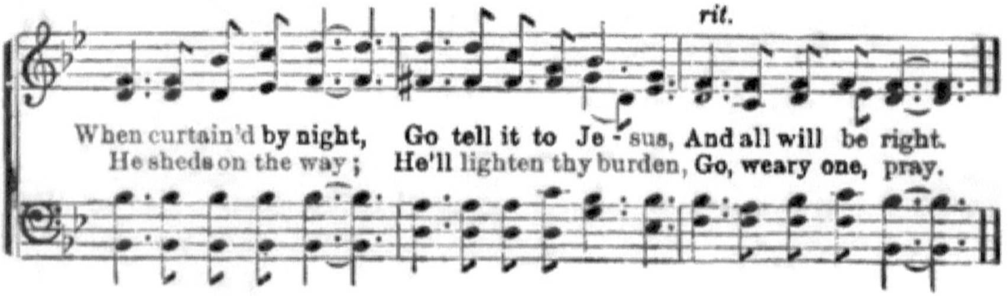

rit.

When curtain'd by night, Go tell it to Je-sus, And all will be right.
He sheds on the way; He'll lighten thy burden, Go, weary one, pray.

3 Hearts growing a-weary
With heavier woe
Now droop 'mid the darkness—
Go comfort them, go!

Go bury thy sorrows,
Let others be blest;
Go give them the sunshine
Tell Jesus the rest.

No. 63. I Hear Thy Welcome Voice.

"Come unto Me, all ye that labor and are heavy-laden, and I will give you rest."—MATT. 11: 28.

Rev. L. HARTSOUGH.   Rev. LEWIS HARTSOUGH, by per.

1. I hear Thy welcome voice That calls me, Lord, to Thee For cleansing in Thy precious blood That flowed on Cal-va-ry.
2. Tho' coming weak and vile, Thou dost my strength assure; Thou dost my vileness fully cleanse, Till spotless all and pure.

CHORUS.
I am coming Lord! Coming now to Thee! Wash me, cleanse me, in the blood That flowed on Cal-va-ry.

3 'Tis Jesus calls me on
   To perfect faith and love,
To perfect hope, and peace, and trust,
   For earth and heaven above.

4 'Tis Jesus who confirms
   The blessed work within,
By adding grace to welcomed grace,
   Where reigned the power of sin.

5 And He the witness gives
   To loyal hearts and free,
That every promise is fulfilled,
   If faith but brings the plea.

6 All hail, atoning blood!
   All hail, redeeming grace!
All hail, the Gift of Christ, our Lord,
   Our Strength and Righteousness!

No. 64. A Sinner Forgiven.

"He said unto her, thy sins are forgiven."—LUKE 7: 48.

JEREMIAH J. CALLAHAN.   Arr. by I. B. WOODBURY.

1. To the hall of the feast came the sin-ful and fair; She heard in the city that Je-sus was there; Un-heed-ing the splendor that blazed on the board, She si-lent-ly knelt at the feet of the Lord, She si-lent-ly knelt at the feet of the Lord.

2. The frown and the murmur went round thro' them all, That one so un-hallowed should tread in that hall; And some said the poor would be ob-jects more meet, As the wealth of her perfume she shower'd on His feet, As the wealth of her per-fume she shower'd on His feet.

3 She heard but the Saviour; she spoke but with sighs,
She dare not look up to the heaven of His eyes;
And the hot tears gush'd forth at each heave of her breast
As her lips to His sandals were throbbingly pressed.

4 In the sky, after tempest, as shineth the bow,—
In the glance of the sunbeam, as melteth the snow
He looked on that lost one "her sins were forgiven,"
And the sinner went forth in the beauty of heaven.

No. 65. Let the Lower Lights be Burning.

"Let your light so shine before men, that they may see your good works, and glorify your Father which is in heaven."—MATT. 5:16.

P. P. BLISS. P. P. BLISS, by per.

1. Bright-ly beams our Father's mer-cy From His light-house ev-er-more, But to us He gives the keeping Of the lights along the shore.

CHORUS.
Let the low-er lights be burning! Send a gleam across the wave! Some poor faint-ing, struggling sea-man; You may res-cue, you may save.

2 Dark the night of sin has settled,
 Loud the angry billows roar;
Eager eyes are watching, longing,
 For the lights along the shore.—*Cho.*

3 Trim your feeble lamp, my brother:
 Some poor sailor tempest-tost,
Trying now to make the harbor,
 In the darkness *may be lost*—*Cho.*

No. 66. Wishing, Hoping, Knowing.

"My beloved is mine, and I am His."—SONGS OF SOLOMON 2: 16.

P. P. BLISS. P. P. BLISS, by per.

1. A long time I wandered in darkness and sin, And wondered if ev-er the light would shine in; I heard Christian friends tell of rap-ture di-vine, And wish'd, how I wish'd, that their Saviour were mine.

2. I heard the glad gospel of "good will to men;" I read "who-so-ev-er" a-gain and a-gain; I said to my soul, "Can that promise be thine?" And then be-gan hop-ing that Je-sus was mine.

CHORUS.

I wish'd He were mine, yes, I wish'd He were mine; I wish'd, how I wish'd, that their Saviour were mine.
I hoped He was mine, yes, I hoped he was mine; I then be-gan hop-ing that Je-sus was mine.

3 Oh, mercy surprising, He saves even me!
"Thy portion forever," He says, "will I be,"
On His word I'm resting—assurance divine—
I'm "hoping" no longer—I know He is mine!

Chorus.—I know He is mine, yes, I know He is mine;
I'm "hoping" no longer—I know He is **mine**!

No. 67. **Varina.** **C. M. D.**

"Thine eyes shall behold the land that is very far off."—ISA. 33: 17.

Rev. I. WATTS. GEO. F. ROOT, by per.

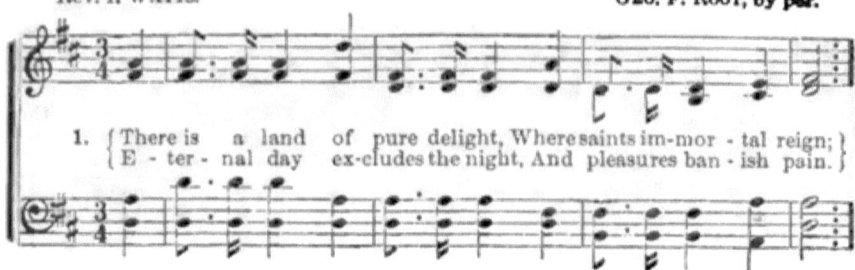

1. { There is a land of pure delight, Where saints im-mor-tal reign; }
   { E-ter-nal day ex-cludes the night, And pleasures ban-ish pain. }

There ev-er-last-ing spring a-bides, And nev-er-with-'ring flowers;

Death, like a nar-row sea, divides This heavenly land from ours.

2 Sweet fields beyond the swelling flood
　Stand dressed in living green ;
So to the Jews old Canaan stood,
　While Jordan rolled between.
Could we but climb where Moses stood,
　And view the landscape o'er, [flood,
Not Jordan's stream, nor death's cold
　Should fright us from the shore.

No. 68. RATHBUN. 8s & 7s.
　　　　　Key C.

1 In the cross of Christ I glory,
　Towering o'er the wrecks of time ;
All the light of sacred story,
　Gathers round its head sublime.

2 When the woes of life o'ertake me,
　Hopes deceive and fears annoy,
Never shall the cross forsake me ;
　Lo! it glows with peace and joy.

3 When the sun of bliss is beaming
　Light and love upon my way,
From the cross the radiance streaming,
　Adds new luster to the day.

4 Bain and blessing, pain and pleasure,
　By the cross are sanctified ;
Peace is there, that knows no measure,
　Joys that through all time abide.

No. 69. Till He Come.

"For yet a little while and He that shall come will come, and will not tarry."—HEB. 10: 37.

Rev. ED. H. BICKERSTETH.   Dr. LOWELL MASON, 1840.

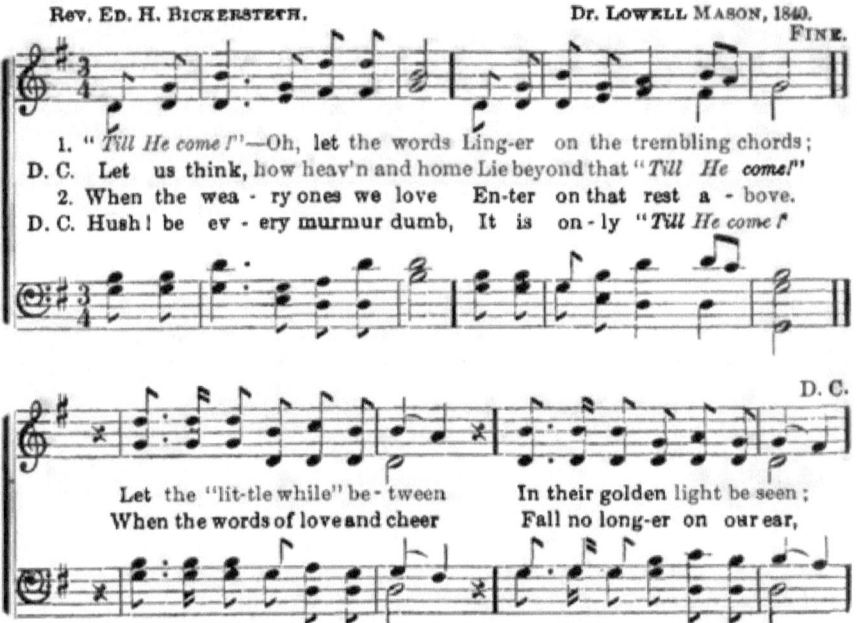

1. "*Till He come!*"—Oh, let the words Linger on the trembling chords;
D.C. Let us think, how heav'n and home Lie beyond that "*Till He come!*"
2. When the weary ones we love Enter on that rest above.
D.C. Hush! be ev-ery murmur dumb, It is only "*Till He come!*"

Let the "lit-tle while" be-tween In their golden light be seen;
When the words of love and cheer Fall no longer on our ear,

3 Clouds and darkness round us press;
Would we have one sorrow less?
All the sharpness of the cross,
All that tells the world is loss.
Death, and darkness, and the tomb,
Pain us only "*Till He come!*"

4 See the feast of love is spread,
Drink the wine and eat the bread;
Sweet memorials, till the Lord
Call us round His heavenly board,
Some from earth, from glory some,
Severed only "*Till He come!*"

No. 70.
DENNIS S. M.
Key F.

1 How solemn are the words,
   And yet to faith how plain,
Which Jesus uttered while on earth—
   "*Ye must be born again!*"

2 "*Ye must be born again!*"
   For so hath God decreed;
No reformation will suffice —
   'Tis *life* poor sinners need.

3 "*Ye must be born again!*"
   And life *in Christ* must have;
In vain the soul may elsewhere go—
   'Tis He *alone* can save.

4 "*Ye must be born again!*"
   Or never enter heaven;
'Tis only blood-washed ones are there,
   The ransomed and forgiven.
ANON.

No. 71.
ORTONVILLE. C. M.
Key B♭.

1 How sweet the name of Jesus sounds
   In a believer's ear;
It soothes His sorrows, heals His wounds
   And drives away His fear.

2 It makes the wounded spirit whole,
   And calms the troubled breast;
'Tis manna to the hungry soul,
   And to the weary, rest.

3 Dear Name, the Rock on which I build
   My shield and hiding-place;
My never-failing treasure, filled
   With boundless stores of grace.

4 Jesus my Shepherd, Saviour, Friend,
   My Prophet, Priest, and King,
My Lord, my Life, my Way, my End,
   Accept the praise I bring.

5 I would Thy boundless love proclaim
   With every fleeting breath;
So shall the music of Thy name
   Refresh my soul in death.
Rev. JOHN NEWTON.

No. 72. The Precious Name.

"And blessed be His glorious name for ever."—PSA. 72:19.

Mrs. LYDIA BAXTER.   W. H. DOANE, by per.

1. Take the name of Jesus with you, Child of sorrow and of woe—
It will joy and comfort give you, Take it then where'er you go.

2. Take the name of Jesus ever, As a shield from every snare;
If temptations 'round you gather, Breathe that holy name in pray'r.

CHORUS.
Precious name, O how sweet! Hope of earth and joy of heav'n,
Precious name, O how sweet— Hope of earth and joy of heav'n.

3 Oh! the precious name of Jesus;
How it thrills our souls with joy,
When His loving arms receive us,
And His songs our tongues employ! *Cho.*

4 At the name of Jesus bowing,
Falling prostrate at His feet,
King of kings in heav'n we'll crown Him,
When our journey is complete. *Cho.*

No. 73. "It Passeth Knowledge."

"The love of Christ, which passeth knowledge."—EPH. 3: 19.

MARY SHEKLETON.   IRA D. SANKEY, by per.

1. It pass-eth knowledge! that dear love of Thine, My Je-sus! Sav-iour! Yet this soul of mine Would of that love, in all its depth and length, Its height, and breadth, and ev-er-last-ing strength, Know more and more.

2.
It passeth *telling!* that dear love of Thine,
My Jesus! Saviour! Yet these lips of mine
Would fain proclaim to sinners, far and
    near,
A love which can remove all guilty fear,
    And love beget.

3.
It passeth *praises!* that dear love of Thine,
My Jesus! Saviour! Yet this heart of mine
Would sing a love so rich, so full, so free,
Which brought an undone sinner, such as
    Right home to God.   [me,

4.
But, ah! I cannot tell, or sing, or know
The fulness of that love whilst here below;
Yet my poor vessel I may freely bring,
O Thou, who art of love the living spring,
    My vessel fill.

5.
I *am* an empty vessel! scarce one thought
Or look of love to Thee I've ever brought,
Yet, I *may* come, and come again to Thee
With this—the contrite sinner's truthful
    "Thou lovest me!"   [plea—

6.
Oh! *fill* me, Jesus! Saviour! with Thy love!
May woes but drive me to the fount above;
Thither may I in childlike faith draw nigh,
And never to another fountain fly,
    But unto Thee!

7.
And when, my Jesus! Thy dear face I see,
When at Thy lofty throne I bend the knee,
Then of Thy love—in all its breadth and
    length,   [strength—
Its height, and depth, and everlasting
    My soul shall sing.

No. 74. Oh, to be Nothing.

"Neither is he that planteth anything, neither he that watereth."—1 Cor. 3: 7.

GEORGIANA M. TAYLOR, 1869.   R. GEO. HALLS. Arr. by P. P. BLISS.

Very slow.

1. Oh, to be nothing, nothing, Only to lie at His feet,
CHO. Oh, to be nothing, nothing, Only to lie at His feet,

A broken and emptied vessel, For the Master's use made meet.
A broken and emptied vessel, For the Master's use made meet.

Emptied that He might fill me As forth to His service I go;

D. C. CHORUS.

Broken, that so unhindered, His life through me might flow.

2 Oh, to be nothing, nothing,
    Only as led by His hand ;
  A messenger at His gateway,
    Only waiting for His command
  Only an instrument ready
    His praises to sound at His will,
  Willing, should He not require me,
    In silence to wait on Him still. *Cho.*

3 Oh, to be nothing, nothing,
    Painful the humbling may be,
  Yet low in the dust I'd lay me
    That the world might my Saviour see
  Rather be nothing, nothing,
    To Him let our voices be raised,
  He is the Fountain of blessing,
    He only is meet to be praised. *Cho.*

No. 75. Almost Persuaded.

"Almost Thou persuadest me to be a Christian."—Acts 26: 28.

P. P. Bliss. P. P. Bliss, by per.

1. "Al - most per - suad - ed" Now to be - lieve;
2. "Al - most per - suad - ed" Come, come to - day;

"Al - most per - suad - ed" Christ to re - ceive;
"Al - most per - suad - ed" Turn not a - way;

Seems now some soul to say, "Go, Spir - it, go Thy way,
Je - sus in - vites you here, An - gels are lingering near,

Some more con - ven - ient day On Thee I'll call."
Prayers rise from hearts so dear: O wanderer, come.

3 "Almost persuaded," harvest is past!
"Almost persuaded," doom comes at last!
"Almost" can not avail;
"Almost" is but to fail!
Sad, sad, that bitter wail—
"Almost—*but lost!*"

No. 76. **Fully Persuaded.**

"Believe on the Lord Jesus Christ and thou shalt be saved."—Acts 16: 31.

Rev. J. B. Atchinson.   Wm. F. Sherwin, by per.

1. Fully persuaded, Lord, I believe!
Fully persuaded, Thy Spirit give;
I will obey Thy call; Low at Thy feet I fall;
Now I surrender all, Christ to receive.

2. Fully persuaded—Lord, hear my cry!
Fully persuaded—Pass me not by;
Just as I am I come, I will no longer roam,
O make my heart Thy home; Save, or I die!

3.
Fully persuaded, no more opprest,
Fully persuaded, now I am blest:
  Jesus is now my Guide,
  I will in Christ abide;
  My soul is satisfied
    In Him to rest!

4.
Fully persuaded, Jesus is mine;
Fully persuaded, Lord, I am Thine!
  O make my love to Thee
  Like Thine own love to me,
  So rich, so full and free,
    Saviour divine!

No. 77. Sweet Hour of Prayer.

"Evening, and morning, and at noon will I pray."—PSALM 4:17.

Rev. W. W. WALFORD, 1846.   WM. B. BRADBURY, 1859.

1. Sweet hour of prayer! sweet hour of prayer! That calls me from a world of care, And bids me at my Father's throne Make all my wants and wishes known: In seasons of distress and grief, My soul has oft-en found relief;
D.C. And oft escaped the tempter's snare, By thy return, sweet hour of prayer, And oft escaped the tempter's snare, By thy return, sweet hour of prayer!

2.
Sweet hour of prayer! sweet hour of prayer!
Thy wings shall my petition bear
To Him whose truth and faithfulness
Engage the waiting soul to bless.
And since He bids me seek His face,
Believe His word, and trust His grace,
‖: I'll cast on Him my every care
And wait for thee, sweet hour of prayer!:‖

3.
Sweet hour of prayer! sweet hour of prayer!
May I thy consolation share,
Till, from Mount Pisgah's lofty height,
I view my home and take my flight;
This robe of flesh I'll drop, and rise
To seize the everlasting prize,
‖:And shout, while passing through the air,
Farewell, farewell, sweet hour of prayer!:‖

No. 78. No Other Name.

"Neither is there salvation in any other."—Acts 4. 12

P. P. Bliss. P. P. Bliss, by per.

1. One of-fer of sal-va-tion, To all the world make known;
The on-ly sure foun-da-tion is Christ the Cor-ner-Stone.

CHORUS.
No oth-er name is giv-en, No oth-er way is known, 'Tis
Je-sus Christ the First and Last, He saves, and He a-lone.

2 One only door of heaven
  Stands open wide to-day,
  One sacrifice is given,
  'Tis Christ, the living way.—Cho.

3 My only song and story
  Is—Jesus died for me;
  My only hope of glory,
  The Cross of Calvary.—Cho.

No. 79. What Shall the Harvest Be?

"Whatsoever a man soweth, that shall he also reap."—GAL. 6. 8.

Mrs. EMILY S. OAKEY, 1850. *Alt.* P. P. BLISS, by per.

1. Sowing the seed by the daylight fair, Sowing the seed by the noon-day glare,
2. Sowing the seed by the wayside high, Sowing the seed on the rocks to die,
3. Sowing the seed of a lingering pain, Sowing the seed of a maddened brain.

Sowing the seed by the fad-ing light, Sowing the seed in the solemn night;
Sowing the seed where the thorns will spoil, Sowing the seed in the fer-tile soil;
Sow-ing the seed of a tarnished name, Sowing the seed of e-ternal shame.

Oh, what shall the harvest be?.... .... Oh, what shall the harvest be?......

What Shall the Harvest Be?—Concluded.

4 Sowing the seed with an aching heart,
  Sowing the seed while the tear-drops start,
  Sowing in hope till the reapers come,
  Gladly to gather the harvest home:
  Oh, what shall the harvest be?
  Oh, what shall the harvest be?

No. 80. There is Life for a Look.

"Look unto Me and be ye saved, all the ends of the earth."—ISAIAH 45 22.

AMELIA M. HULL.   Rev. E. G. TAYLOR, by per.

1. There is life for a look at the Cru-ci-fied One, There is life at this moment for thee; Then look, sinner, look unto Him and be saved, Unto Him who was nailed to the tree.

REFRAIN.
Look! look! look and live! There is life for a look at the Cru-cified One, There is life at this moment for thee.

2. Oh, why was He there as the Bearer of sin,
If on Jesus thy guilt was not laid?
Oh, why from His side flowed the sin-cleansing blood,
If His dying thy debt has not paid?

3. It is not thy tears of repentance and prayers,
But the *Blood*, that atones for the soul;
On Him, then, who shed it, thou may-est at once
Thy weight of iniquities roll.

4. Then doubt not thy welcome, since God has declared
There remaineth no more to be done;
That once in the end of the world He appeared,
And completed the work He begun.

5. Then take with rejoicing from Jesus at once
The life everlasting He gives;
And know with assurance thou never canst die
Since Jesus thy righteousness, lives.

No. 81. Yet There is Room.

"Yet there is room."—LUKE 14:22.

HORATIUS BONAR, D. D., 1873.   IRA D. SANKEY, by per.

Slow, with expression.

1. Yet there is room! The Lamb's bright hall of song,
With its fair glo-ry, beck-ons thee a-long;

REFRAIN. *Very slow.*
Room, room, still room! Oh, en-ter, en-ter now!

2 Day is declining, and the sun is low;
The shadows lengthen, light makes haste to go:
Room, room, still room! oh, enter, enter now!

3 The bridal hall is filling for the feast:
Pass in, pass in, and be the Bridegroom's guest:
Room, room, still room! oh, enter, enter now!

4 It fills, it fills, that hall of jubilee!
Make haste, make haste; 'tis not **too** full for thee:
Room, room, still room! oh, enter, enter now!

5 **Yet there** is room! Still open **stands the gate,**
The gate of love; it is not yet too late:
Room, room, still room! oh, enter, enter now;

6 Pass in, pass in! **That** banquet is for thee;
That cup of everlasting love is free:
Room, room, still room! oh, enter, enter now!

7 All heaven is there, all joy! Go in, go in;
The angels beckon thee the prize to win:
Room, room, still room! oh, enter, enter now;

8 Louder and sweeter sounds the loving call;
Come, lingerer, come; enter that festal hall:
Room, room, still room! oh, enter, enter now!

9 Ere night that gate may close, and seal thy doom;
Then the last, low, long cry:—"No room, no room!"
No room, no room:—oh, woful cry, "No room!"

No. 82. Only an Armour-Bearer.

"Now it came to pass upon a day, that Jonathan the son of Saul said unto the young man that bare his armour, Come, and let us go over to the Philistines' garrison that is on the other side; it may be that the LORD will work for us: for there is no restraint to the LORD to save by many or by few. And his armour-bearer said unto him, Do all that is in thine heart: turn thee; behold, I am with thee according to thine heart. And Jonathan climbed up upon his hands and upon his feet, and his armour-bearer after him: and they fell before Jonathan; and his armour-bearer slew after him. So the LORD saved Israel that day: and the battle passed over unto Beth-aven."—1 SAM. 14:1, 6, 7, 13, 23.

P. P. BLISS.　　　　　　　　　　　　　　　　　P. P. BLISS, by per.

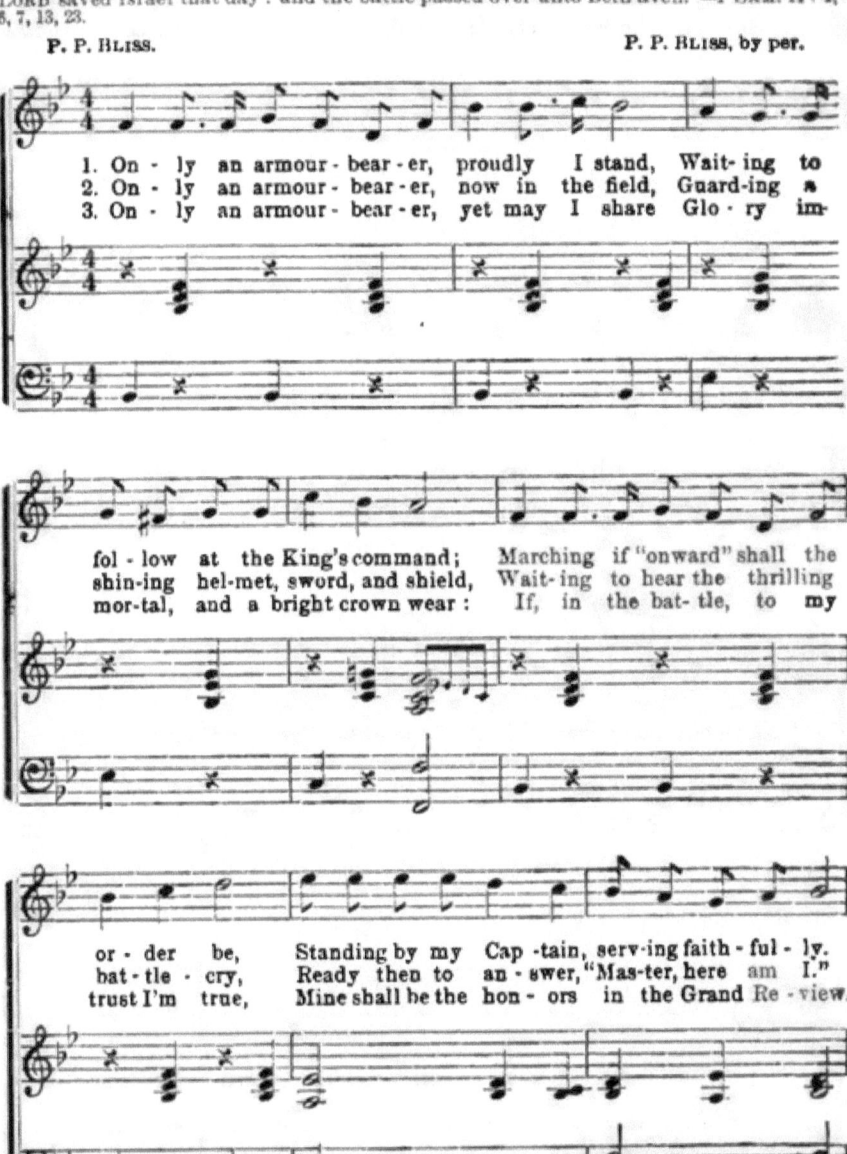

1. On-ly an armour-bear-er, proudly I stand, Wait-ing to fol-low at the King's command; Marching if "onward" shall the or-der be, Standing by my Cap-tain, serv-ing faith-ful-ly.
2. On-ly an armour-bear-er, now in the field, Guard-ing a shin-ing hel-met, sword, and shield, Wait-ing to hear the thrilling bat-tle-cry, Ready then to an-swer, "Mas-ter, here am I."
3. On-ly an armour-bear-er, yet may I share Glo-ry im-mor-tal, and a bright crown wear: If, in the bat-tle, to my trust I'm true, Mine shall be the hon-ors in the Grand Re-view.

Only an Armour-Bearer.—Concluded.

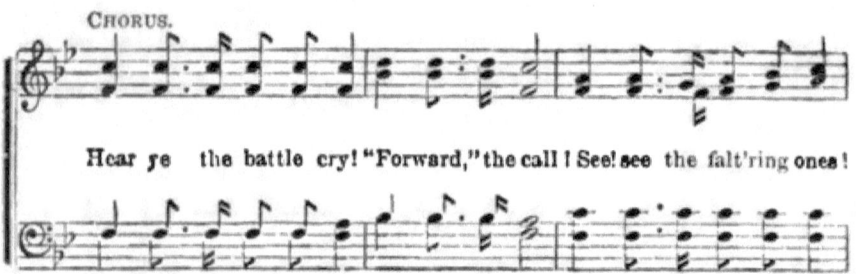

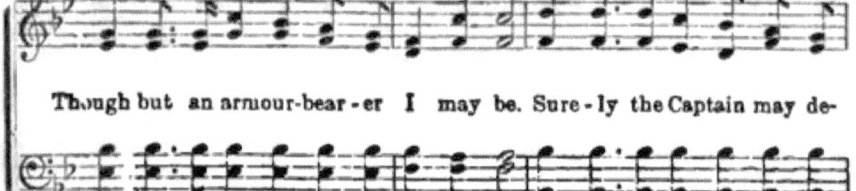

Pull for the Shore.—Concluded.

Pull for the shore, sail-or, pull for the shore!
Heed not the roll-ing waves, but bend to the oar,
Safe in the life-boat, sail-or, cling to self no more!
Leave the poor old stranded wreck, and pull for the shore.

2 Trust in the life-boat, sailor, all else will fail,
Stronger the surges dash and fiercer the gale,
Heed not the stormy winds, though loudly they roar;
Watch the " bright and morning star," and pull for the shore.
    Pull for the shore, &c.

3 Bright gleams the morning, sailor, up lift the eye;
Clouds and darkness disappearing, **glory is nigh!**
Safe in the life-boat, sailor, sing evermore;
" Glory, glory, hallelujah !" pull for the shore.
    Pull for the shore, &c.

No. 84. Sun of My Soul.

"The Lord God is a sun."—PSA. 74: 11.

J. KEBLE, 1827. German. AIR. by W. H. MONK.

1. Sun of my soul, Thou Sav-iour dear, It is not night if Thou be near;
2. When the soft dews of kind-ly sleep My wearied eye-lids gen-tly steep,

Oh, may no earth-born cloud a-rise, To hide Thee from Thy servant's eyes.
Be my last thought, how sweet to rest Forev-er on my Saviour's breast.

3 Abide with me from morn till eve,
For without Thee I cannot live;
Abide with me when night is nigh,
For without Thee I dare not die.

4 If some poor wandering child of Thine
Have spurned to-day the voice divine—
Now, Lord, the gracious work begin;
Let him no more lie down in sin.

5 Watch by the sick; enrich the poor
With blessings from Thy boundless store;
Be every mourner's sleep to-night,
Like infant's slumbers, pure and light.

6 Come near and bless us when we wake,
Ere through the world our way we take,
Till in the ocean of Thy love
We lose ourselves in heaven above.

No. 85. Jesus, Lover of My Soul.

"The Lord will be a refuge in times of trouble."—PSALM 9: 9.

REV. CH. WESLEY, 1740. SIMEON B. MARSH, 1834.

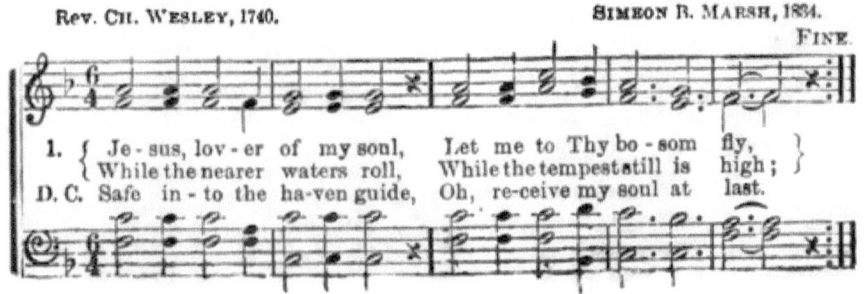

1. { Je-sus, lov-er of my soul, Let me to Thy bo-som fly,
{ While the nearer waters roll, While the tempest still is high;
D. C. Safe in-to the ha-ven guide, Oh, re-ceive my soul at last.

Jesus, Lover of My Soul.—Concluded.

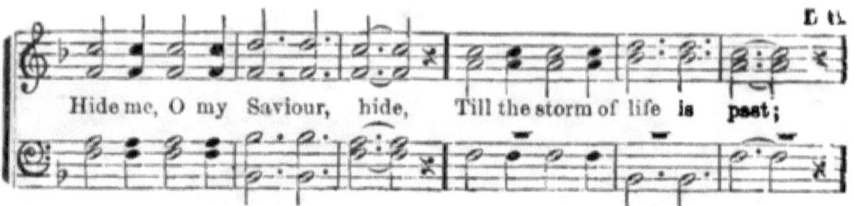

2 Other refuge have I none,
　　Hangs my helpless soul on Thee:
　Leave, oh, leave me not alone,
　　Still support and comfort me.
　All my trust on Thee is stayed
　　All my help from Thee I bring;
　Cover my defenceless head
　　With the shadow of Thy wing.

3 Thou, O Christ, art all I want;
　　More than all in Thee I find:
　Raise the fallen, cheer the faint,
　　Heal the sick, and lead the blind.

Just and holy is Thy Name,
　I am all unrighteousness:
Vile, and full of sin I am,
　Thou art full of truth and grace

4 Plenteous grace with Thee is found
　　Grace to cover all my sin:
　Let the healing streams abound;
　　Make me, keep me, pure within.
　Thou of life the Fountain art,
　　Freely let me take of Thee;
　Spring Thou up within my heart,
　　Rise to all eternity.

No. 86.　　Rock of Ages.

"The Lord is my defence, and my God is the Rock of my refuge."—PSA. M. 22.

Rev. A. M. TOPLADY, 1776.　　　　　　　Dr. THOS. HASTINGS, 1830.

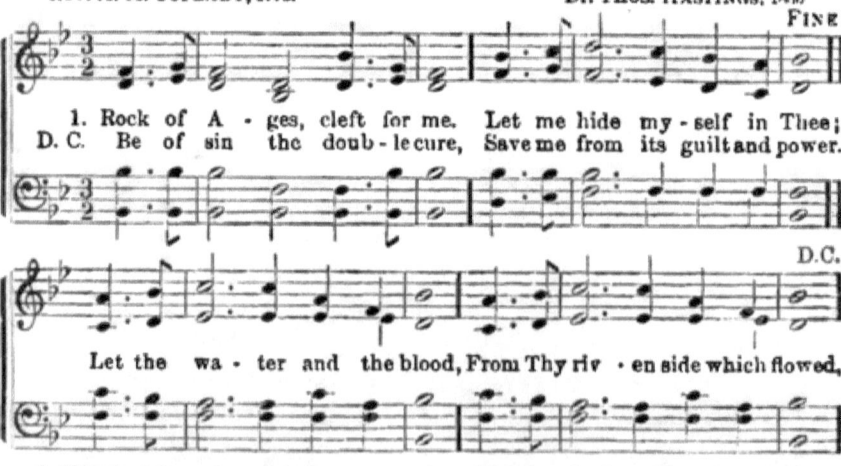

2 Not the labor of my hands
　Can fulfil Thy law's demands;
　Could my zeal no respite know,
　Could my tears forever flow,
　All for sin could not atone;
　Thou must save, and Thou alone.

3 Nothing in my hand I bring,
　Simply to Thy cross I cling;
　Naked, come to Thee for dress,

Helpless, look to Thee for grace;
Foul, I to the fountain fly,
Wash me, Saviour, or I die.

4 While I draw this fleeting breath,
　When mine eyes shall close in death
　When I soar to worlds unknown,
　See Thee on Thy judgment throne,
　Rock of Ages, cleft for me,
　Let me hide myself in Thee.

No. 90. I Left it All with Jesus.

"Casting all your care upon Him; for He careth for you."—1 Peter 5:7

Miss ELLEN H. WILLIS.   English.

1. I left it all with Je-sus Long a-go; All my sins I brought Him,
2. I leave it all with Je-sus, For He knows How to steal the bit-ter

And my woe, When by faith I saw Him On the tree, Heard His small, still whisper,
From life's woes; How to gild the tear-drop With His smile, Make the desert garden

'Tis for thee,' From my heart the bur-den Rolled a-way—Hap-py day!
Bloom a-while: When my weakness lean-eth On His might, All seems light.

From my heart the bur-den Rolled a-way—Hap-py day!
When my weak-ness lean-eth On His might, All seems light.

3 I leave it all with Jesus
   Day by day;
Faith can firmly trust Him
   Come what may.
Hope has dropped her anchor,
   Found her rest
In the calm, sure haven
   Of His breast :
Love esteems it heaven
To abide At His side.

6 Oh, leave it all with Jesus,
   Drooping soul!
Tell not half thy story,
   But the whole.
Worlds on worlds are hanging
   On His hand,
Life and death are waiting
   His command;
Yet His tender bosom
Makes thee room—Oh, come home.

3
E'er since by faith I saw the stream
Thy flowing wounds supply,
Redeeming love has been my theme
And shall be till I die.—*Ref.*

4
Then in a nobler, sweeter song
I'll sing thy power to save,
When this poor, lisping, stammering tongue
Lies silent in the grave.—*Ref.*

No. 93. **My Prayer.**

"Be ye therefore perfect."—MATT. 5: 48.

P. P. Bliss.
P. P. Bliss, by per.

1. More ho-li-ness give me, More striv-ings with-in;
2. More grat-i-tude give me, More trust in the Lord;
3. More pu-ri-ty give me, More strength to o'er-come;

More pa-tience in suff-'ring, More sor-row for sin;
More pride in His glo-ry, More hope in His word;
More free-dom from earth-stains, More long-ings for home;

More faith in my Sav-iour, More sense of His care;
More tears for His sor-rows, More pain at His grief;
More fit for the king-dom, More used would I be;

rit.

More joy in His ser-vice, More pur-pose in prayer.
More meek-ness in tri-al, More praise for re-lief.
More bless-ed and ho-ly, More, Sav-iour, *like Thee.*

No. 94.   Only Trust Him.

"Take My yoke upon you, and learn of Me; and ye shall find rest unto your souls."—MATT. 11 : 29.

Rev. J. H. S.   Rev. J. H. STOCKTON, by per.

1. Come, ev-ery soul by sin oppressed, There's mercy with the Lord,
And He will sure-ly give you rest, By trust-ing in His word.

CHORUS.
On-ly trust Him, on-ly trust Him, On-ly trust Him now;
He will save you, He will save you, He will save you now.

2 For Jesus shed His precious blood
  Rich blessings to bestow;
  Plunge now into the crimson flood
  That washes white as snow.

3 Yes, Jesus is the Truth, the Way
  That leads you into rest;
  Believe in Him without delay,
  And you are fully blest.

4 Come then, and join this holy band,
  And on to glory go,
  To dwell in that celestial land,
  Where joys immortal flow.

No. 96. **Nothing but Leaves.**

"And when He came to it He found nothing but leaves."—MARK 11

Lucy Evelina Akerman. Silas J. Vail, by per

1. Nothing but leaves! The Spirit grieves O'er years of wasted life; O'er sins indulged while conscience slept, O'er vows and promises un-kept, And reap from years of strife— Nothing but leaves! Nothing but leaves!

2 Nothing but leaves! No gathered sheaves,
   Of life's fair ripening grain:
   We sow our seeds; lo! tares and weeds,—
   Words, *idle* words, for earnest deeds—
   Then reap, with toil and pain,
   Nothing but leaves! nothing but leaves!

3 Nothing but leaves! Sad mem'ry weaves
   No veil to hide the past:
   And as we trace our weary way,
   And count each lost and misspent day
   We sadly find at last—
   Nothing but leaves! nothing but leaves!

4 Ah, who shall thus the Master meet,
   And bring but withered leaves?
   Ah, who shall at the Saviour's feet,
   Before the awful judgment-seat
   Lay down for golden sheaves,
   Nothing but leaves! nothing but leaves!

No. 97. Jewels.

"And they shall be Mine, saith the Lord of hosts, in that day when I make up My jewels."—MALACHI 3: 17.

Rev. W. O. CUSHING.   GEO. F. ROOT, by per.
Moderato.

1. When He com-eth, when He com-eth To make up His jew-els, All His jew-els, precious jew-els, His loved and His own.

CHORUS.
Like the stars of the morn-ing, His bright crown a-dorn-ing, They shall shine in their beauty, Bright gems for His crown.

2 He will gather, He will gather
The gems for His kingdom:
All the pure ones, all the bright ones,
His loved and His own.—*Cho.*

3 Little children, little children
Who love their Redeemer,
Are the jewels, precious jewels,
His loved and His own.—*Cho.*

Go Work in My Vineyard.—Concluded.

work,............ go work,...............

work in My vineyard, go work in My vineyard, go work in My vineyard; there's

Go work,...... go work,

plenty to do, Go work, work, work, work, The harvest is great and the lab'rers are few.

3 "Go work in My vineyard;" oh, "work while 'tis day,"
The bright hours of sunshine are hastening away;
And night's gloomy shadows are gathering fast;
Then the time for our labor shall **ever** be past.
Begin **in the morning, and** toil **all the day,**
Thy strength I'll supply **and** thy wages I'll **pay;**
And blessed, thrice blessed **the** diligent **few,**
Who finish the labor I've given them **to do.**

No. 99.   Seymour. 7s.

"A broken and a contrite heart, O God, thou wilt not despise."—Ps. 51; 17.

Rev. CHAS. WESLEY, 1740.   C. M. VON WEBER.

1. Depth of mer - cy! can there be Mer - cy still reserved for me?
2. I have long withstood His grace; Long provoked Him to His face;
3. Now, in - cline me to re - pent; Let me now my sins la - ment;

Can my God His wrath for - bear? Me, **the chief of** sin - ners, spare?
Would not hearken to His calls, Grieved **Him by a** thousand falls.
Now my foul re - volt de - plore, Weep, be - **lieve, and** sin no more.

No. 100. When the Comforter Came.

"He shall give you another Comforter."—John 14:16.

WILLIAM MOORE.   Rev. R. LOWRY, by per.

1. My heart, that was heavy and sad, Was made to re-joice and be glad,
2. To sin and to e-vil in-clined, With darkness per-vad-ing my mind,
3. The voice of thanksgiving I raised, The Lord, my Re-deemer, I praised;

And peace without measure I had,   When the Com-fort-er came.
No rest I could a-ny-where find,   Till the Com-fort-er came.
I was at His mer-cy a-maz'd,   When the Com-fort-er came.

REFRAIN.

Peace, sweet peace, Peace when the Comfort-er came! My heart that was heav-y and sad, Was made to re-joice and be glad, And peace without measure I had, When the Com-fort-er came.

No. 101. Coronation. C. M.

Rev. E. Perronet, 1786. O. Holden, 1793.

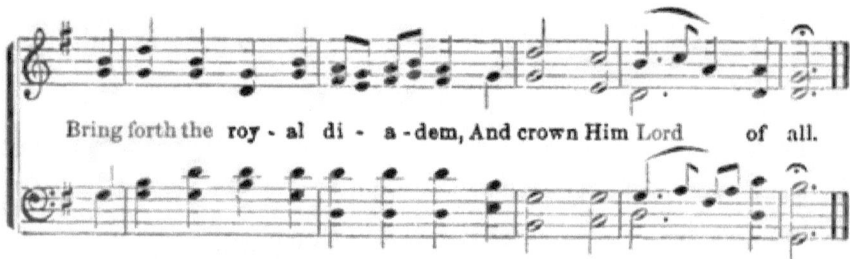

2 Let every kindred, every tribe,
　On this terrestrial ball,
　To Him all majesty ascribe,
　And crown Him Lord of all.

3 Oh, that with yonder sacred throng
　We at His feet may fall;
　We'll join the everlasting song,
　And crown Him Lord of all.

No. 102.

1 O for a thousand tongues to sing
　My great Redeemer's praise;
　The glories of my God and King,
　The triumphs of His grace.

2 My gracious Master, and my God,
　Assist me to proclaim,—
　To spread, through all the earth abroad
　The honors of Thy Name.

3 Jesus!—the Name that charms our fear,
　That bids our sorrows cease;
　'Tis music in the sinner's ears,
　'Tis life, and health, and peace.

4 He breaks the power of cancell'd sin,
　He sets the pris'ner free;
　His blood can make the foulest clean
　His blood avail'd for me.
　　　　　Rev. Chas. Wesley, 1740.

No. 103. ROCKINGHAM. L. M.
WM. COWPER, 1779. Dr. LOWELL MASON, 1832.

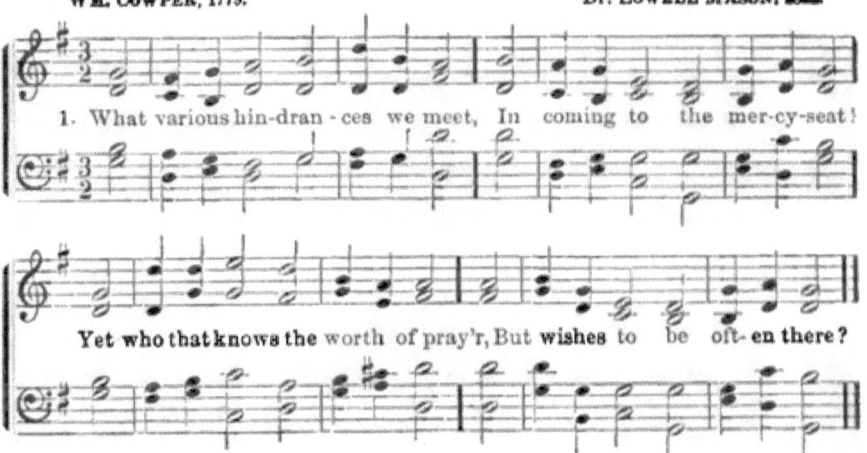

1. What various hin-dran-ces we meet, In coming to the mer-cy-seat!
Yet who that knows the worth of pray'r, But wishes to be oft-en there?

2 Prayer makes the darkened clouds withdraw;
  Prayer climbs the ladder Jacob saw,
  Gives exercise to faith and love,
  Brings every blessing from above.

3 Restraining prayer, we cease to **fight**;
  Prayer makes the Christian's armor bright;
  And Satan trembles when he sees
  The weakest saint upon his knees.

No. 104. L. M.

1 So **let** our lips and lives express
  The holy gospel we profess;
  So let our works and virtues shine;
  To **prove the** doctrine all divine.

2 Thus shall we best proclaim abroad
  The honors of our Saviour God;
  When His salvation reigns within,
  And **grace** subdues the power of sin.

3 Religion bears our spirits up,
  While we expect that blessed hope,—
  The bright appearance of the Lord
  And faith stands leaning on His word.
  Rev. I. WATTS, 1709.

No. 105. RETREAT. L. M. Key C.

1 From every stormy **wind that blows**,
  From every swelling **tide of woes**,
  There is a calm, a sure retreat;
  'Tis found beneath the mercy-seat.

2 There is a place, where Jesus sheds
  The oil of gladness on our heads;
  A place than all besides more sweet,—
  It is the blood-bought mercy-seat.

3 There is a scene where spirits blend,
  Where friend holds fellowship with friend;
  Though sunder'd **far, by faith we meet**,
  Around one common mercy-seat.
  Rev. HUGH STOWELL, 1827.

No. 106. BENEVENTO. 7s. 8 lines. Key F.

1 Sinners, turn; why will ye die?
  God, your Maker, asks you why?
  God, who did your being give,
  Made you with himself to live;
  He the fatal cause demands,—
  Asks the work of His own hands,—
  Why, ye thankless creatures, why
  Will ye cross His **love**, and die?

2 Sinners, turn; why will ye die?
  God, your Saviour, asks you why?
  He, who did your souls retrieve,
  Died Himself, that ye might live.
  Will ye let Him die in vain?
  Crucify your Lord again?
  Why, ye ransomed sinners, why
  Will ye slight His grace and die?

3 Sinners, turn, why will ye die?
  God, the Spirit, asks you why?
  He who all your lives hath strove,
  Urged you to embrace His love.
  Will ye not His grace receive?
  Will ye still refuse to live?
  O ye dying sinners, why,
  Why will ye forever die?
  Rev. C. WESLEY, 1741.

No. 107. Evan. C. M.
"Rouse's Version," 1843.   Psalm 23.   Wm. H. Havergal, 1847.

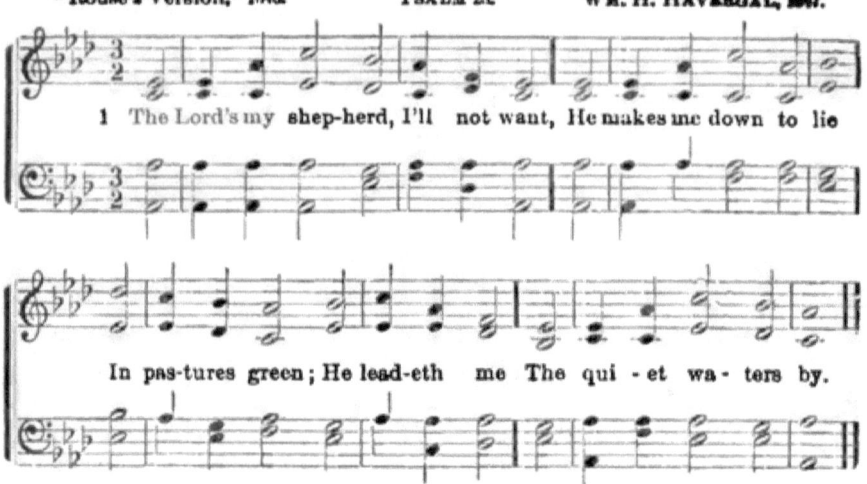

1 The Lord's my shep-herd, I'll not want, He makes me down to lie
In pas-tures green; He lead-eth me The qui-et wa-ters by.

2 My soul He doth restore again,
   And me to walk doth make
Within the paths of righteousness,
   Ev'n for His own name's sake.

3 Yea, though I walk in death's dark vale,
   Yet will I fear none ill;
For Thou art with me; and Thy rod
   And staff me comfort still.

4 My table Thou hast furnished
   In presence of my foes;
My head Thou dost with oil anoint,
   And my cup overflows.

5 Goodness and mercy all my life
   Shall surely follow me;
And in God's house for evermore,
   My dwelling place shall be.

No. 108.   C. M.

1 O for a faith that will not shrink,
   Though press'd by every foe,
That will not tremble on the brink
   Of any earthly woe;

2 That will not murmur or complain
   Beneath the chast'ning rod,
But, in the hour of grief or pain,
   Will lean upon its God;

3 A faith that shines more bright and clear
   When tempests rage without;
That when in danger knows no fear,
   In darkness feels no doubt;—

4 Lord, give us such a faith as this,
   And then, whate'er may come,

We'll taste, e'en here, the hallow'd bliss
   Of an eternal home.
                    Rev. W. H. Bathurst, 1831.

No. 109.   Azmon. C. M.   Key A.

1 Salvation! O the joyful sound!
   What pleasure to our ears;
A sovereign balm for every wound,
   A cordial for our fears.

2 Salvation! let the echo fly
   The spacious earth around,
While all the armies of the sky
   Conspire to raise the sound.

3 Salvation! O Thou bleeding Lamb!
   To Thee the praise belongs;
Salvation shall inspire our hearts,
   And dwell upon our tongues.
                    Rev. I. Watts, 1709.

No. 110.   Antioch.   Key E♭.

1 Joy to the world, the Lord is come!
   Let earth receive her King;
Let every heart prepare Him room,
   And heaven and nature sing.

2 Joy to the world, the Saviour reigns,
   Let men their songs employ;
While fields and floods, rocks, hills, and
   Repeat the sounding joy.   [plains,

3 He rules the world with truth and grace,
   And makes the nations prove
The glories of His righteousness,
   And wonders of His love.
                    Rev. I. Watts, 1719.

No. 111. Dundee. C. M.

Rev. Isaac Watts, 1709. Guillaume Franc, 1543.

A-las! and did my Saviour bleed, And did my Sov'reign die?
Would He de-vote that sa-cred head For such a worm as I?

2 Was it for crimes that I have done,
   He groan'd upon the tree?
  Amazing pity! grace unknown!
   And love beyond degree!

3 Well might the sun in darkness hide,
   And shut his glories in,
  When Christ, the mighty Maker died,
   For man, the creature's sin.

4 Thus might I hide my blushing face
   While His dear cross appears;
  Dissolve my heart in thankfulness,
   And melt mine eyes to tears.

5 But drops of grief can ne'er repay
   The debt of love I owe:
  Here, Lord, I give myself away,—
   'Tis all that I can do.

No. 112. Laban. S. M.

Geo. Heath, 1781. Dr. Lowell Mason, 1830.

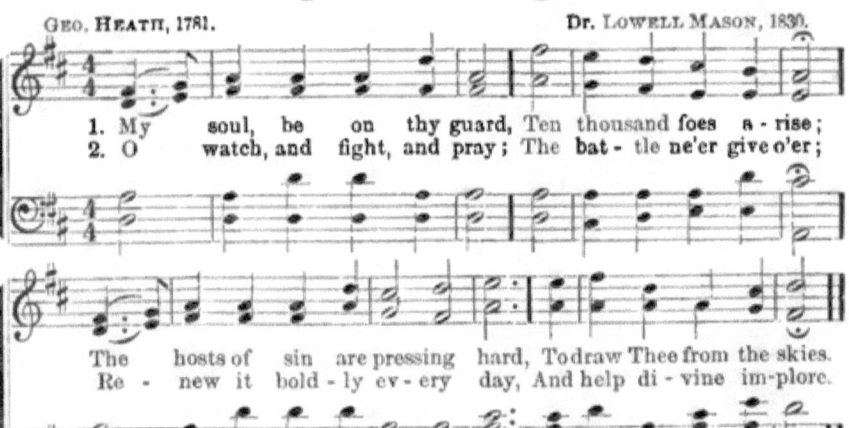

1. My soul, be on thy guard, Ten thousand foes a-rise;
   The hosts of sin are pressing hard, To draw Thee from the skies.
2. O watch, and fight, and pray; The bat-tle ne'er give o'er;
   Re-new it bold-ly ev-ery day, And help di-vine im-plore.

3 Ne'er think the vict'ry won,
   Nor lay thine armor down:
  The work of faith will not be done,
   Till thou obtain the crown.

4 Then persevere till death
   Shall bring thee to thy God;
  He'll take thee, at thy parting breath,
   To His divine abode.

No. 113. **Boylston.** **S. M.**

Rev. Isaac Watts, 1709.   Dr. Lowell Mason, 1832.

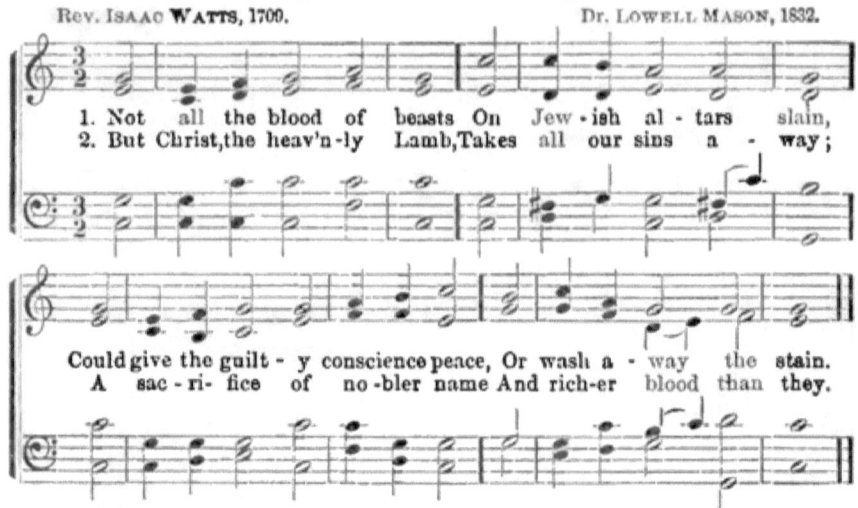

1. Not all the blood of beasts On Jewish altars slain, Could give the guilty conscience peace, Or wash away the stain.
2. But Christ, the heav'nly Lamb, Takes all our sins away; A sacrifice of nobler name And richer blood than they.

3 My faith would lay her hand
  On that dear head of thine,
While like a penitent I stand
  And there confess my sin.

4 My soul looks back to see
  The burden thou didst bear,
While hanging on the cursed tree,
  And knows her guilt was there.

No. 114. **Dennis.** **S. M.**

Rev. John Fawcett, 1772.   From H. G. Nageli.

1. Blest be the tie that binds Our hearts in Christian love; The fellowship of kindred minds Is like to that above.
2. Before our Father's throne, We pour our ardent prayers; Our fears, our hopes, our aims are one, Our comforts and our cares.

3 We share our mutual woes;
  Our mutual burdens bear;
And often for each other flows
  The sympathizing tear.

4 When we asunder part,
  It gives us inward pain;
But we shall still be join'd in heart,
  And hope to meet again.

No. 115. Arlington. C. M.

Rev. Isaac Watts, 1720.   Thos. A. Arne, 1744.

1. Am I a soldier of the cross—A foll'wer of the Lamb,
And shall I fear to own His cause, Or blush to speak His name?

2. Must I be carried to the skies On flowery beds of ease;
While others fought to win the prize, And sail'd thro' bloody seas?

3 Are there no foes for me to face?
   Must I not stem the flood?
Is this vile world a friend to grace
   To help me on to God?

4 Since I must fight if I would reign,
   Increase my courage, Lord;
I'll bear the toil, endure the pain,
   Supported by Thy word.

No. 116. Nettleton. 8s & 7s.

Rev. R. Robinson, 1758.   Old Melody, 1812.

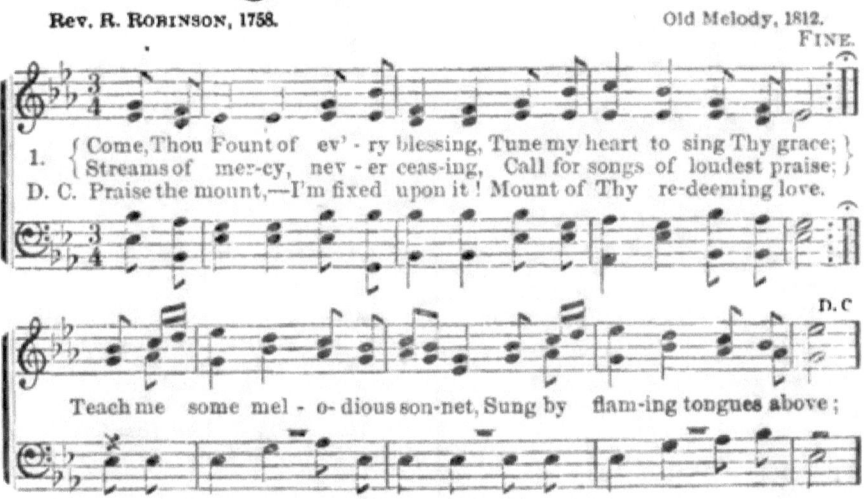

1. { Come, Thou Fount of ev'ry blessing, Tune my heart to sing Thy grace; }
   { Streams of mercy, never ceasing, Call for songs of loudest praise; }
D. C. Praise the mount,—I'm fixed upon it! Mount of Thy redeeming love.

Teach me some melodious sonnet, Sung by flaming tongues above;

2 Here I'll raise my Ebenezer,
   Hither by Thy help I'm come;
And I hope by Thy good pleasure,
   Safely to arrive at home.
Jesus sought me when a stranger,
   Wandering from the fold of God!
He, to rescue me from danger,
   Interposed His precious blood.

3 Oh, to grace how great a debtor,
   Daily I'm constrained to be!
Let Thy goodness as a fetter,
   Bind my wandering heart to Thee
Prone to wander, Lord, I feel it—
   Prone to leave the God I love—
Here's my heart, oh, take and seal it,
   Seal it for Thy courts above.

No. 117. New Haven. 6s & 4s.

Rev. Ray Palmer, D.D., 1830. Dr. Thos. Hastings, 1833.

1. My faith looks up to Thee, Thou Lamb of Calvary; Saviour divine; Now hear me while I pray; Take all my guilt away; O, let me, from this day, Be wholly Thine.

2. May Thy rich grace impart
   Strength to my fainting heart;
     My zeal inspire;
   As Thou hast died for me,
   O may my love to Thee
   Pure, warm, and changeless be—
     A living fire.

3. While life's dark maze I tread,
   And griefs around me spread,
     Be Thou my guide;
   Bid darkness turn to day;
   Wipe sorrow's tears away,
   Nor let me ever stray
     From Thee aside.

4. When ends life's transient dream;
   When death's cold sullen stream
     Shall o'er me roll;
   Blest Saviour, then in love,
   Fear and distrust remove;
   O bear me safe above,—
     A ransom'd soul.

No. 118. Bethany. 6s & 4s. Key G.

1. Nearer, my God, to Thee,
     Nearer to Thee!
   E'en though it be a cross
     That raiseth me;
   Still all my song shall be—
   Nearer, my God, to Thee!
     Nearer to Thee!

2. Though, like the wanderer,
     The sun gone down,
   Darkness be over me,
     My rest a stone;
   Yet in my dreams I'd be—
   Nearer, my God, to Thee!
     Nearer to Thee!

3. There let the way appear,
     Steps unto heaven;
   All that Thou sendest me,
     In mercy given;
   Angels to beckon me
   Nearer, my God, to Thee—
     Nearer to Thee!

4. Then with my waking thoughts,
     Bright with Thy praise,
   Out of my stony griefs,
     Bethel I'll raise;
   So by my woes to be
   Nearer, my God, to Thee!
     Nearer to Thee!

5. Or if on joyful wing,
     Cleaving the sky,
   Sun, moon, and stars **forgot**,
     Upward I fly;
   Still all my song shall be—
   Nearer, my God, to Thee!
     Nearer to Thee!

Mrs. Sarah F. Adams, 1840.

No. 119. Lenox. 6s & 8s.

Rev. Ch. Wesley, 1742. Lewis Edson, 1782.

1. A-rise, my soul, arise, Shake off thy guilty fears, The bleeding sacri-fice
In my be-half ap-pears; Be-fore the throne my Sure-ty stands,
Be-fore the throne my Surety stands, My name is written on His hands.

2 He ever lives above,
  For me to intercede,
His all redeeming love,
  His precious blood to plead;
His blood atoned for all our race,
And sprinkles now the throne of grace.

3 Five bleeding wounds He bears,
  Received on Calvary;
They pour effectual prayers,
  They strongly plead for me;
Forgive him, oh, forgive, they cry,
Nor let that ransomed sinner die.

4 My God is reconciled;
  His pardoning voice I hear;
He owns me for His child;
  I can no longer fear;
With confidence I now draw nigh,
And Father, Abba, Father, cry.

No. 120. "Your Mission." Key F.

1 Hark! the voice of Jesus crying,—
  "Who will go and work to-day?
Fields are white and harvest waiting,
  Who will bear the sheaves away?"
Loud and strong the Master calleth,
  Rich reward He offers thee:
Who will answer, gladly saying,
  "Here am I; send me, send me!"

2 If you cannot cross the ocean,
  And the heathen lands explore,
You can find the heathen nearer,
  You can help them at your door.
If you cannot give your thousands,
  You can give the widow's mite;
And the least you do for Jesus,
  Will be precious in His sight.

No. 120.—Concluded.

If you cannot speak like angels,
  If you cannot preach like Paul,
You can tell the love of Jesus,
  You can say He died for all.
If you cannot rouse the wicked
  With the judgment's dread alarms,
You can lead the little children
  To the Saviour's waiting arms.

4 If you cannot be the watchman,
  Standing high on Zion's wall
Pointing out the path to heaven,
  Offering life and peace to all; [ties
With your prayers and with your boun-
  You can do what heaven demands;
You can be like faithful Aaron,
  Holding up the prophet's hands.

5 If among the older people,
  You may not be apt to teach; [herd,
"Feed my lambs," said Christ, our Shep-
  " Place the food within their reach."
And it may be that the children
  You have led with trembling hand,
Will be found among your jewels,
  When you reach the better land.

6 Let none hear you idly saying,
  "There is nothing I can do,"
While the souls of men are dying,
  And the Master calls for you.
Take the task He gives you gladly,
  Let His work your pleasure be;
Answer quickly when He calleth,
  "Here am I; send me, send me!"
       Rev. Dan'l. March, 1869.

No. 121.   WEBB. 7s & 6s.
       Key Bb.

1 Stand up! stand up for Jesus!
  Ye soldiers of the cross;
Lift high His royal banner,
  It must not suffer loss;
From victory unto victory
  His army He shall lead,
Till every foe is vanquished,
  And Christ is Lord indeed.

2 Stand up! stand up for Jesus!
  Stand in his strength alone;
The arm of flesh will fail you—
  Ye dare not trust your own;
Put on the gospel armor,
  And, watching unto prayer,
Where duty calls, or danger,
  Be never wanting there.

3 Stand up! stand up for Jesus!
  The strife will not be long;
This day the noise of battle,
  The next the victor's song;

To him that overcometh,
  A crown of life shall be;
He with the King of Glory
  Shall reign eternally.
       Rev. Geo. Duffield, Jr., 1858.

No. 122.   TUNE—WORK, FOR THE NIGHT.
       Key F

1 Work, for the night is coming;
  Work through the morning hours;
Work, while the dew is sparkling;
  Work, 'mid springing flowers;
Work, when the day grows brighter
  Work, in the glowing sun;
Work, for the night is coming,
  When man's work is done.

2 Work, for the night is coming;
  Work through the sunny noon;
Fill brightest hours with labor;
  Rest comes sure and soon.
Give every flying minute
  Something to keep in store;
Work, for the night is coming,
  When man works no more.

3 Work, for the night is coming,
  Under the sunset skies;
While their bright tints are glowing,
  Work, for daylight flies.
Work, till the last beam fadeth,
  Fadeth to shine no more;
Work, while the night is dark'ning,
  When man's work is o'er.
       Annie L. Walker, 1860.

No. 123.   EVAN. C. M.
       Key Ab.

1 I heard the voice of Jesus say,
  "Come unto Me and rest;
Lay down, thou weary one, lay down
  Thy head upon My breast."

2 I came to Jesus as I was—
  Weary, and worn, and sad;
I found in Him a resting-place,
  And He has made me glad.

3 I heard the voice of Jesus say,
  " Behold I freely give
The living water—thirsty one,
  Stoop down, and drink, and live."

4 I came to Jesus, and I drank
  Of that life-giving stream:
My thirst was quench'd, my soul revived
  And now I live in Him.

5 I heard the voice of Jesus say,
  " I am this dark world's light,
Look unto Me, thy morn shall rise,
  And all thy day be bright."

6 I look'd to Jesus, and I found
  In Him my Star, my Sun;
And in that light of life I'll walk
  'Till trav'ling days are done.
       Rev. H. Bonar, 1857.

No. 124. THE BEAUTIFUL RIVER.
Key E♭.

1 Shall we gather at the river
  Where bright angel feet have **trod**;
  With its **crystal** tide for ever
  Flowing by the throne of God.

CHO.—Yes, we'll gather at **the river,**
  The beautiful, the beautiful river—
  Gather with the saints at the river,
  That flows by the throne of God.

2 On **the** margin of the river,
  Washing up its silver spray,
  We **will walk aud** worship ever,
  All the happy golden day.
CHO.—Yes, we'll gather at the river, &c.

3 Ere we reach the shining river,
  Lay we every burden down;
  Grace our spirits will deliver,
  And provide a robe and crown.
CHO.—Yes, we'll gather at the river, &c.

4 At the smiling of the river,
  Mirror of the Saviour's face,
  Saints whom death will never sever,
  Lift their songs of saving grace.
CHO.—Yes, we'll gather at the river, &c.

5 Soon we'll reach the silver river,
  Soon our pilgrimage will cease;
  Soon **our happy hearts will quiver,**
  With the melody of peace.
CHO.—Yes, we'll gather at the river, &c.
        Rev. ROBERT LOWRY, 1864.

No. 125. 40th PSALM. C. M.

1 I waited for the Lord my God,
  And patiently did bear;
  At length to me He did incline
  My voice and cry to hear.

2 He took me from a fearful pit,
  And from the miry clay,
  And on a **rock** He set my feet,
  Establishing **my way.**

3 He put a new song in my mouth,
  Our God to magnify;

Many shall see it, and shall fear,
  And on the Lord rely.

4 O blessed is the man whose trust
  Upon the Lord relies;
  Respecting not the proud, nor such
  As turn aside to lies.
        SCOTCH VERSION.

No. 126. SAVIOUR, LIKE A SHEPHERD.
8s, 7s & 4. Key E♭.

1 **Saviour,** like a shepherd lead us,
  Much we need Thy tend'rest care
  In Thy pleasant pastures feed us
  For our use Thy folds prepare;
    Blessed Jesus, blessed Jesus,
    Thou hast bought us, Thine we are;
    Blessed Jesus, blessed Jesus,
    Thou hast bought us, Thine we are.

2 We are Thine, do Thou befriend **us,**
  Be the Guardian of our way;
  Keep Thy flock, from sin defend us,
  Seek us when we go astray;
    Blessed Jesus, blessed Jesus,
    Hear, O hear us, when we pray
    Blessed Jesus, blessed Jesus,
    Hear, O **hear us, when** we pray.

3 Thou hast promised to receive us,
  Poor and sinful though we be;
  Thou hast mercy to relieve us,
  Grace to cleanse, and power to free;
    Blessed Jesus, blessed Jesus,
    We will early turn to Thee;
    Blessed Jesus, blessed Jesus,
    We will early **turn to Thee.**

4 Early let us seek **Thy favor,**
  Early let us do Thy will;
  Blessed Lord and only Saviour,
  With Thy love our bosoms fill.
    Blessed Jesus, blessed Jesus,
    Thou hast loved us, love us still
    Blessed Jesus, blessed Jesus,
    Thou hast loved us, love us still.
        DOROTHY THRUPP, 1836.

No. 127. ZION. 8s, 7s & 4.
Key D.

1 Come, ye sinners, poor and needy,
　Weak and wounded, sick and sore;
Jesus ready stands to save you,
　Full of pity, love, and power:
　　He is able,
　He is willing: doubt no more;
　　He is able,
　He is willing: doubt no more.

2 Now, ye needy, come and welcome;
　God's free bounty glorify;
True belief and true repentance,—
　Every grace that brings you nigh,—
　　Without money,
　Come to Jesus Christ and buy;
　　Without money,
　Come to Jesus Christ and buy.

3 Let not conscience make you linger;
　Nor of fitness fondly dream:
All the fitness He requireth
　Is to feel your need of Him:
　　This He gives you,—
　'Tis the Spirit's glimm'ring beam;
　　This He gives you,—
　'Tis the Spirit's glimm'ring beam.

4 Come, ye weary, heavy-laden,
　Bruised and mangled by the fall;
If you tarry 'till you're better,
　You will never come at all;
　　Not the righteous,—
　Sinners, Jesus came to all;
　　Not the righteous,—
　Sinners, Jesus came to call.
　　　　　　Rev. JOS. HART, 1759.

No. 128. MARLOW. C. M.

1 Come, Holy Spirit, Heavenly Dove!
　With all Thy quickening powers;
Kindle a flame of heavenly love
　In these cold hearts of ours.

2 Dear Lord! and shall we ever live
　At this poor dying rate?
Our love so faint, so cold to Thee,
　And Thine to us so great?

3 Come, Holy Spirit, Heavenly Dove,
　With all Thy quickening powers;
Come, shed abroad a Saviour's love,
　And that shall kindle ours.
　　　　　　I. WATTS, 1709.

No. 129. HE LOVED ME.
(*Tune on page 75.*)

1 Once I was dead in sin,
　And hope within me died;
But now I'm dead to sin—
　With Jesus crucified.
CHO.—And can it be that "He loved me,
　And gave himself for me?"

2 Oh height I cannot reach,
　Oh depth I cannot sound,
Oh love, O boundless love,
　In my Redeemer found!
　CHO.—And can it be, &c.

3 Oh cold, ungrateful heart
　That can from Jesus turn,
When living fires of love
　Should on His altar burn.
　CHO.—And can it be, &c.

4 I live—and yet, not I,
　But Christ that lives in me;
Who from the law of sin
　And death hath made me free.
　CHO.—And can it be, &c.
　　　　　　Rev. A. T. PIERSON

No. 130. THE CHRISTIAN'S HOME. P. M.
Key C.

1 In the Christian's home in glory
　There remains a land of rest;
There my Saviour's gone before me,
　To fulfil my soul's request,
CHO.—There is rest for the weary,
　There is rest for the weary,
　There is rest for the weary,
　　There is rest for you;
　On the other side of Jordan,
　　In the sweet fields of Eden,
　Where the tree of life is blooming
　　There is rest for you.

2 He is fitting up my mansion,
   Which eternally shall stand;
For my stay shall not be transient
   In that holy, happy land.
     CHO.—There is rest, &c.

3 Sing, O sing ye, heirs of glory!
   Shout your triumphs as you go
Zion's gates will open for you,
   You shall find an entrance through.
     CHO.—There is rest, &c.
          Rev. SAM'L Y. HARMER, 1856.

No. 131. BOYLSTON. S. M. Key C.

1 Did Christ o'er sinners weep,
   And shall our cheeks be dry?
Let floods of penitential grief
   Burst forth from every eye.

2 The Son of God in tears
   The wondering angels see;
Be thou astonished, O my soul!
   He shed those tears for thee.

3 He wept that we might weep;
   Each sin demands a tear:
In heaven alone no sin is found,
   And there's no weeping there.
          Rev. BENJ. BEDDOME, 1787.

No. 132. COME TO JESUS. Key F.

1 Come to Jesus, come to Jesus,
   Come to Jesus just now;
Just now come to Jesus,
   Come to Jesus, just now.

2 He will save you, He will save you,
   He will save you just now;
Just now He will save you,
   He will save you just now.

3 He is able, He is able,
   He is able just now;
Just now He is able,
   He is able just now.

4 He is willing, He is willing,
   He is willing just now;
Just now He is willing,
   He is willing just now.

5 He is waiting, He is waiting,
   He is waiting just now;

Just now He is waiting,
   He is waiting just now.

6 He will hear you, He will hear you,
   He will hear you just now;
Just now He will hear you,
   He will hear you just now.

7 He will cleanse you, He will cleanse
     you,
He will cleanse you just now;
Just now He will cleanse you,
He will cleanse you just now.

8 He'll renew you, He'll renew you,
   He'll renew you just now;
Just now He'll renew you,
   He'll renew you just now.

9 He'll forgive you, etc.

10 If you trust Him, etc.

11 He will save you, etc.
                   ENGLISH.

No. 133. HAPPY DAY. L. M. Key G.

1 O happy day, that fixed my choice
   On Thee, my Saviour and my God!
Well may this glowing heart rejoice,
   And tell its raptures all abroad.
CHO.—Happy day, happy day,
   When Jesus washed my sins away;
He taught me how to watch and pray
   And live rejoicing every day,
Happy day, happy day,
   When Jesus washed my sins away.

2 'Tis done, the great transaction's done—
   I am my Lord's, and He is mine;
He drew me, and I followed on,
   Charmed to confess the voice divine.
     CHO.—Happy day, &c.

3 Now rest, my long divided heart;
   Fixed on this blissful centre, rest;
Nor ever from thy Lord depart,
   With Him of every good possessed.
     CHO.—Happy day, &c.

4 High heaven, that heard the solemn vow,
   That vow renewed shall daily hear,
Till in life's latest hour I bow,
   And bless in death a bond so dear.
     CHO.—Happy day, &c.
          PHILIP DODDRIDGE, D.D., 1755

No. 134. Salvation.

"For the grace of God that bringeth salvation to all men hath appeared.—Titus 2: 11.

P. P. Bliss.   P. P. Bliss, by per.

1. Come, sing the gospel's joyful sound, Salvation full and free;
Proclaim to all the world around, The year of jubilee!

CHORUS.
Salvation, Salvation, The grace of God doth bring;
Salvation, Salvation, Thro' Christ our Lord and King.

2 Ye mourning souls, aloud rejoice;
  Ye blind, your Saviour see!
Ye pris'ners, sing with thankful voice,
  The Lord hath made you free!—*Cho.*

3 With rapture swell the song again,
  Of Jesus' dying love;
'Tis peace on earth, good will to men,
  And praise to God above.—*Cho.*

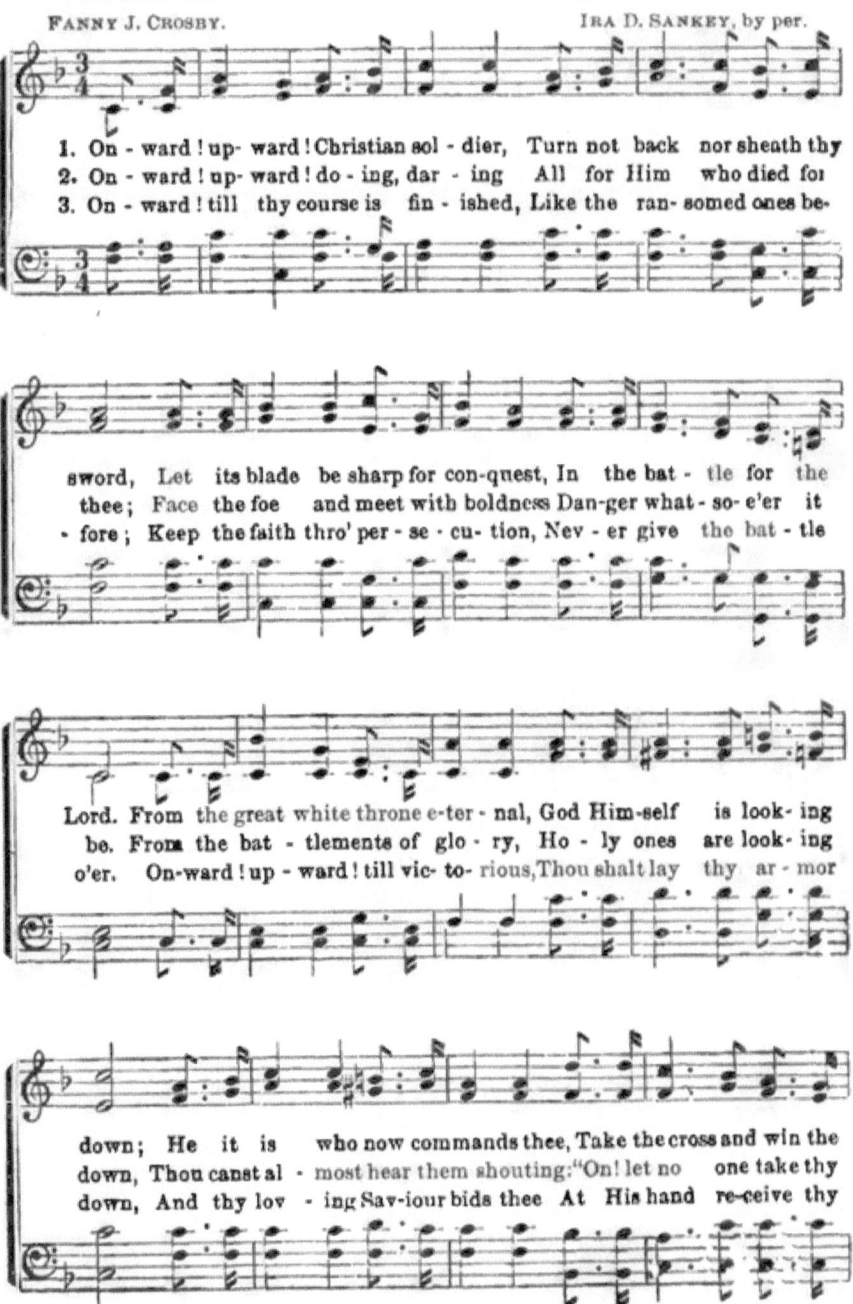

Onward, Upward!—Concluded.

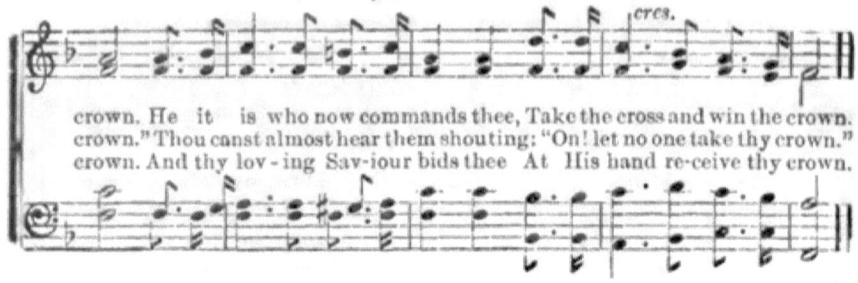

crown. He it is who now commands thee, Take the cross and win the crown.
crown." Thou canst almost hear them shouting: "On! let no one take thy crown."
crown. And thy lov-ing Sav-iour bids thee At His hand re-ceive thy crown.

No. 136. More Love to Thee, O Christ.

"Continue ye in my love."—JOHN 15: 9.

Mrs. ELIZABETH PRENTISS. W. H. DOANE, by per.

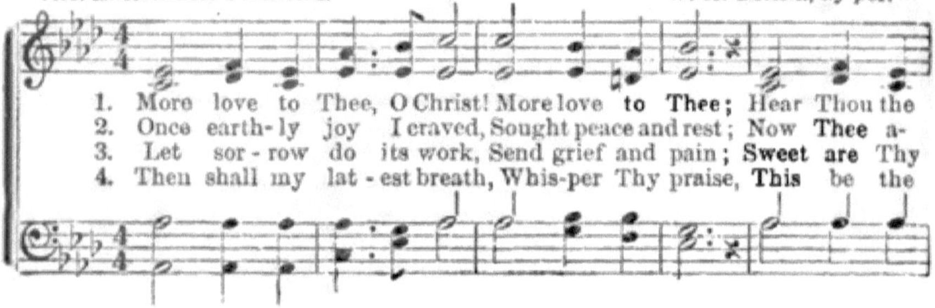

1. More love to Thee, O Christ! More love to Thee; Hear Thou the pray'r I make On bend-ed knee; This is my earn-est plea,
2. Once earth-ly joy I craved, Sought peace and rest; Now Thee a-lone I seek, Give what is best: This all my pray'r shall be,
3. Let sor-row do its work, Send grief and pain; Sweet are Thy mes-sen-gers, Sweet their re-frain, When they can sing with me,—
4. Then shall my lat-est breath, Whis-per Thy praise, This be the part-ing cry My heart shall raise; This still its pray'r shall be:

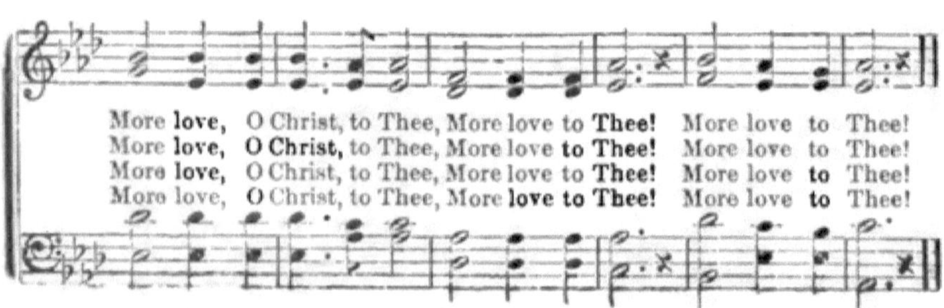

More love, O Christ, to Thee, More love to Thee! More love to Thee!
More love, O Christ, to Thee, More love to Thee! More love to Thee!
More love, O Christ, to Thee, More love to Thee! More love to Thee!
More love, O Christ, to Thee, More love to Thee! More love to Thee!

No. 137.

Wholly Thine.

"The God of peace sanctify you wholly."—Thes. 5: 23.

Mrs. Annie S. Hawkes. Rev. Robert Lowry, by per.

1. Thine, most gra - cious Lord, O make me whol - ly Thine—
2. Whol - ly Thine, my Lord, To go when Thou dost call;
3. Whol - ly Thine, O Lord, In ev - ery pass - ing hour;

Thine in thought, in word, and deed, For thou, O Christ, art mine.
Thine to yield my ver - y self In all things, great and small.
Thine in si - lence, Thine to speak, As Thou dost grant the power.

REFRAIN.

Whol - ly Thine, whol - ly Thine; Thou hast bought me, I am Thine;

Bless - ed Sav - iour, Thou art mine; Make me whol - ly Thine.

4.
Wholly Thine, O Lord,
 To fashion as Thou wilt,—
Strengthen, bless, and keep the soul
 Which Thou hast saved from guilt.—*Ref.*

5.
Thine, Lord, wholly Thine,
 For ever one with Thee—
Rooted, grounded in Thy love,
 Abiding, sure, and free.—*Ref.*

5 When He comes, our **glorious** King,
All His ransomed home to bring,
Then anew this song we'll sing:
Hallelujah, what a Saviour!

To the Work.—Concluded.

No. 146. All for Me.

"And when they had platted a crown of thorns, they put it on His head, and a reed in His hand."—MATT. 27 : 29.

ANON.   IRA. D. SANKEY, by per.
Tenderly.

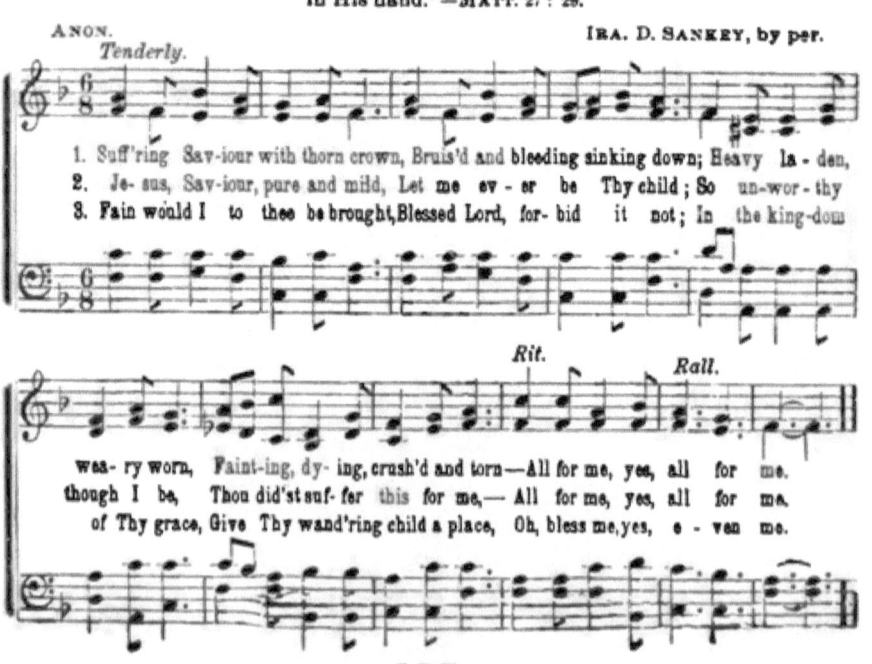

No. 148. Dark is the Night.

"Thou shalt compass me about with songs of deliverance."—Ps. xi. 7.

FANNY J. CROSBY.   T. E. PERKINS, by per.

1. { Dark is the night, and cold the wind is blow-ing, Near-er and nearer comes the breakers' roar; }
   { Where shall I go, or whith-er fly for ref-uge? Hide me, my Father, till the storm is o'er; }

CHORUS.

{ With His loving hand to guide, let the clouds a-bove me roll, And the bil-lows in their fu-ry dash a-round me. }
{ I can brave the wildest storm, with His glo-ry in my soul, I can (Omit...............) sing a-midst the tem-pest—Praise the Lord!

2 Dark is the night, but cheering is the promise;
  He will go with me o'er the troubled wave;
Safe He will lead me through the pathless waters,
  Jesus, the mighty one, and strong to save.

3 Dark is the night, but lo! the day is breaking,
  Onward my bark, unfurl thy every sail;
Now at the helm I see my Father standing,
  Soon will my anchor drop within the vail.

No. 150. Ho! Reapers of Life's Harvest.

"The harvest truly is plenteous, but the laborers are few."—MATT. 9: 37.

I. B. W.
I. B. WOODBURY, by per.

1. Ho! reapers of life's harvest, Why stand with rusted blade, Until the night draws round thee, And day begins to fade? Why stand ye idle, waiting, For reapers more to come? The golden morn is passing, Why sit ye idle, dumb?

2. Thrust in your sharpened sickle, And gather in the grain, The night is fast approaching, And soon will come again. The Master calls for reapers, And shall He call in vain? Shall sheaves lie there ungathered, And waste upon the plain?

3 Come down from hill and mountain
  In morning's ruddy glow,
Nor wait until the dial
  Points to the noon below;
And come with stronger sinew,
  Nor faint in heat or cold,
And pause not till the evening
  Draws round its wealth of gold.

4 Mount up the heights of Wisdom,
  And crush each error low;
Keep back no words of knowledge
  That human hearts should know.
Be faithful to thy mission,
  In service of thy Lord,
And then a golden chaplet
  Shall be thy just reward.

Joy in Sorrow.—Concluded.

3 An Elim with its coolness,
    Its fountains and its shade;
  A blessing in its fulness,
    When buds of promise fade.
  O'er tears of soft contrition
    I've seen a rainbow light;
  A glory and fruition,
    So near!—yet out of sight.

4 My Saviour, Thee possessing,
    I have the joy, the balm,
  The healing and the blessing,
    The sunshine and the psalm;
  The promise for the fearful,
    The Elim for the faint;
  The rainbow for the tearful,
    The glory for the saint!

No. 152. The Heavenly Land.

"*A better country, that is an heavenly.*"—HEB. 11: 16.

Rev. LEWIS HARTSOUGH, 1858.   WM. B. BRADBURY, by per.

2 I love to think of the heavenly land,
    Where my Redeemer reigns,
  Where rapturous songs of triumph rise,
    In endless, joyous strains.—*Ref.*

3 I love to think of the heavenly land,
    The saints eternal home.
  Where palms, and robes, and crowns ne'er fade,
    And all our joys are one.—*Ref.*

4 I love to think of the heavenly land,
    The greetings there we'll meet,
  The harps—the songs forever ours—
    The walks—the golden streets.—*Ref.*

5 I love to think of the heavenly land,
    That promised land so fair,
  Oh, how my raptured spirit longs
    To be forever there.—*Ref.*

No. 153. Call Them in.

"Go out into the highways and hedges, and compel them to come in."—LUKE 11

Miss ANNA SHIPTON.   IRA. D. SANKEY, by per.
Moderato.

1. "Call them in"—the poor, the wretched, Sin-stained wand'rers from the fold; Peace and par-don free-ly of-fer; Can you weigh their worth with gold? "Call them in"—the weak, the wea-ry, Lad-en with the doom of sin; Bid them come and rest in Je-sus; He is waiting—"Call them in."

2. "Call them in"—the Jew, the Gen-tile; Bid the stran-ger to the feast; "Call them in"—the rich, the no-ble, From the high-est to the least: Forth the Fa-ther runs to meet them, He hath all their sor-rows seen; Robe, and ring, and roy-al sandals, Wait the lost ones—"Call them in."

3 "Call them in"—the mere professors,
   Slumbering, sleeping, on death's brink;
Nought of life are they possessors,
   Yet of safety vainly think:
Bring them in—the careless scoffers,
   Pleasure seekers of the earth:
Tell of God's most gracious offers,
   And of Jesus' priceless worth.

4 "Call them in"—the broken-hearted,
   Cowering 'neath the brand of shame;
Speak Love's message low and tender,
   'Twas for sinners Jesus came:
See, the shadows lengthen round us,
   Soon the day-dawn will begin;
Can you leave them lost and lonely?
   Christ is coming—"Call them in."

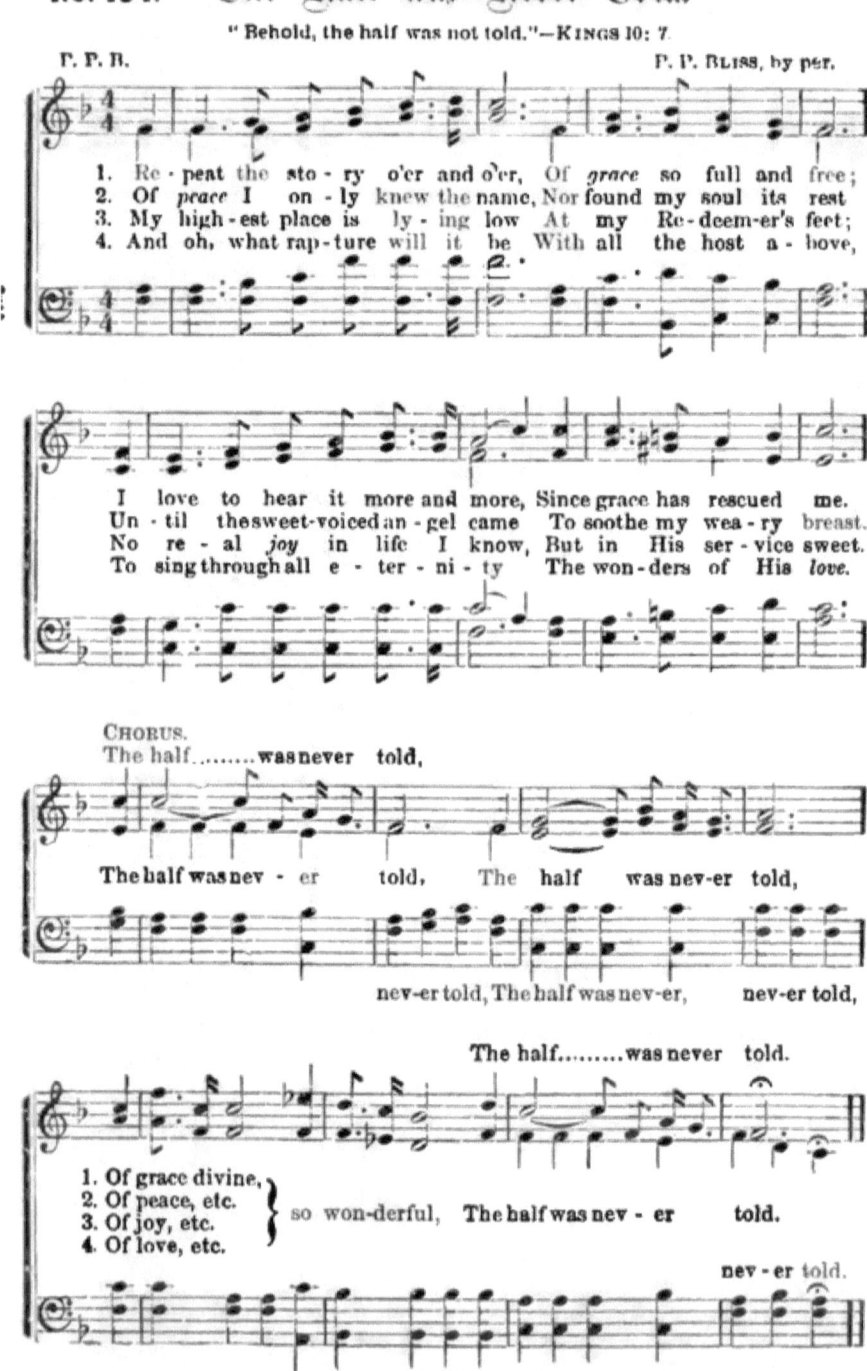

No. 156. **I Bring my Sins to Thee.**

"In returning and rest ye shall be saved."—Isa. 30:15.

FRANCES RIDLEY HAVERGAL. P. P. BLISS, by per.

1. I bring my *sins* to Thee, The sins I can-not count,
   That all may cleansed be In Thy once o-pened Fount;
   I bring them Sav-iour, all to Thee; The bur-den is too
   great for me, The bur-den is too great for me.

2. I bring my *grief* to Thee, The grief I can-not tell;
   No words shall need-ed be, Thou know-est all so well;
   I bring the sor-row laid on me, O suff-'ring Sav-iour,
   all to Thee, O suff-'ring Sav-iour, all to Thee.

3 My *joys* to Thee I bring,
  The joys thy love has given,
  That each may be a wing
  To lift me nearer heaven,
  I bring them, Saviour, all to Thee,
  Who hast procured them all for me.

4 My *life* I bring to Thee,
  I would not be my own;
  O Saviour, let me be
  Thine ever, Thine alone,
  My heart, my life, my all I bring
  To Thee, my Saviour and my King

Song of Salvation.—Concluded.

1. "This is a faithful saying and worthy of all acceptation, that Christ Jesus came into the world to save sinners."—1 Tim. 1 : 15.—*Cho.*

2. "He was wounded for our transgressions, He was bruised for our iniquities. And with His stripes we are healed."—Isa. 53 : 5.—*Cho.*

3. "In my Father's house are many mansions......I go to prepare a place for you...... That where I am, there ye may be also."—John 14 : 2, 3.—*Cho.*

4. "I will give unto him that is athirst of the fountain of the water of life freely. He that overcometh shall inherit all things, and I will be his God, and he shall be my son." —Rev. 21 : 6, 7.—*Cho.*

No. 158. Dare to be a Daniel.

"But Daniel purposed in his heart that he would not defile himself with the portion of the king's meat, nor with the wine which he drank."—Dan. 1 : 8.

P. P. B.   P. P. Bliss, by per.

1. Standing by a pur-pose true, Heed-ing God's com-mand,
2. Ma-ny might-y men are lost, Dar-ing not to stand,
3. Ma-ny gi-ants, great and tall, Stalk-ing thro' the land,
4. Hold the gos-pel ban-ner high! On to vic-t'ry grand!

Hon-or them, the faith-ful few! All hail to Dan-iel's Band!
Who for God had been a host, By join-ing Dan-iel's Band.
Head-long to the earth would fall, If met by Dan-iel's Band.
Sa-tan and his host de-fy, And shout for Dan-iel's Band.

CHORUS

Dare to be a Dan-iel, Dare to stand a-lone!
Dare have a pur-pose firm! Dare to make it known!

No. 159.   Tune—Greenville.   8s, 7s & 4.

1 Lord, dismiss us with Thy blessing,
   Fill our hearts with joy and peace;
Let us each, Thy love possessing,
   Triumph in redeeming grace;
    O, refresh us, O, refresh us,
   Traveling through this wilderness.

2 Thanks we give, and adoration,
   For Thy gospel's joyful sound:
May the fruits of Thy salvation
   In our hearts and lives abound;
    Ever faithful, Ever faithful,
   To the truth may we be found.

3 So, whene'er the signal's given,
   Us from earth to call away,
Borne on angel's wings to heaven,
   Glad the summons to obey,
    May we ever, May we ever
   Reign with Christ in endless day!

John Fawcett D.D., 1774.

No. 160. At the Feet of Jesus.

"Mary which also sat at Jesus' feet, and heard his word."—LUKE 10. 39.

P. P. B.
P. P. BLISS, by per.

Moderato.

1. At the feet of Jesus, List'ning to His word:
2. At the feet of Jesus, Pour-ing perfume rare,
3. At the feet of Jesus, In that morn-ing hour,

Learn-ing wis-dom's les-son From her lov-ing Lord:
Ma-ry did her Sav-iour, For the grave pre-pare:
Lov-ing hearts re-ceiv-ing Res-ur-rec-tion power:

Ma-ry, led by heav'n-ly grace, Chose the meek dis-ci-ple's place.
And, from love the "good work" done, She her Lord's ap-prov-al won.
Haste with joy to preach the word:"Christ is ris-en, Praise the Lord!"

CHORUS.

At the feet of Je-sus is the place for me,
At the feet of Je-sus is the place for me,
At the feet of Je-sus, ris-en now for me,

There a hum-ble *learn-er* would I choose to be.
There in sweet-est *ser-vice* would I ev-er be.
I shall sing His *prais-es* through e-ter-ni-ty.

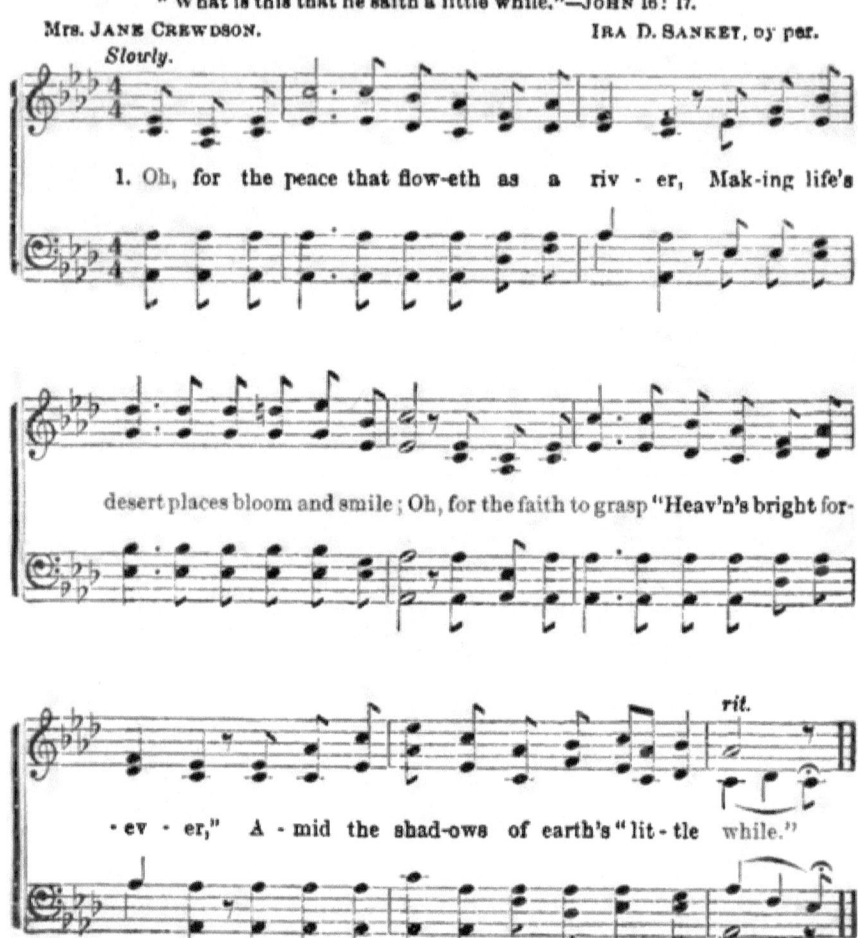

No. 161. A Little While.

"What is this that he saith a little while."—JOHN 16: 17.

Mrs. JANE CREWDSON. IRA D. SANKEY, by per.

1. Oh, for the peace that flow-eth as a riv-er, Mak-ing life's desert places bloom and smile; Oh, for the faith to grasp "Heav'n's bright for-ev-er," A-mid the shad-ows of earth's "lit-tle while."

2 "A little while" for patient vigil-keeping,
   To face the storm and wrestle with the strong;
 "A little while" to sow the seed with weeping,
   Then bind the sheaves and sing the harvest song.

3 "A little while" the earthern pitcher taking,
   To wayside brooks, from far off fountains fed;
 Then the parched lip its thirst forever slacking
   Beside the fulness of the Fountain-head.

4 "A little while" to keep the oil from failing,
 "A little while" faith's flickering lamp to trim;
 And then the Bridegroom's coming footsteps hailing,
   We'll haste to meet Him with the bridal hymn.

No. 162. The Solid Rock.

"The Lord is my defence, and rock of my refuge."—Ps. 94:22.

Rev. Edward Mote, 1825.   Wm. B. Bradbury, by per.

1. My hope is built on nothing less Than Jesus' blood and righteousness; I dare not trust the sweetest frame, But wholly lean on Jesus' name.

2. When darkness veils His lovely face, I rest on His unchanging grace; In every high and stormy gale, My anchor holds within the vail.

CHORUS.
On Christ, the Solid Rock I stand; All other ground is sinking sand, All other ground is sinking sand.

3 His oath, His covenant, His blood,
Support me in the whelming flood;
When all around my soul gives way,
He then is all my hope and stay.

4 When He shall come with trumpet sound,
O, may I then in Him be found;
Drest in His righteousness alone,
Faultless to stand before the throne!

4
Now just a word for Jesus;
Let not the time be lost;
The heart's neglected duty
Brings sorrow to its cost.—*Ref.*

5
Now just a word for Jesus;
And if your faith be dim,
Arise in all your weakness,
And leave the rest to Him.—*Ref.*

No. 164. **Look Away to Jesus.**

"Looking unto Jesus."—HEB. 12: 2.

Rev. HENRY BURTON.   P. P. BLISS, by per.

1. Look away to Jesus, Soul by woe oppress'd;
'Twas for Thee He suffer'd, Come to Him and rest,
All thy griefs He carried, All thy sins He bore;
Look away to Jesus; Trust Him evermore.

2. Look away to Jesus, Soldier in the fight;
When the battle thickens Keep thine armor bright;
Though thy foes be many, Tho' thy strength be small,
Look away to Jesus; He shall conquer all.

3. Look away to Jesus, When the skies are fair;
Calm seas have their dangers; Mariner, beware!
Earthly joys are fleeting, Going as they came,
Look away to Jesus, Evermore the same.

4 Look away to Jesus,
  'Mid the toil and heat;
Soon will come the resting
  At the Master's feet;
For the guests are bidden,
  And the feast is spread;
Look away to Jesus,
  In His footsteps tread.

4 When, amid the music
  Of the endless feast.
Saints will sing His praises,
  Thine shall not be least;
Then, amid the glories
  Of the crystal sea,
Look away to Jesus,
  Through eternity.

Who's on the Lord's Side?—Concluded.

true and the tried, Who'll stand by his col-ors—who's on the Lord's side?

3 Who is there among us yet under the rod,
   Who knows not the pardoning mercy of God?
   Oh, bring to Him humbly the heart in its pride;
   Oh, haste, while He's waiting and seek the Lord's side.—*Cho.*

4 Oh, heed not the sorrow, the pain and the wrong,
   For soon shall our sighing be changed into song;
   So, bearing the cross of our convenant Guide,
   We'll shout, as we triumph, "*I'm on the Lord's side.*"—*Cho.*

---o---

No. 167. **Remember Me.**

"O Lord, Thou knowest; remember."—JER. 15:15.

ISAAC WATTS. ASA HULL, by per.

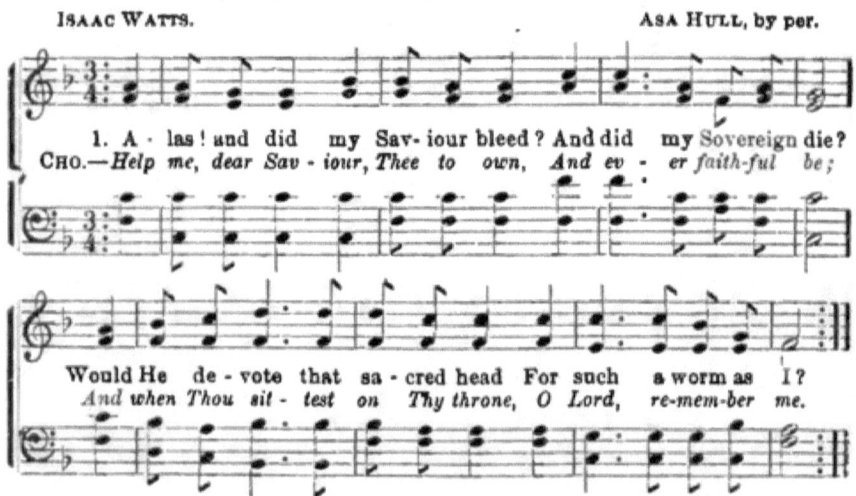

1. A-las! and did my Sav-iour bleed? And did my Sovereign die?
CHO.—*Help me, dear Sav-iour, Thee to own, And ev-er faith-ful be;*

Would He de-vote that sa-cred head For such a worm as I?
And when Thou sit-test on Thy throne, O Lord, re-mem-ber me.

2 Was it for crimes that I had done
    He groaned upon the tree?
  Amazing pity! grace unknown!
    And love beyond degree.—*Cho.*

3 Well might the sun in darkness hide,
    And shut his glories in,
  When Christ, the mighty Maker died
    For man, the creature's sin.—*Cho.*

4 Thus might I hide my blushing face,
    Whilst His dear cross appears,
  Dissolve my heart in thankfulness,
    And melt mine eyes to tears.—*Cho.*

5 But drops of grief can ne'er repay
    The debt of love I owe;
  Here, Lord, I give myself away;
    'Tis all that I can do.—*Cho.*

143

No. 169. **Whiter than Snow.**

"Wash me, and I shall be whiter than snow."—Ps. 51: 7.

JAMES NICHOLSON.   WM. G. FISCHER, 1872, by per.

1. Lord Je-sus, I long to be per-fect-ly whole; I want Thee for-
2. Lord Je-sus, look down from Thy throne in the skies, And help me to
3. Lord Je-sus, for this I most humbly en-treat; I wait, bless-ed
4. Lord Je-sus, Thou seest I pa-tient-ly wait; Come now, and with-

-ev - er, to live in my soul; Break down ev'-ry i-dol, cast
make a com-plete sac-ri-fice; I give up my-self, and what
Lord, at Thy cru-ci-fied feet, By faith, for my cleansing. I
-in me a new heart cre-ate; To those who have sought Thee, Thou

out ev'-ry foe; Now wash me, and I shall be whit-er than snow.
-ev - er I know—Now wash me, and I shall be whit-er than snow.
see Thy blood flow—Now wash me, and I shall be whit-er than snow.
nev-er said'st No—Now wash me, and I shall be whit-er than snow.

CHORUS.

Whit - er than snow, yes, whit - er than snow;

Now wash me, and I shall be whit - er than snow.

No. 170. **Blessed River.**

"And he shewed me a pure river of water of life."—REV. 22: 1.

HORATIUS BONAR, D. D.   Rev. ROBERT LOWRY, by per.

1. Fresh from the throne of glory Bright in its crystal gleam,
Bursts out the living fountain, Swells on the living stream;
Blessed River, Let me ever Feast my eyes on thee,
Blessed River, Let me ever Feast my eyes on thee.

2. Stream full of life and gladness, Spring of all health and peace,
No harps by thee hang silent, Nor happy voices cease;
Tranquil River, Let me ever Sit and sing by thee,
Tranquil River, Let me ever Sit and sing by thee.

3. River of God, I greet thee, Not now afar, but near;
My soul to thy still waters Hastes in its thirstings here;
Holy River, Let me ever Drink of only thee,
Holy River, Let me ever Drink of only thee.

Scatter Seeds of Kindness.—Concluded.

3 If we knew the baby fingers,
  Pressed against the window pane,
 Would be cold and stiff to-morrow—
  Never trouble us again—
 Would the bright eyes of our darling
  Catch the frown upon our brow?
 Would the prints of rosy fingers
  Vex us then as they do now?

4 Ah! those little ice-cold fingers,
  How they point our memories back
 To the hasty words and actions
  Strewn along our backward track!
 How those little hands remind us,
  As in snowy grace they lie,
 Not to scatter thorns—but roses—
  For our reaping by and by.

No. 175. Onward, Christian Soldiers.

"Take unto you the whole armor of God."—EPH. 6:13.

Rev. S. BARING-GOULD.   JOS. HAYDN, arr.

1. Onward, Christian soldiers, Marching as to war, With the Cross of Jesus
2. Like a mighty army Moves the Church of God; Brothers, we are treading
3. Crowns and thrones may perish, Kingdoms rise and wane, But the Church of Jesus
4. Onward, then, ye people, Join the happy throng, Blend with ours your voices

Going on be-fore. Christ the Royal Master Leads against the foe,
Where the saints have trod; We are not di-vid-ed, All one bod-y we;
Constant will remain; Gates of hell can nev-er 'Gainst that Church prevail;
In the triumph song; Glo-ry, laud, and hon-or, Un-to Christ the King,

CHORUS.

Forward in-to bat-tle, See, His banners go. Onward, Christian sol-diers,
One in hope and doctrine, One in char-i-ty.
We have Christ's own promise, And that cannot fail.
This thro' countless a-ges Men and angels sing.

Marching as to war, With the Cross of Je-sus Going on be-fore.

I am Sweeping through the Gate.—Concluded.

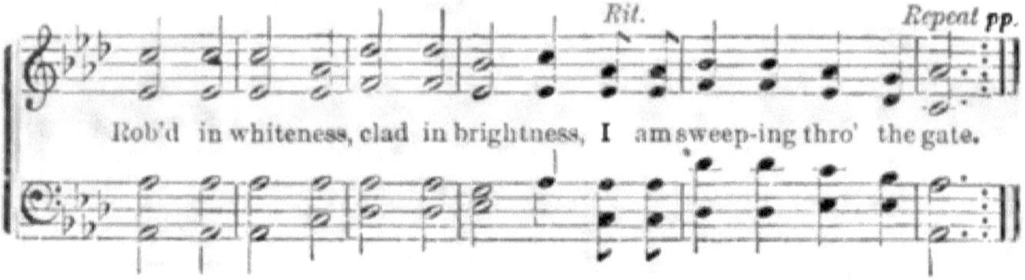

Rob'd in whiteness, clad in brightness, I am sweep-ing thro' the gate.

No. 179. Jesus is Mine.

"My beloved is mine."—SONG OF SOLOMON 2: 16.

Mrs. CATHERINE J. BONAR, 1843.   T. E. PERKINS, by per.

1. Fade, fade each earth-ly joy, Je - sus is mine! Break ev'-ry
2. Tempt not my soul a-way, Je - sus is mine! Here would I
3. Fare-well, ye dreams of night, Je - sus is mine! Lost in this
4. Fare-well, mor-tal-i-ty, Je - sus is mine! Wel-come e-

ten - der tie, Je - sus is mine! Dark is the wil-der-ness,
ev - er stay, Je - sus is mine! Per - ish-ing things of clay,
dawn-ing light, Je - sus is mine! All that my soul has tried,
ter - ni - ty, Je - sus is mine! Wel-come, O loved and blest,

Earth has no rest-ing place, Jesus a-lone can bless, Je - sus is mine!
Born but for one brief day, Pass from my heart away, Je - sus is mine!
Left but a dis-mal void, Je-sus has sat-is-fied, Je - sus is mine!
Welcome, sweet scenes of rest, Welcome, my Saviour's breast, Je - sus is mine!

3 Hallelujah, He is risen!
Death for aye hath lost his sting,
Christ, Himself the Resurrection,
From the grave His own will bring:
||: He is risen,
Living Lord and coming King. :||

No. 181. O Crown of Rejoicing.

"Henceforth there is laid up for me a crown of righteousness." —2 Tim. 4: 8

Rev. J. B. ATCHINSON. P. P. BLISS, by per.

DUET.

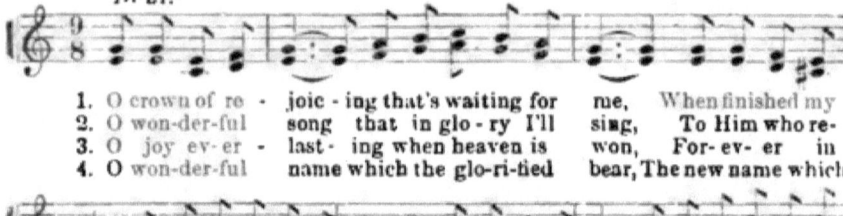

1. O crown of re - joic - ing that's waiting for me, When finished my
2. O won-der-ful song that in glo - ry I'll sing, To Him who re-
3. O joy ev - er - last - ing when heaven is won, For - ev - er in
4. O won-der-ful name which the glo-ri-fied bear, The new name which

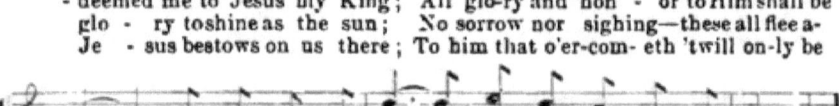

course, and when Jesus I see, And when from my Lord comes the sweet sounding
- deemed me to Jesus my King; All glo-ry and hon - or to Him shall be
glo - ry to shine as the sun; No sorrow nor sighing—these all flee a-
Je - sus bestows on us there; To him that o'er-com- eth 'twill on-ly be

word: "Re-ceive, faith-ful ser - - vant, the joy of thy Lord."
given, And prais- es un - ceas - ing for - ev - er in heaven.
- way, No night there, no shad - ows—'tis one end-less day.
given, Blest sign of ap - prov - al, our wel-come to heaven.

CHORUS.

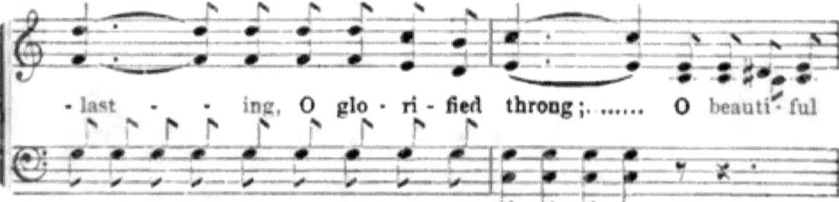

O crown of re- joic - - - ing, O wonderful song;...... O joy ev-er-
Crown of rejoicing, O wonderful, wonderful song;

- last - - ing, O glo - ri - fied throng;...... O beauti - ful
Joy ev - er- last- ing, O glo - ri - fied, glo - ri-fied throng;

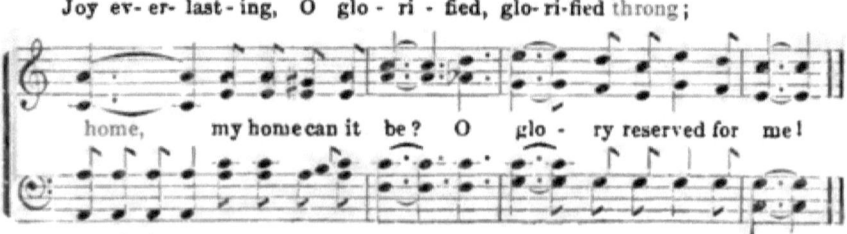

home, my home can it be? O glo - ry reserved for me!
Beautiful home,

No. 182.   **His Word a Tower.**

"As thy days, so shall thy strength be?"—DEUT. 33: 25.

ANON.   P. P. BLISS, by per.

1. While foes are strong and danger near, A voice falls gently on my ear:
2. With such a prom-ise need I fear, For all that now I hold most dear?

My Sav-iour speaks, He says to me, That "as my days my strength shall be."
No, I will nev-er anxious be, For "as my days my strength shall be."

CHORUS

His word a Tower to which I flee, For "as my days my strength shall be."

His word a Tower to which I flee, For "as my days my strength shall be."

3 And when at last I'm called to die,
   Still on Thy promise I'll rely;
   Yes, Lord, I then will trust in Thee,
   That "as my days my strength shall be."
     CHO —His word a Tower, &c.

We shall Sleep.—Concluded.

3 We shall sleep, but not for ever,
　In the lone and silent grave;
　Blessed be the Lord that taketh,
　Blessed be the Lord that gave.
　　　　Cho.

In the bright, eternal city
　Death can never, never come!
In His own good time He'll call us
　From our rest, to Home, sweet Home.
　　　　Cho.

No. 185. **Watchman, Tell Me.**

"Watchman, what of the night."—Isa. 21: 11.

Rev. SIDNEY S. BREWER.   Arr. by WM. B. BRADBURY.

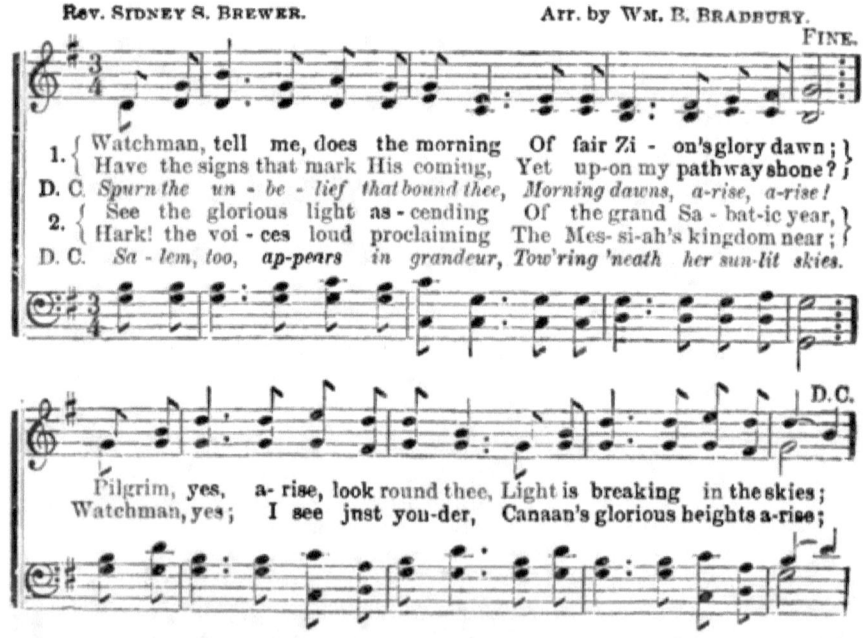

3 Pilgrim in that golden city,
　Seated in the jasper throne,
　Zion's King, arrayed in beauty,
　Reigns in peace from zone to zone;
　There, on verdant hills and mountains,
　Where the golden sunbeams play.
　Purling streams, and crystal fountains,
　Sparkle in th' eternal day.

4 Pilgrim, see! the light is beaming
　Brighter still upon thy way;
　Signs thro' all the earth are gleaming,
　Omens of thy coming day,
　When the last loud trumpet sounding,
　Shall awake from earth to sea,
　All the saints of God now sleeping,—
　Clad in immortality.

No. 186. Give me the Wings of Faith.

"Here we have no continuing city."—HEB. 13: 14.

Rev. I. WATTS, 1709.   Arr. by WALTER KITTREDGE.

1. Give me the wings of faith to rise, Within the vail, and see The saints a-bove, how great their joys, How bright their glo-ries be.
2. Once they were mourners here be-low, And pour'd out cries and tears; They wres-tled hard, as we do now, With sins, and doubts, and fears.

CHORUS.

Many are the friends who are waiting to-day, Happy on the golden strand,
Many are the voices calling us a-way, To join their glorious band.
Calling us a-way, Calling us a-way, Calling to the bet-ter land.

Repeat pp.

3.
I asked them whence their victory came:
They, with united breath,
Ascribe their conquest to the Lamb,
Their triumph to His death.
    Cho.—Many are the friends, &c.

162

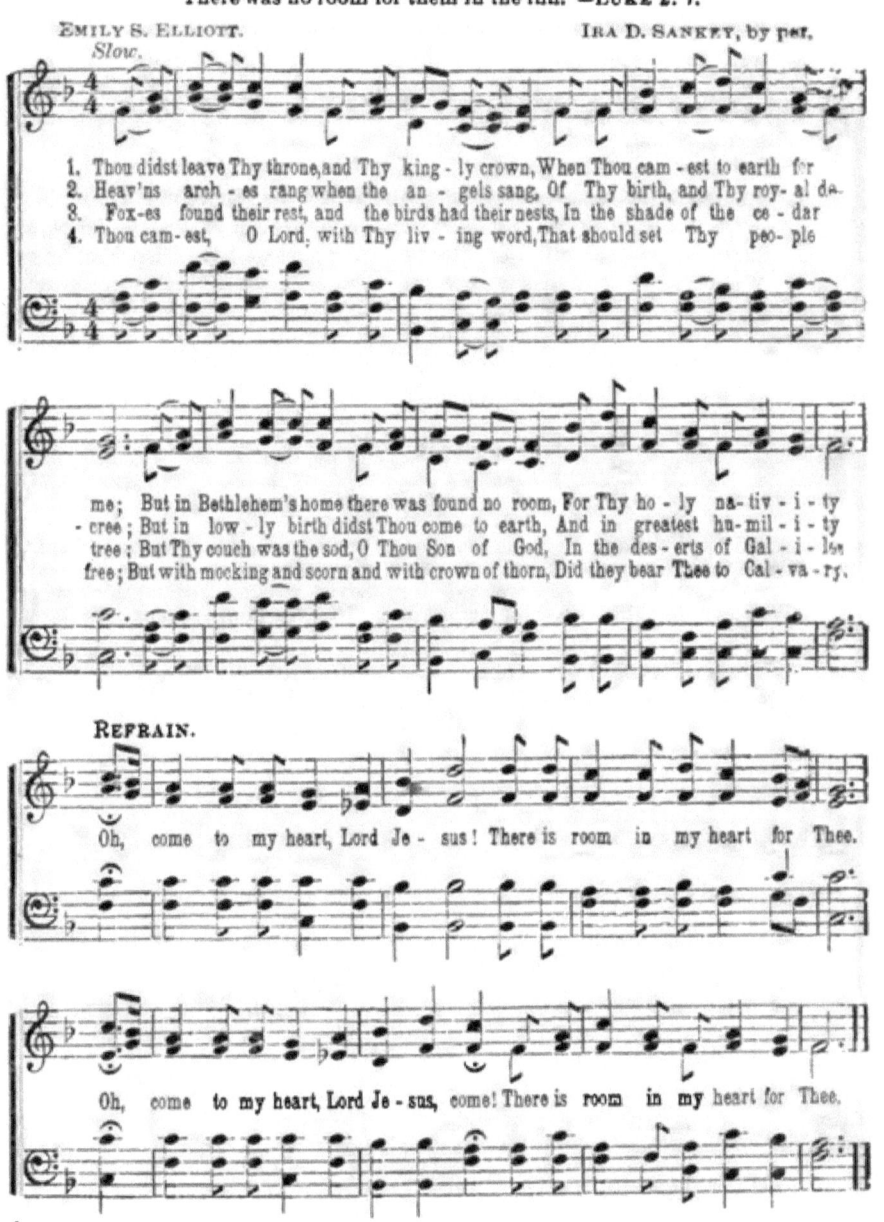

5 Heaven's arches shall ring, and its choirs shall sing,
    At Thy coming to victory,
  Thou wilt call me home, saying "yet there is room,"
    There is room at My side for thee.—Ref.

No. 189. **Home at Last.**

"In my Father's house are many mansions—I go to prepare a place for you."—John 14:2.
"And there shall be no more death, neither sorrow nor crying."—Rev. 21: 4.

Mrs. MARIA P. A. CROZIER.   IRA D. SANKEY, by per.

1. "Home at last" on heavenly mountains, Heard the "Come and en-ter in;"
2. Free at last from all tempta-tion, No more need of watch-ful care;
3. Saved to greet on hills of glo-ry Loved ones we have missed so long;
4. Welcomed at the pearl-y por-tal, Ev-er more a wel-come guest;

Saved by life's fair flowing fountains, Saved from earthly taint and sin.
Joy-ful in complete sal-va-tion, Given the vic-tor's crown to wear.
Saved to tell the sin-ner's sto-ry, Saved to sing redemption's song.
Welcome to the life im-mor-tal, In the man-sions of the blest.

REFRAIN.

"Home, sweet home," our home for-ev-er; All the pil-grim jour-ney past;

Slow.

Welcome home to wan-der, nev-er, Saved thro' Jesus—"Home at last."

No. 191. Come; for the Feast is Spread.

"Come; for all things are now ready."—LUKE 14: 17.

Rev. HENRY BURTON.   P. P. BLISS, by per

1. Come, for the feast is spread; Hark to the call!
Come to the Living Bread, Broken for all;
Come to His house of wine, Low on His breast recline,
All that He hath is thine; Come, sinner, come.

2. Come where the fountain flows— River of life—
Healing for all thy woes, Doubting and strife;
Millions have been supplied, No one was e'er denied;
Come to the crimson tide, Come, sinner, come.

3. Come to the throne of grace, Boldly draw near;
He who would win the race Must tarry here;
What-e'er thy want may be, Here is the grace for thee,
Jesus thy only plea, Come, Christian, come.

4 Come to the Better Land,
   Pilgrim, make haste!
Earth is a foreign strand—
   Wilderness waste!
Here are the harps of gold,
Here are the joys untold—
Crowns for the young and old;
   Come, pilgrim, come.

5 Jesus, we come to Thee,
   Oh, take us in!
Set Thou our spirits free;
   Cleanse us from sin!
Then, in yon land of light,
Clothed in our robes of white
Resting not day nor night,
   Thee will we sing.

No. 193. Refuge. 7s.

"The Lord also will be a refuge......in times of trouble."—Ps. 9: 9.

Rev. Charles Wesley, 1740.   Jos. P. Holbrook, by per.

1. Je-sus, lov-er of my soul, Let me to Thy bo-som fly,
While the near-er wa-ters roll, While the tem-pest still is high;
Hide me, oh, my Sav-iour hide, Till the storm of life is past;
Safe in-to the ha-ven guide, Oh, re-ceive my soul at last.

2. Oth-er ref-uge have I none, Hangs my help-less soul on Thee;
Leave, oh, leave me not a-lone, Still sup-port and comfort me:
All my trust on Thee is stayed, All my help from Thee I bring;
Cov-er my de-fenceless head With the shad-ow of Thy wing.

3 Thou, O Christ, art all I want;
  More than all in Thee I find:
Raise the fallen, cheer the faint,
  Heal the sick, and lead the blind:
Just and holy is Thy name,
  I am all unrighteousness;
Vile, and full of sin I am,
  Thou art full of truth and grace.

4 Plenteous grace with Thee is found—
  Grace to cover all my sin:
Let the healing streams abound;
  Make me, keep me, pure within,
Thou of life the Fountain art,
  Freely let me take of Thee:
Spring Thou up within my heart,
  Rise to all eternity.

Oh, what are You Going to Do?—Concluded.

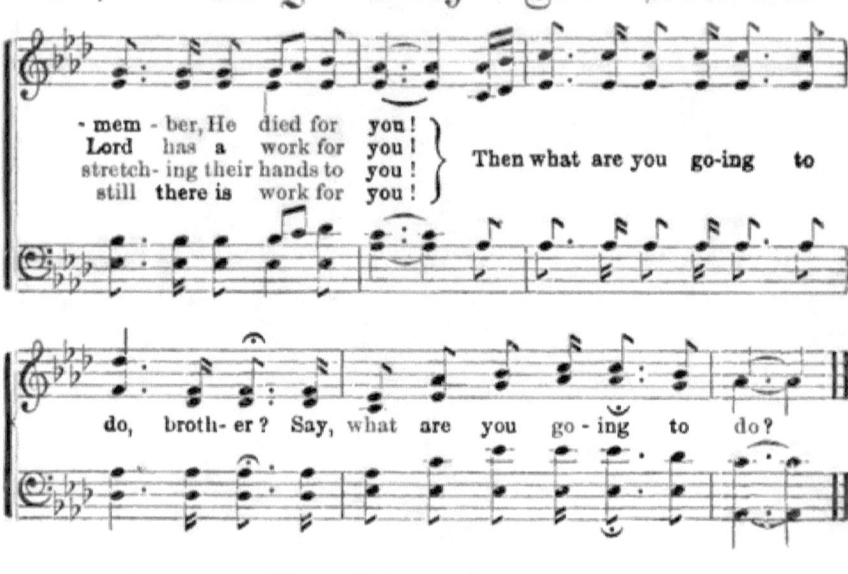

-mem - ber, He died for you!
Lord has a work for you!
stretch-ing their hands to you!
still there is work for you!

Then what are you go-ing to do, broth-er? Say, what are you go-ing to do?

No. 195. Art Thou Weary?

"Come unto me, and I will give you rest."—MATT. 11:28.

Rev. J. M. NEALE, trans.   Rev. HENRY W. BAKER, 1868.

1. Art thou wea-ry, art thou lan-guid? Art thou sore dis-tress'd?
2. Hath He marks to lead me to Him If He be my guide?

"Come to Me," saith One, and com-ing, Be at rest." A-MEN.
"In His feet and hands are wound-prints, And His side."

3 Is there diadem as monarch,
    That His brow adorns?
"Yes, a crown in very surety,
    But of thorns!"

4 If I find Him, if I follow,
    What my future here?
"Many a sorrow, many a labor,
    Many a tear."

5 If I still hold closely to Him,
    What hath He at last?
"Sorrow vanquished, labor ended,
    Jordan past."

6 If I ask Him to receive me,
    Will He say me nay?
"Not till earth and not till heaven
    Pass away."

No. 196. The Valley of Blessing.

"The valley of Berachah."—2 CHR. 20: 26.

Mrs. ANNIE WITTENMYER. WM. G. FISCHER, by per.

1. I have en-tered the val-ley of bless-ing so sweet, And Je-sus a-bides with me there; And His spir-it and blood make my cleansing complete, And His per-fect love cast-eth out fear.
2. There is peace in the val-ley of bless-ing so sweet, And plen-ty the land doth im-part, And there's rest for the weary-worn trav-el-er's feet, And joy for the sor-row-ing heart.
3. There is love in the val-ley of bless-ing so sweet, Such as none but the blood-wash'd may feel, When heaven comes down redeemed spir-its to greet, And Christ sets His cov-e-nant seal.
4. There's a song in the val-ley of bless-ing so sweet, That an-gels would fain join the strain, As with rap-tur-ous prais-es we bow at His feet, Cry-ing, Wor-thy the Lamb that was slain.

CHORUS.

Oh, come to this val-ley of blessing, blessing so sweet, Where Jesus will fullness bestow— And be-lieve, and re-

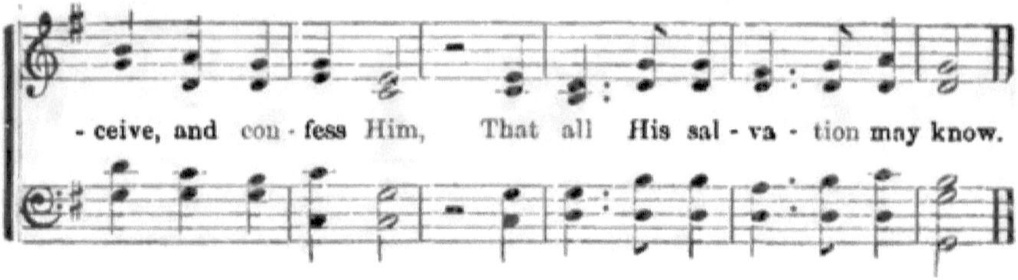

The Valley of Blessing.—Concluded.

-ceive, and con-fess Him, That all His sal-va-tion may know.

No. 197. Come, ye Disconsolate.

"Come unto me and I will give you rest."—MATT. 11:28.

THO'S. MOORE & THO'S. HASTINGS.   SAMUEL WEBBE.

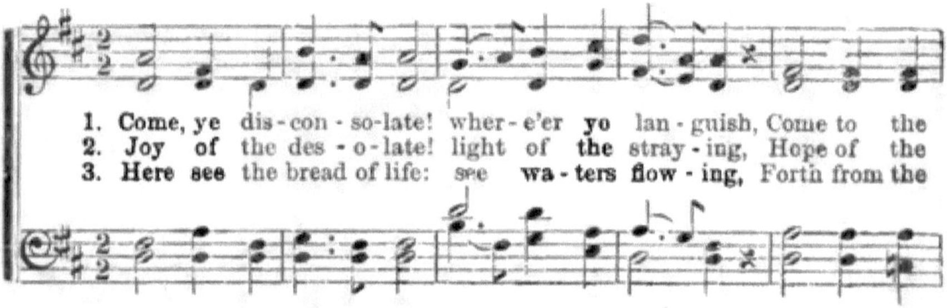

1. Come, ye dis-con-so-late! wher-e'er yo lan-guish, Come to the
2. Joy of the des-o-late! light of the stray-ing, Hope of the
3. Here see the bread of life: see wa-ters flow-ing, Forth from the

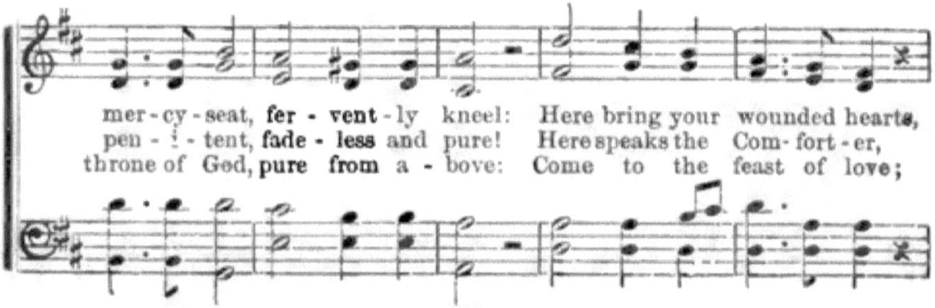

mer-cy-seat, fer-vent-ly kneel: Here bring your wounded hearts,
pen-i-tent, fade-less and pure! Here speaks the Com-fort-er,
throne of God, pure from a-bove: Come to the feast of love;

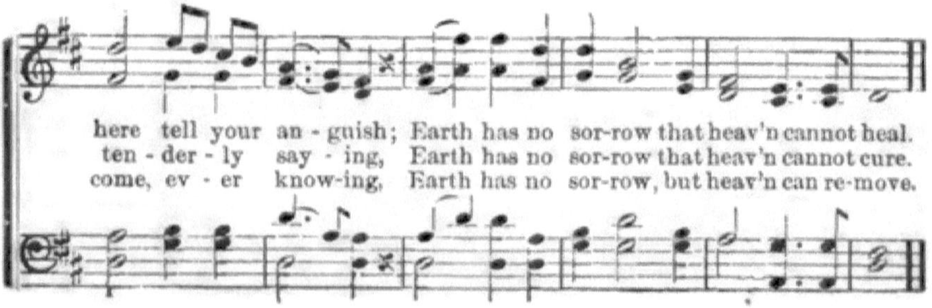

here tell your an-guish; Earth has no sor-row that heav'n cannot heal.
ten-der-ly say-ing, Earth has no sor-row that heav'n cannot cure.
come, ev-er know-ing, Earth has no sor-row, but heav'n can re-move.

No. 203.

Eternity!

"Remember how short my time is."—Ps. 89: 47.

Mrs. ELLEN M. H. GATES.   P. P. BLISS, by per.

1. Oh, the clanging bells of Time! Night and day they nev-er cease;
2. Oh, the clanging bells of Time! How their changes rise and fall,

We are wea-ried with their chime, For they do not bring us peace;
But in un-der tone sub-lime, Sounding clear-ly through them all,

And we hush our breath to hear, And we strain our eyes to see
Is a voice that must be heard, As our mo-ments on-ward flee,

Rit.   *Rallentando.*

If thy shores are drawing near,— E-ter-ni-ty! E-ter-ni-ty!
And it speak-eth aye one word,— E-ter-ni-ty! E-ter-ni-ty!

3 Oh, the clanging bells of Time!
   To their voices, loud and low,
In a long, unresting line
   We are marching to **and fro**;
And we yearn for sight **or sound**,
   Of the life that is to be,
For thy breath doth wrap us round,—
   Eternity! Eternity!

4 Oh, the clanging bells of **Time**!
   Soon their notes will all **be dumb**,
And in joy and peace sublime,
   We shall feel the silence come;
And our souls their thirst **will slake**
   And our eyes the King **will see**,
When thy glorious morn **shall break**
   Eternity! Eternity!

No. 205. **Expostulation.**

"Turn ye, turn ye—for why will ye die?"—Ezk. 33: 11.

J. H.   Rev. Josiah Hopkins, 1830.

1. Oh, turn ye, oh, turn ye, for why will ye die? When God in great
2. How vain the de-lu-sion, that while you de-lay, Your hearts may grow
3. The con-trite in heart He will free-ly receive, Oh! why will you

mer-cy is com-ing so nigh? Now Je-sus in-vites you, the
bet-ter your chains melt a-way; Come guilt-y, come wretched, come
not the glad mes-sage be-lieve? If sin be your bur-den, why

Spirit says, "Come," And an-gels are wait-ing to welcome you home
just as you are All help-less and dy-ing, to Je-sus re-pair.
will you not come? 'Tis you He makes welcome; He bids you come home

No. 206. **Cross and Crown.**

"And he bearing his cross, went forth."—John 19: 17.

Tho's. Shepherd.   Geo. N. Allen, 1849.

1. Must Je-sus bear the cross a-lone, And all the world go free?
2. The con-se-cra-ted cross I'll bear, Till death shall set me free;
3. Up-on the crys-tal pavement, down At Je-sus' piercéd feet,
4. O precious cross! O glorious crown! O res-ur-rec-tion day!

No, there's a cross for ev'-ry one, And there's a cross for me.
And then go home my crown to wear, For there's a crown for me.
With joy I'll cast my gold-en crown, And His dear name re-peat.
Ye an-gels, from the stars come down, And bear my soul a-way.

No. 207. There's a Light in the Valley.

"Though I walk through the valley • • • I will fear no evil."—Psa. 23: 4.

P. P. B.   P. P. Bliss, by per.

With Expression.

1. Through the val-ley of the shad-ow I must go, Where the cold waves of Jor-dan roll; But the promise of my Shepherd will I know, Be the rod and the staff to my soul. *(Slower.)* E-ven now down the val-ley as I glide, I can hear my Sav-iour *(A tempo.)* say, "Fol-low me!" And with Him I'm not a-fraid to cross the

There's a Light in the Valley.—Concluded.

2 Now the rolling of the billows I can hear,
   As they beat on the turf-bound shore;
   But the beacon light of love so bright and clear,
   Guides my bark, frail and lone safely o'er.
   I shall find down the valley no alarms,
   For my Saviour's blessed smile I can see;
   He will bear me in His loving, mighty arms,
   There's a light in the valley for me,
   There's a light, &c.

Out of the Ark.—Concluded.

3 O sinners, the heralds of mercy implore,
   They cry like the patriarch, "Come;"
The Ark of salvation is moored to your shore,
   Oh, enter while yet there is room!
The storm-cloud of Justice rolls dark over head,
   And when by its fury you're tossed,
Alas, of your perishing souls 'twill be said,
   "They heard—they refused—*and were lost!*"—*Cho.*

Waiting and Watching for Me.—Concluded.

4 Oh, should I be brought there by the bountiful grace
Of Him who delights to forgive,
Though I bless not the weary about in my path,
Pray only for self while I live,—
Methinks I should mourn o'er my sinful neglect,
If sorrow in heaven can be,
∥: Should no one I love, at the beautiful gate,
Be waiting and watching for me! :∥—Cha.

No. 211. Shirland. S. M.

TIMOTHY DWIGHT, D.D., 1800.　　　　　SAMUEL STANLEY, 1800.

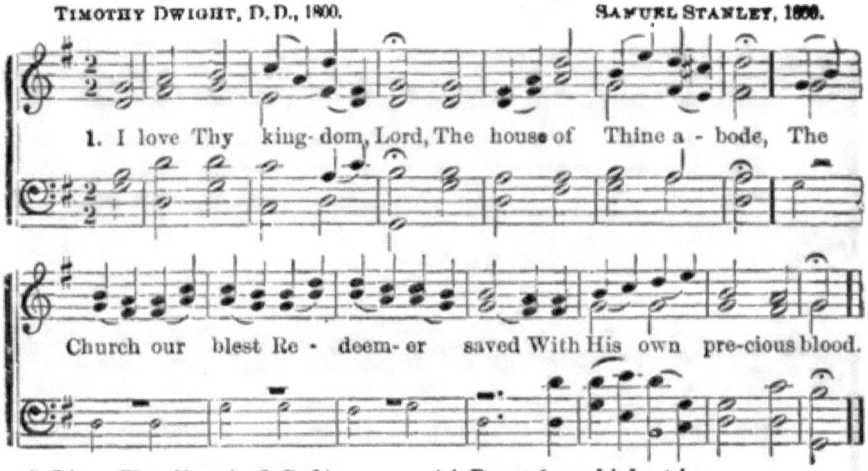

1. I love Thy king-dom, Lord, The house of Thine a-bode, The Church our blest Re-deem-er saved With His own pre-cious blood.

2 I love Thy Church, O God!
　Her walls before Thee stand,
　Dear as the apple of Thine eye,
　And graven on Thy hand.

3 For her my tears shall fall;
　For her my prayers ascend;
　To her my cares and toils be given,
　Till toils and cares shall end.

4 Beyond my highest joy
　I prize her heavenly ways;
　Her sweet communion, solemn vows,
　Her hymns of love and praise.

5 Sure as Thy truth shall last,
　To Zion shall be given
　The brightest glories earth can yield,
　And brighter bliss of heaven.

No. 212. Hebron. L. M.

TIMOTHY DWIGHT, D.D., 1800.　　　　　Dr. L. MASON, 1839.

1. While life prolongs its precious light, Mer-cy is found, and peace is given; But soon, ah, soon, approaching night Shall blot out ev'-ry hope of heaven.

2 While God invites, how blest the day!
　How sweet the Gospel's charming sound!
　Come, sinners, haste, O haste away,
　While yet a pard'ning God is found.

3 Soon, borne on times's most rapid wing,
　Shall death command you to the grave,—
　Before His bar your spirits bring,
　And none be found to hear or save.

4 In that lone land of deep despair,
　No Sabbath's heavenly light shall rise,—
　No God regard your bitter prayer,
　No Saviour call you to the skies.

5 Now God invites; how blest the day!
　How sweet the Gospel's charming sound!
　Come, sinners, haste, O haste away,
　While yet a pard'ning God is found.

No. 213. 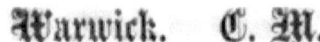 **C. M.**

Rev. JOHN NEWTON, 1779.   SAMUEL STANLEY.

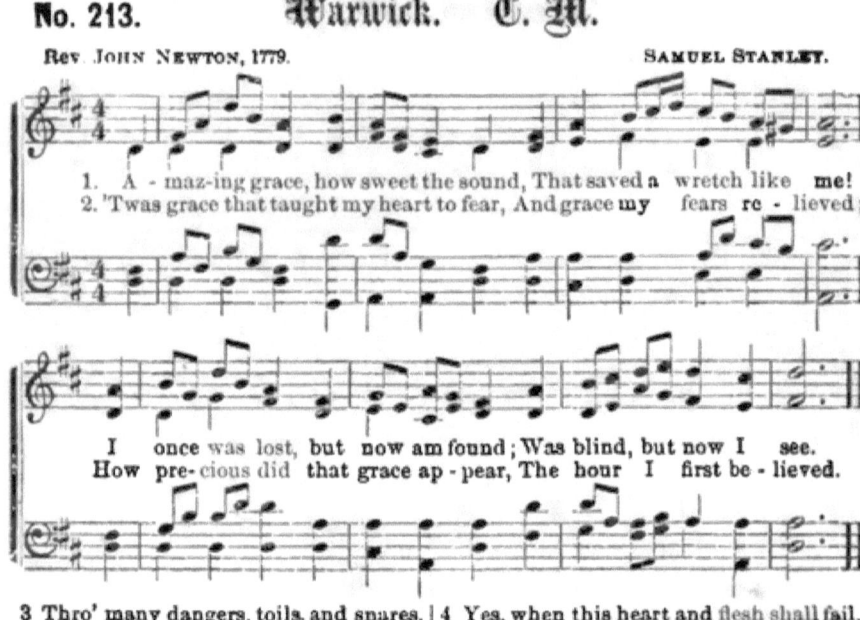

1. A-maz-ing grace, how sweet the sound, That saved a wretch like me! I once was lost, but now am found; Was blind, but now I see.
2. 'Twas grace that taught my heart to fear, And grace my fears re-lieved; How pre-cious did that grace ap-pear, The hour I first be-lieved.

3 Thro' many dangers, toils, and snares,
   I have already come;
'Tis grace that brought me safe thus far,
   And grace will lead me home.

4 Yes, when this heart and flesh shall fail,
   And mortal life shall cease,
I shall possess, within the vail,
   A life of joy and peace.

No. 214.  **7s.**

THOMAS SCOTT, 1773.   IGNACE PLEYEL.

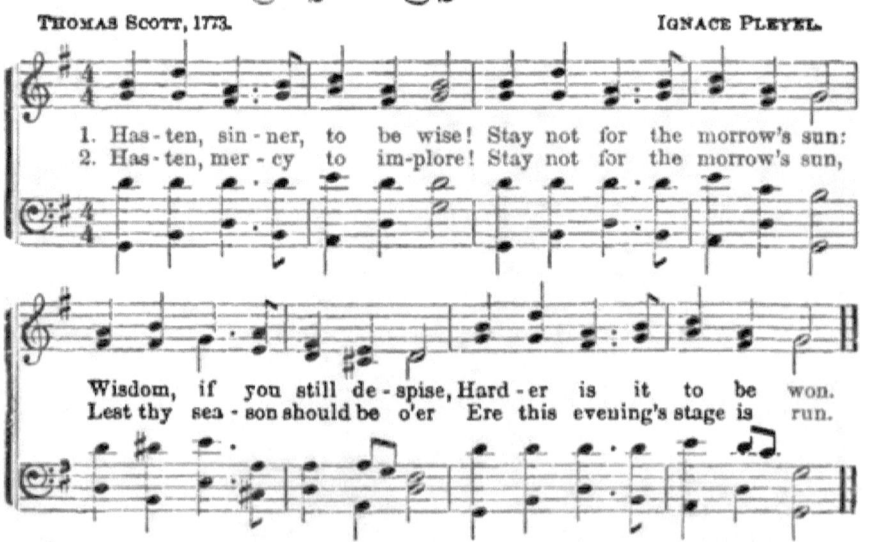

1. Has-ten, sin-ner, to be wise! Stay not for the morrow's sun: Wisdom, if you still de-spise, Hard-er is it to be won.
2. Has-ten, mer-cy to im-plore! Stay not for the morrow's sun, Lest thy sea-son should be o'er Ere this evening's stage is run.

3 Hasten, sinner, to return!
   Stay not for the morrow's sun,
Lest thy lamp should fail to burn
   Ere salvation's work is done.

4 Hasten, sinner, to be blest!
   Stay not for the morrow's sun,
Lest perdition thee arrest
   Ere the morrow is begun.

No. 215. Sessions. L. M.

"That the promise by faith might be given to them that believe."—GAL. 3:

A. D. 1531.   L. O. EMERSON, 1847.

1. Faith is a living pow'r from heaven Which grasps the promise God has giv'n;
   Se-cure-ly fixed on Christ alone, A trust that can-not be o'er-thrown.
2. Faith finds in Christ whate'er we need To save and strengthen, guide and feed;
   Strong in His grace it joys to share His cross, in hope His crown to wear.

3 Faith to the conscience whispers peace;
And bids the mourner's sighing cease;
By faith the children's right we claim,
And call upon our Father's name.

4 Such faith in us, O God, implant,
And to our prayers Thy favor grant
In Jesus Christ, Thy saving Son,
Who is our fount of health alone.

No. 216. Olive's Brow. L. M.

"My soul is exceeding sorrowful, even unto death."—MATT. 26: 38.

Rev. WM. BINGHAM TAPPAN, 1819.   WM. B. BRADBURY, 1855, by per.

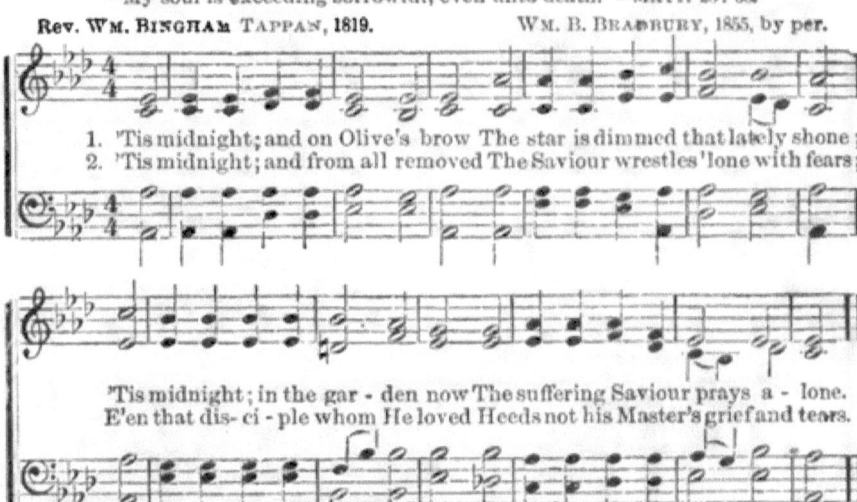

1. 'Tis midnight; and on Olive's brow The star is dimmed that lately shone;
   'Tis midnight; in the gar-den now The suffering Saviour prays a-lone.
2. 'Tis midnight; and from all removed The Saviour wrestles 'lone with fears;
   E'en that dis-ci-ple whom He loved Heeds not his Master's grief and tears.

3 'Tis midnight; and for others' guilt
The Man of Sorrows weeps in blood;
Yet He, who hath in anguish knelt,
Is not forsaken by His God.

4 'Tis midnight; and from ether-plains
Is borne the song that angels know;
Unheard by mortals are the strains
That sweetly soothe the Saviour's woe.

No. 217.   MENDON.   Key D.

1 Come, my soul, thy suit prepare,
  Jesus loves to answer prayer,
  He Himself has bid thee pray,
  Therefore will not say thee, nay.

2 Thou art coming to a King,
  Large petitions with thee bring,
  For His grace and power are such,
  None can ever ask too much.

3 With my burden I begin,
  Lord, remove this load of sin;
  Let Thy blood for sinners spilt,
  Set my conscience free from guilt.

4 Lord, I come to Thee for rest,
  Take possession of my breast,
  There Thy blood-bought right maintain-
  And without a rival reign.

  Rev. JOHN NEWTON, 1779.

No. 218.   P. M.   Key E.

1 There's a beautiful land on high,
  To its glories I fain would fly,—
    When by sorrows pressed down,
    I long for a crown,
  In that beautiful land on high.

CHO.—In that beautiful land I'll be,
    From earth and its cares set free;
      My Jesus is there,
      He's gone to prepare
    A place in that land for me.

2 There's a beautiful land on high,
  I shall enter it by and by;
    There, with friends, hand in hand,
    I shall walk on the strand,
  In that beautiful land on high.

CHO.—In that beautiful land I'll be,
    From earth and its cares set free;
      My Jesus is there,
      He's gone to prepare
    A place in that land for me.

3 There's a beautiful land on high,
  Then why should I fear to die,
    When death is the way
    To the realms of day,
  In that beautiful land on high.

CHO.—In that beautiful land I'll be,
    From earth and its cares set free;
      My Jesus is there,
      He's gone to prepare
    A place in that land for me.

4 There's a beautiful land on high,
  And my kindred its bliss enjoy,
    Methinks I now see
    How they're waiting for me,
  In that beautiful land on high.

CHO.—In that beautiful land I'll be,
    From earth and its cares set free
      My Jesus is there,
      He's gone to prepare
    A place in that land for me.

5 There's a beautiful land on high,
  And though here I oft weep and sigh,
    My Jesus hath said,
    That no tears shall be shed,
  In that beautiful land on high.

CHO.—In that beautiful land I'll be,
    From earth and its cares set free
      My Jesus is there,
      He's gone to prepare
    A place in that land for me.

6 There's a beautiful land on high.
  Where we never shall say " good-by "
    When over the river
    We're happy forever,
  In that beautiful land on high.

CHO.—In that beautiful land I'll be,
    From earth and its cares set free;
      My Jesus is there,
      He's gone to prepare
    A place in that land for me.

    JAMES NICHOLSON. 1852

No. 219.   THE SHINING SHORE.   Key G.

1 My days are gliding swiftly by,
    And I, a pilgrim stranger,
  Would not detain them as they fly
    Those hours of toil and danger.

CHO.—For O, we stand on Jordan's strand
    Our friends are passing over,
  And just before, the shining shore
    We may almost discover.

2 We'll gird our loins, my brethern dear,
   Our heavenly home discerning;
Our absent Lord has left us word,
   Let every lamp be burning.

CHO.—For O, we stand on Jordan's strand,
   Our friends are passing over,
And just before, the shining shore
   We may almost discover.

3 Should coming days be cold and dark,
   We need not cease our singing:
That perfect rest naught can molest,
   Where golden harps are ringing.

CHO.—For O, we stand on Jordan's strand,
   Our friends are passing over,
And just before, the shining shore
   We may almost discover.

4 Let sorrow's rudest tempest blow,
   Each chord on earth to sever;
Our King says Come, and there's our
     home,
   Forever, O forever.

CHO.—For O, we stand on Jordan's strand,
   Our friends are passing over,
And just before, the shining shore
   We may almost discover.
           REV. DAVID NELSON, 1835.

No. 220.   2s & 7s. Key C.

1 We are waiting by the river,
   We are watching by the shore,
Only waiting for the boatman,
   Soon He'll come to bear us o'er.

2 Though the mist hang o'er **the river,**
   And its billows loudly roar,
Yet we hear the song of angels,
   Wafted from the other shore.

3 And the bright celestial city,—
   We have caught such radiant gleams
Of its towers like dazzling sunlight,
   With its sweet and peaceful streams.

4 He has called for many a loved one,
   We have seen them leave our side;
With our Saviour we shall meet them
   When we too have crossed the tide.

5 When we've passed the vale of shadows,
   With its dark and chilling tide,
In that bright and glorious city
   We shall evermore abide.
           MISS MARY P. GRIFFIN.

No. 221.   TUNE—C. Y. V. NO. 24

1 My God I have found
   The thrice blessed ground,
Where life, and where joy, and Cr & comfort abound.

CHO.—Hallelujah! This the glory!
   Hallelujah! Amen!
   Hallelujah! Thine the glory!
   Revive us again

2 'Tis found in the blood
   Of Him who once stood
My refuge and safety, my surety with God.

CHO.—Hallelujah! Thine the glory!
   Hallelujah! Amen!
   Hallelujah! Thine the glory!
   Revive us again.

3 He bore on the tree
   The sentence for me,
And now both the surety and sinners are free.

CHO.—Hallelujah! Thine the glory!
   Hallelujah! Amen!
   Hallelujah! Thine the glory!
   Revive us again.

4 And though here **below**
   'Mid sorrow and woe,
My place is in heaven with Jesus I know

CHO.—Hallelujah! Thine the glory!
   Hallelujah! Amen!
   Hallelujah! Thine the glory!
   Revive us again.

5 And this I shall find
   For such is His mind,
"He'll not be in glory and leave me behind."

CHO.—Hallelujah! Thine the glory!
   Hallelujah! Amen!
   Hallelujah! Thine the glory!
   Revive us again.
           REV. JOHN CAMPBELL

No. 224. I've Found a Friend.

"A friend that sticketh closer than a brother."—Prov. 18: 24.

ANON.
GEO. C. STEBBINS, by per.

1. I've found a Friend; oh, such a Friend! He loved me ere I knew Him;
   He drew me with the cords of love, And thus He bound me to Him.
   And 'round my heart still close-ly twine Those ties which naught can sever,
   For I am His, and He is mine, For-ev-er and for-ev-er.

2. I've found a Friend; oh, such a Friend! He bled, He died to save me;
   And not a-lone the gift of life, But His own self He gave me.
   Naught that I have my own I call, I hold it for the Giv-er:
   My heart, my strength, my life, my all, Are His, and His for-ev-er.

3. I've found a Friend; oh, such a Friend! All pow-er to Him is given;
   To guard me on my on-ward course, And bring me safe to heav-en.
   Th' e-ter-nal glo-ries gleam a-far, To nerve my faint en-deav-or:
   So now to watch, to work, to war, And then to rest for-ev-er.

4. I've found a Friend; oh, such a Friend! So kind, and true, and ten-der,
   So wise a Coun-sel-lor and Guide, So might-y a De-fend-er!
   From Him, who loves me now so well, What pow'r my soul can sev-er?
   Shall life or death, or earth or hell? No; I am His for-ev-er.

He will Hide Me.—Concluded.

hide me In the shadow of His hand.
safely hide me In the shadow of His hand

No. 226. **Thine, Jesus, Thine.**

"I am thine."—Ps. 119: 94.

ENGLISH.   P. P. BLISS, by per.

1. Thine, Jesus, Thine, No more this heart of mine Shall seek its joy apart from Thee; The world is crucified to me, And I am Thine, And I am Thine.
2. Thine, Thine alone, My joy, my hope, my crown; Now earthly things may fade and die, They charm my soul no more, for I Am Thine alone, Am Thine alone.
3. Thine, ever Thine, Forever to recline On love eternal, fixed and sure, Yes, I am Thine forevermore, Lord, Jesus, Thine, Lord, Jesus, Thine.
4. Thine, Jesus, Thine, Soon in Thy crown to shine, When from the glory Thou shalt come And with Thy saints shall take me home, Lord, Jesus, come, Lord, Jesus, come.

My Redeemer.—Concluded.

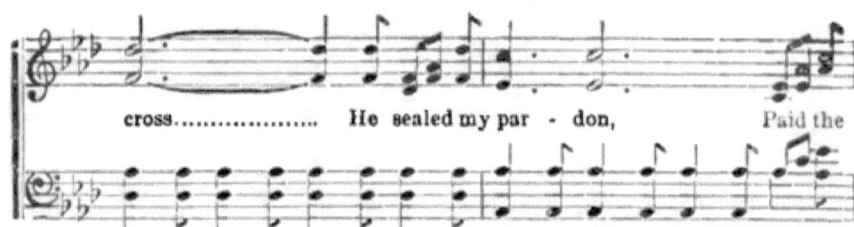

No. 230. Jesus Christ is Passing by.

"He heard that it was Jesus of Nazareth."—MARK 10: 47.

J. DENHAM SMITH. Mrs. JOS. F. KNAPP, by per.

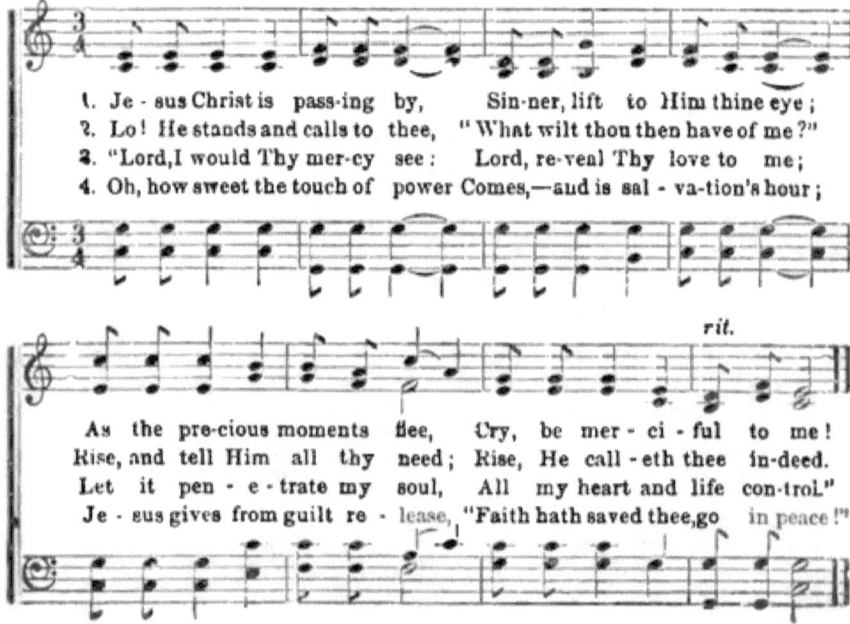

A Light upon the Shore.—Concluded.

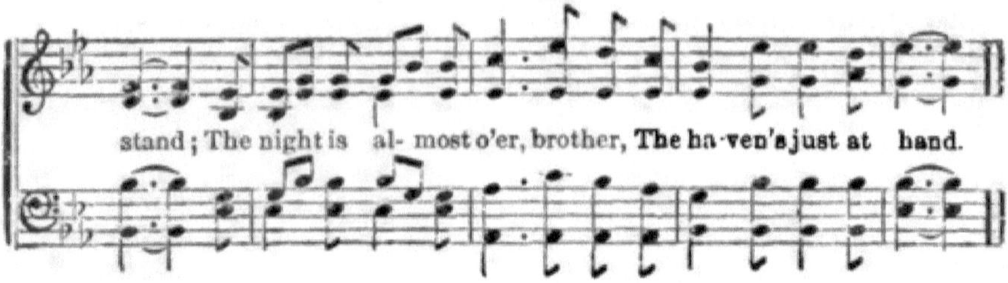

stand; The night is al-most o'er, brother, The ha-ven's just at hand.

No. 234.   **Consecration.**

"Ye are not your own."—1 Cor. 6: 19.

Miss Frances R. Havergal.   P. P. Bliss, by per.

1. Take my life and let it be Con- se- cra- ted, Lord, to Thee;
2. Take my feet and let them be Swift and beau- ti- ful for Thee;
3. Take my lips and let them be Fill'd with mes- sa- ges from Thee;
4. Take my mo-ments and my days, Let them flow in end- less praise;
5. Take my will and make it Thine, It shall be no lon- ger mine;
6. Take my love, my God, I pour At Thy feet its treas- ure store;

Take my hands and let them move At the im- pulse of Thy love.
Take my voice and let me sing Al- ways—on- ly—for my King.
Take my sil- ver and my gold, Not a mite would I with-hold.
Take my in- tel- lect and use Ev'- ry pow'r as Thou shalt choose.
Take my heart, it is Thine own, It shall be Thy roy- al throne.
Take my- self, and I will be Ev- er, on- ly, all for Thee.

Chorus, *after each stanza.*

All to Thee, all to Thee, Con- se- cra- ted, Lord, to Thee.

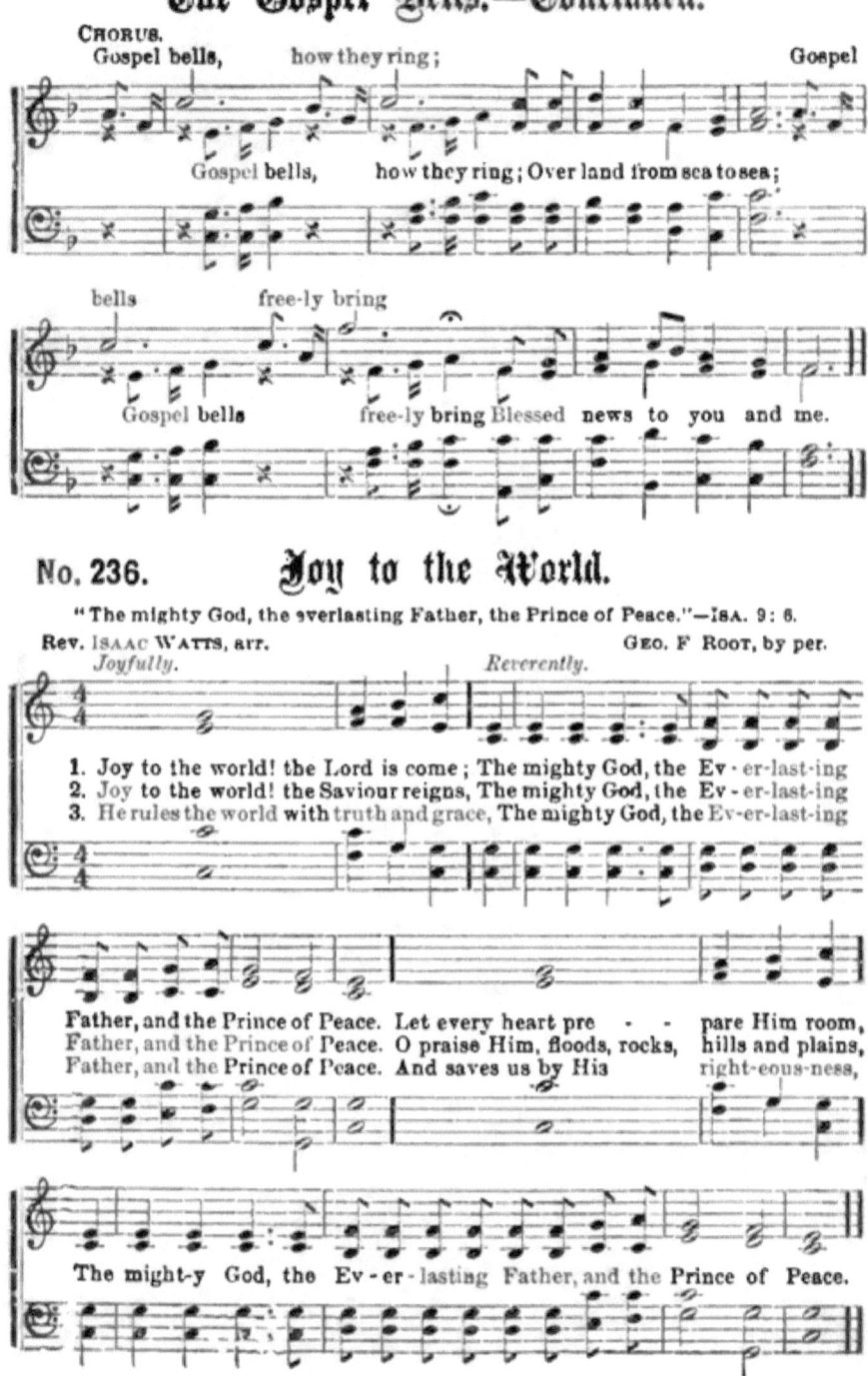

Ye must be Born again.—Concluded.

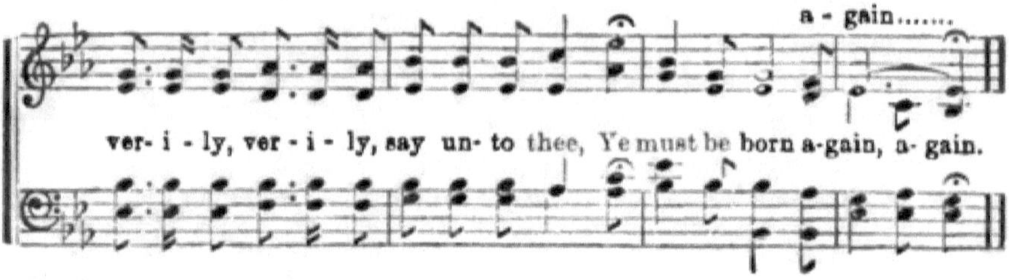

ver-i-ly, ver-i-ly, say un-to thee, Ye must be born a-gain, a-gain.

No. 238. **Cut it Down.**

"Cut it down, why cumbereth it the ground?"—LUKE 13: 7.

P. P. BLISS.   P. P. BLISS, by per.

Slow.

1. *Justice.* Cut it down, cut it down, Spare not the fruit-less tree!
2. *Mercy.* One year more, one year more, Oh, spare the fruit-less tree!
3. *Justice.* Cut it down, cut it down, And burn the worth-less tree!
4. *Mercy.* One year more, one year more, For mer-cy spare the tree!
5. Still it stands, still it stands, A fair, but fruit-less tree!

It spreads a harm-ful shade around, It spoils what else were useful ground,
Behold its branches broad and green, Its spreading leaves have hopeful been,
For oth-er use the soil prepare, Some oth-er tree will flour-ish there,
An-oth-er year of care bestow, On its fair form some fruit may grow,
The Mas-ter, seek-ing fruit thereon Has come—but, griev'd at finding none,

No fruit for years on it I've found, Cut it down, cut it down.
Some fruit thereon may yet be seen, One year more, one year more.
And in my vine-yard much fruit bear, Cut it down, cut it down.
If not—then lay the cumb'rer low, One year more, one year more.
Now speaks to Justice—Mer-cy flown—Cut it down, cut it down.

No. 239. **Christ Returneth.**

"I will come again, and receive you unto Myself."—JOHN 16: 3.

H. L. TURNER.   JAMES McGRANAHAN, by per.

1. It may be at morn, when the day is a-waking, When sunlight thro' darkness and shadow is breaking, That Jesus will come in the fullness of glory, To receive from the world "His own."
2. It may be at mid-day, it may be at twilight, It may be, perchance, that the blackness of mid-night Will burst into light in the blaze of His glory, When Jesus receives "His own."
3. While its hosts cry Ho-san-na, from heaven descending, With glorified saints and the angels attending With grace on His brow, like a halo of glory, Will Jesus receive "His own."
4. Oh, joy! oh, delight! should we go without dying, No sickness, no sadness, no dread and no crying, Caught up thro' the clouds with our Lord into glory, When Jesus receives "His own."

CHORUS.

O Lord Jesus, how long, how long Ere we shout the glad song, Christ returneth, Hal-le-lu-jah! hal-le-lu-jah! A-men, Hal-le-lu-jah! A-men.

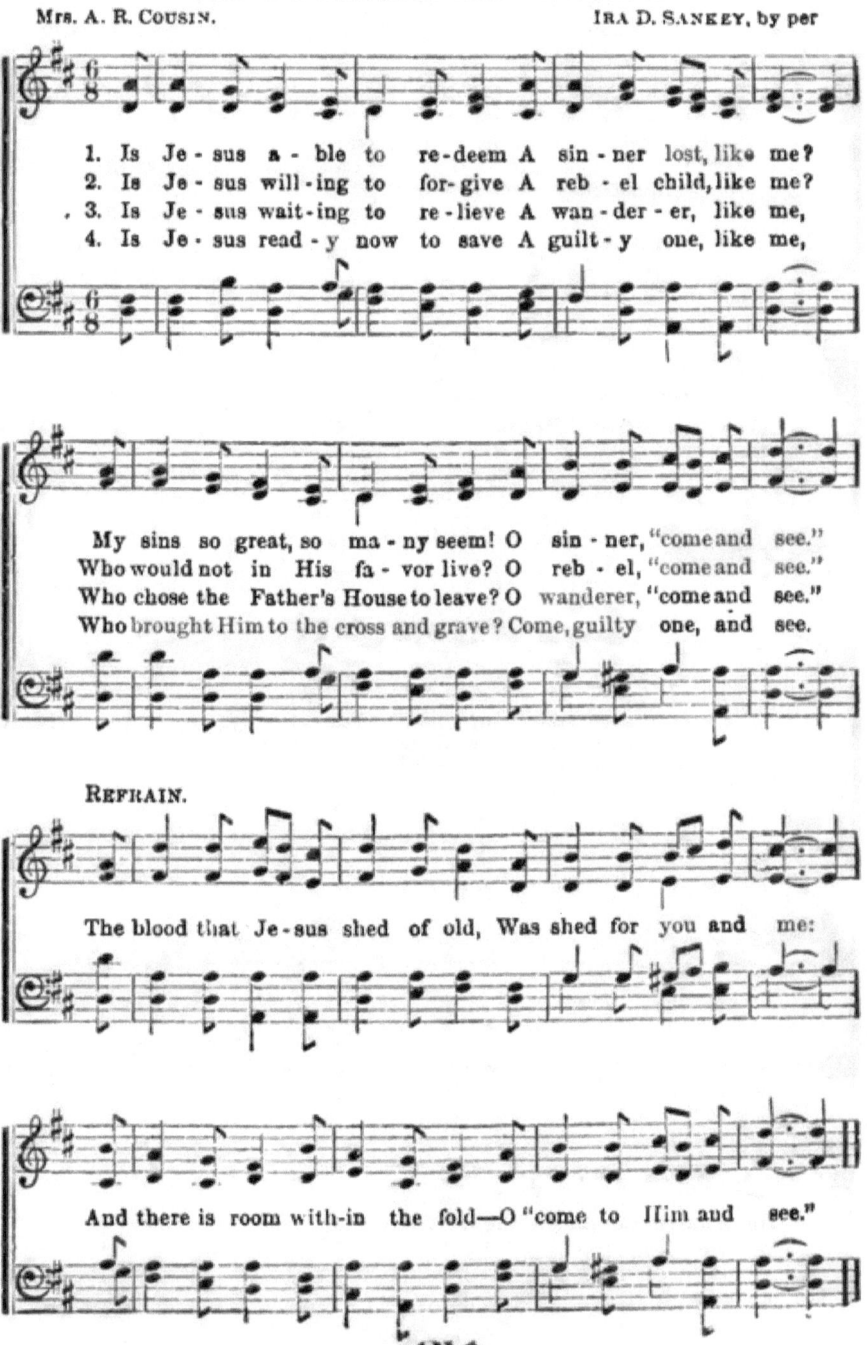

No. 244. How Happy are We.

"He that keepeth the law, happy is he."—Prov. 29: 18.

P. P. B.　　　　　　　　　　　　　　　　　　　　P. P. Bliss, by per.

1. Oh, how hap-py are we, Who in Je-sus a-gree, And ex-pect His re-turn from a-bove; We sit 'neath His vine, and de-light-ful-ly join In the praise of His ex-cel-lent love.

2. When u-nit-ed to Him, We par-take of the stream Ev-er flow-ing in peace from the throne, We in Je-sus be-lieve, and the spir-it re-ceive, That pro-ceeds from the Fa-ther and Son.

3. We re-mem-ber the word Of our cru-ci-fied Lord, When He went to pre-pare us a place, "I will come in that day and will take you a-way, And ad-mit to a sight of my face."

4. Come, Lord, from the skies And com-mand us to rise To the man-sions of glo-ry a-bove; With Thee to as-cend and e-ter-ni-ty spend, In a rap-ture of heav-en-ly love.

Chorus.

Oh, how happy are we Who in Je-sus a-gree, How happy, how happy are we.

No. 245. Blessed Hope.

"That ye sorrow not even as others which have no hope."—1 Thess. 4:13.

W. W. D.
James McGranahan, by per.

1. Bless-ed hope that in Jesus is giv-en, In our sor-row to cheer and sus-tain, That soon in the mansions of Heav-en, We shall meet with our lov'd ones a-gain.
2. Bless-ed hope in the word God has spo-ken, All our peace by that word we ob-tain; And as sure as God's word was ne'er bro-ken, We shall meet with our lov'd ones a-gain.
3. Bless-ed hope! how it shines in our sor-row, Like the star o-ver Beth-le-hem's plain, That it may be, with Him, ere the mor-row, We shall meet with our lov'd ones a-gain.
4. Bless-ed hope! the bright star of the morn-ing, That shall her-ald His com-ing to reign; Oh, the glo-ry that waits its fair dawn-ing, When we meet with our lov'd ones a-gain.

CHORUS.

Blessed hope,...... blessed hope,...... We shall meet with our lov'd ones again,

Blessed hope,...... blessed hope,...... We shall meet with our lov'd ones again.

Over the Line.—Concluded.

chant-ing the heav-en-ly strain: "O - ver the line,"—Why
should I re-main With a step between me and Je - sus?

4th v. "O - ver the line,"—I
will not re-main, I'll cross it and go to Je - sus?

No. 248. **Save, Jesus, Save!**

"Lord, save me."—MATT. 14: 30.

ANON.   GEO. C. STEBBINS.

1. Save, Je - sus, save! Thy bless-ing now we crave; For ev'-ry anx-ious
2. Save, Je - sus, save! Thy ban-ner o'er us wave, Of love e - ter - nal
3. Save, Je - sus, save! Thou conqueror o'er the grave, Give ev'-ry fet - tered
4. Save, Je - sus, save! And Thou a - lone shalt have The glo - ry of the

sin-ner here, Oh, let Thy mer-cy now appear, Lord Je-sus, save, Lord Je-sus, save!
and di-vine; O Lord, let each one here be Thine, Lord Jesus, &c.
soul re-lease, And to the troubled whisper "Peace." Lord Jesus, &c.
work di-vine, Yea, endless prais-es shall be Thine! Lord Jesus, &c.

3 The hill of Zion yields
   A thousand sacred sweets,
||: Before we reach the heavenly fields, :||
|: Or walk the golden streets. :||

4 Then let our songs abound,
   And every tear be dry;
||: We're marching thro' Immanuel's ground, :||
|: To fairer worlds on high. :||

No. 253. **I'll Stand by You.**

This song was suggested by a thrilling incident of a wreck and rescue at sea.
W. W. D.   JAMES McGRANAHAN, by per.

1. Fierce and wild the storm is rag-ing Round a help-less bark,
2. Wea-ry, helpless, hopeless sea-men Faint-ing on the deck,
3. On a wild and storm-y o-cean, Sink-ing neath the wave,
4. Dar-ing death thy soul to res-cue, He in love has come,

On to doom 'tis swift-ly driv-ing, O'er the wa-ters dark!
With what joy they hail their Sav-iour, As he hails the wreck!
Souls that per-ish heed the mes-sage, Christ has come to save!
Leave the wreck and in Him trust-ing, Thou shalt reach thy home!

CHORUS.
Joy,...... behold the Sav-iour, Joy,...... the message hear,

Joy, O joy, be-hold the Saviour, Joy, O joy, the message hear,

"I'll stand by un-til the morning, I've *come* to save you, do not fear," Yes,

I'll Stand by You.—Concluded.

I'll stand by until the morning, I've come to save you, do not fear, do not fear.

No. 254. **Saved by the Blood.**

"The blood of Christ cleanseth us from all sin."—1 John 1: 7.

FANNY J. CROSBY.   V. H. DOANE, by per.

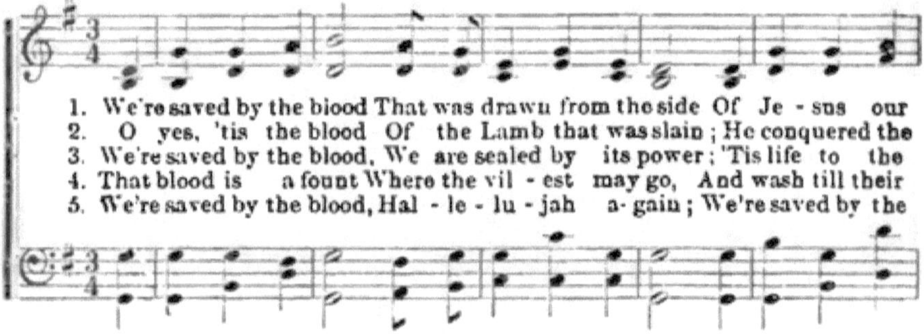

1. We're saved by the blood That was drawn from the side Of Je-sus our
2. O yes, 'tis the blood Of the Lamb that was slain; He conquered the
3. We're saved by the blood, We are sealed by its power; 'Tis life to the
4. That blood is a fount Where the vil-est may go, And wash till their
5. We're saved by the blood, Hal-le-lu-jah a-gain; We're saved by the

REFRAIN.

Lord, When He languished and died. Hal - le - lu - jah to God, For re-
grave, And He liv - eth a - gain.
soul, And its hope ev' - ry hour.
souls Shall be whi - ter than snow.
blood, Hal - le - lu - jah, A - men.

-demption so free; Hal-le-lu-jah, Hal-le-lu-jah, Dear Saviour, to Thee.

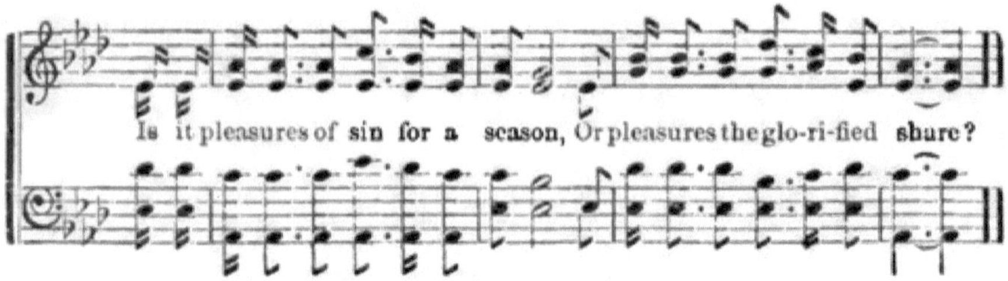

Come now saith the Lord.—Concluded.

Is it pleasures of sin for a season, Or pleasures the glo-ri-fied share?

No. 256.   **I'm going Home.**

"In my Father's house are many mansions."—JOHN 14: 2.

Rev. WILLIAM HUNTER.   Arr. by WILLIAM MILLER, M.D.

1. { My heav'nly home is bright and fair; Nor pain, nor death can en-ter there;
    { Its glitt'ring tow'rs the sun out-shine; That heav'nly man-sion shall be mine.
2. { My Fa-ther's house is built on high; Far, far a-bove the star-ry sky;
    { When from this earth-ly pris-on free, That heav'nly man-sion mine shall be.
3. { Let oth-ers seek a home be-low, Which flames devour, or waves o'er-flow,
    { Be mine a hap-pier lot, to own A heav'nly man-sion near the throne.
4. { Then fail this earth, let stars de-cline, And sun and moon re-fuse to shine,
    { All na-ture sink and cease to be, That heav'nly man-sion stands for me.

CHORUS.

I'm go-ing home, I'm go-ing home, I'm go-ing home to die no more,

To die no more, to die no more, I'm go-ing home to die no more.

No. 258.

Christ for Me.

"The Lord is my helper."—HEB. 13: 6.

R. G. H.   R. GEO. HALLS, by per.
Moderato—bold.

1. Whom have I, Lord, in heav'n but Thee? None but Thee! None but Thee!
2. I en-vy not the rich their joys, Christ for me! Christ for me!
3. Tho' with the poor be cast my lot, Christ for me! Christ for me!

And this my song thro' life shall be, Christ for me! Christ for me!
I cov-et not earth's glitt'ring toys, Christ for me! Christ for me!
"He know-eth best,"—I mur-mur not, Christ for me! Christ for me!

mf

He hath for me the wine-press trod, He hath redeemed me "by His blood,"
Earth can no last-ing bliss be-stow, "Fading" is stamped on all be-low;
Tho' "Vine and Fig-tree" blight assail, The "la-bor of the Ol-ive fail,"

f

And rec-on-ciled my soul to God, Christ for me! Christ for me!
Mine is a joy no end can know, Christ for me! Christ for me!
And death o'er flocks and herds pre-vail, Christ for me! Christ for me!

4 Tho' I am now on hostile ground,
   Christ for me! Christ for me!
And sin beset me all around,
   Christ for me! Christ for me!
Let earth her fiercest battles wage,
And foes against my soul engage,
Strong in His strength I scorn their rage,
   Christ for me! Christ for me!

5 And when my life draws to its close,
   Christ for me! Christ for me!
Safe in His arms I shall repose,
   Christ for me! Christ for me!
When sharpest pains my frame pervade,
And all the powers of nature fade,
Still will I sing thro' death's cold shade,
   Christ for me! Christ for me!

No. 259. Will Jesus Find us Watching?

"Watch therefore; for ye know not what hour your Lord doth come."—MATT 24:42.

FANNY J. CROSBY.   W. H. DOANE, by per.

1. When Jesus comes to reward His servants, Whether it be noon or night, Faithful to Him will He find us watching, With our lamps all trimm'd and bright?
2. If at the dawn of the early morning, He shall call us one by one, When to the Lord we restore our talents, Will He answer thee—Well done?
3. Have we been true to the trust He left us? Do we seek to do our best? If in our hearts there is naught condemns us, We shall have a glorious rest.
4. Blessed are those whom the Lord finds watching, In His glory they shall share; If He shall come at the dawn or midnight, Will He find us watching there?

REFRAIN.

Oh, can we say we are ready, brother? Ready for the soul's bright home? Say will He find you and me still watching, Waiting, waiting when the Lord shall come?

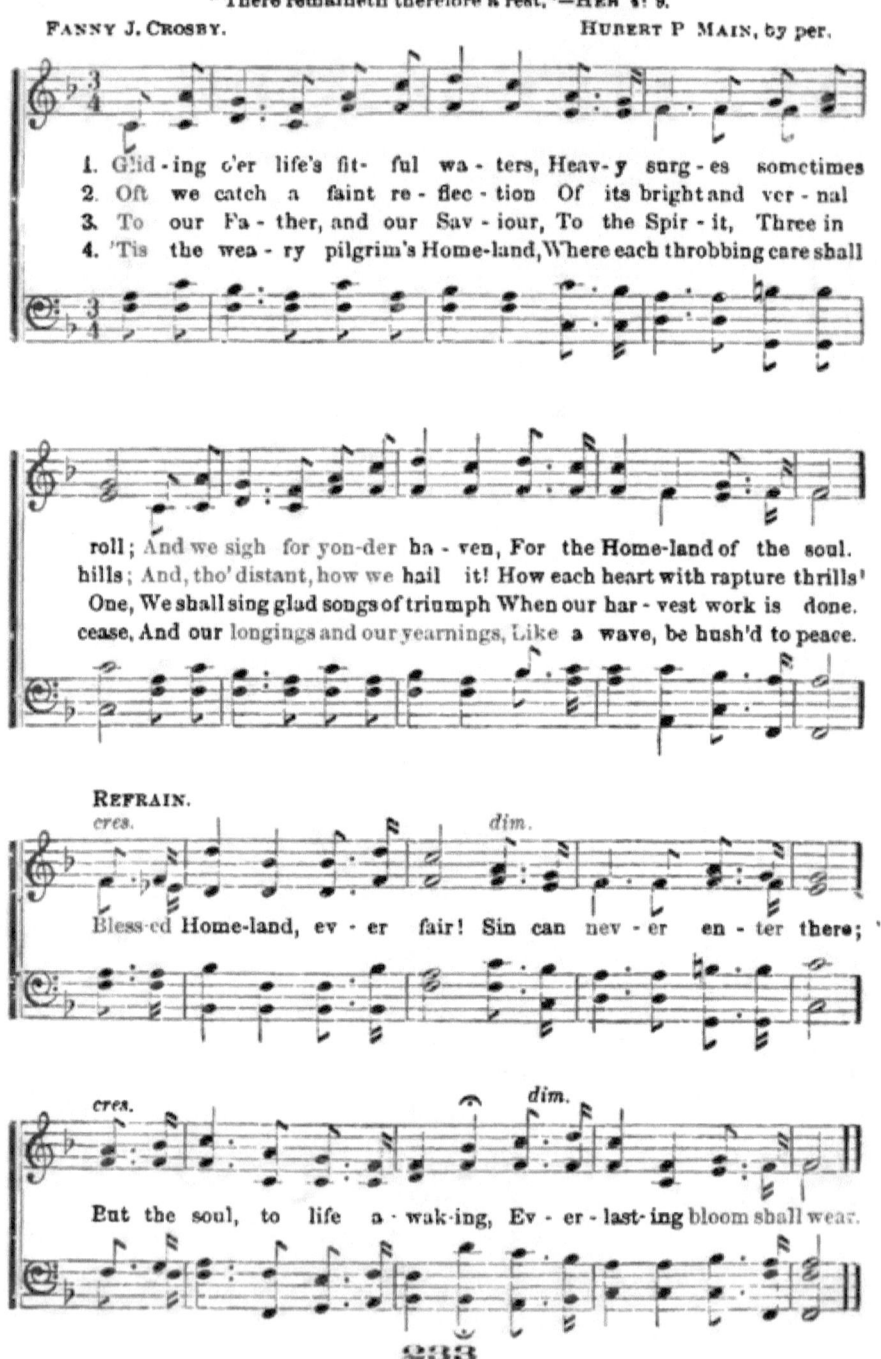

No. 264. The Heavenly Canaan.

"Thine eyes shall behold the land that is very far off."—ISA. 33: 17.

Rev. ISAAC WATTS.   WILLIAM HENRY OAKLEY, by per.

1. There is a land of pure de-light, Where saints immor-tal reign
2. Sweet fields, be-yond the swelling flood, Stand dress'd in liv-ing green
3. O could we make our doubts remove,—Those gloomy doubts that rise,—

E - ter - nal day ex-cludes the night, And pleas - ures ban - ish pain.
So to the Jews fair Ca- naan stood, While Jor- dan rolled between.
And see the Ca- naan that we love, With un - be-cloud - ed eyes,—

There ev - er-last - ing spring a- bides, And nev - er - fad-ing flow'rs ;
But tim' - rous mor- tals start and shrink To cross this nar- row sea,
Could we but climb where Mo- ses stood, And view the landscape o'er,—

Death, like a nar - row sea, di - vides That heavenly land from ours.
And lin - ger, trem-bling on the brink, And fear to launch a-way.
Not Jordan's stream, nor death's cold flood, Should fright us from the shore.

No. 267. The Hem of His Garment.

"If I may but touch his garment, I shall be whole."—MATT. 9: 21.

G. F. R.
GEO. F. ROOT, by per.

1. She on-ly touch'd the hem of His gar-ment As to His side she stole, A-mid the crowd that gath-er'd a-round Him, And straightway she was whole.
2. She came in fear and trem-bling be-fore Him, She knew her Lord had come, She felt that from Him vir-tue had healed her, The might-y deed was done.
3. He turn'd with "daugh-ter be of good com-fort, Thy faith hath made thee whole," And peace that pass-eth all un-der-stand-ing With glad-ness filled her soul.

CHORUS.

Oh, touch the hem of His gar-ment And thou, too, shall be free, His sav-ing pow'r this ver-y hour Shall give new life to thee.

No. 270. The Smitten Rock.

"They drank of that spiritual rock that followed them, and that rock was Christ."—1 Cor. 10: 4.

GEO. C. NEEDHAM.   IRA D. SANKEY, by per.

1. From the riv-en Rock there floweth, Liv-ing wa-ter ev-er clear;
2. "With-out mon-ey, with-out mer-it," Je-sus calls, "Come un-to Me."
3. Faint-ing in the des-ert, drear-y, Guilt-y sin-ner, hark! 'tis He!

Wea-ry pilgrim, journeying onward, Know you not that Fount is near?
Thirsty traveller, be en-couraged, Know you not the Fount is free?
'Tis the Sav-iour still en-treat-ing, Know you not He call-eth thee?

CHORUS.

Je-sus is the Rock of A-ges—Smitten, stricken, lo! He dies;
From His side a liv-ing fountain, Know you not it sat-is-fies?

No. 273. There is a Green Hill far away.

"And they took Jesus and led him away."—JOHN 19: 16.

Mrs. CECIL F. ALEXANDER.　　　　　　　　　　GEO. C. STEBBINS, by per.

1. There is a green hill far a-way, With-out a cit-y wall;
   Where the dear Lord was cru-ci-fied, Who died to save us all.
2. We may not know, we can-not tell What pains He had to bear;
   But we be-lieve it was for us He hung and suffered there.
3. He died that we might be forgiven, He died to make us good,
   That we might go at last to heav'n, Sav'd by His precious blood.
4. There was no oth-er good enough, To pay the price of sin;
   He on-ly could un-lock the gate Of heav'n and let us in.

CHORUS.

Oh! dear-ly, dear-ly has He loved, And we must love Him too;
And trust in His re-deem-ing blood, And try His works to do.

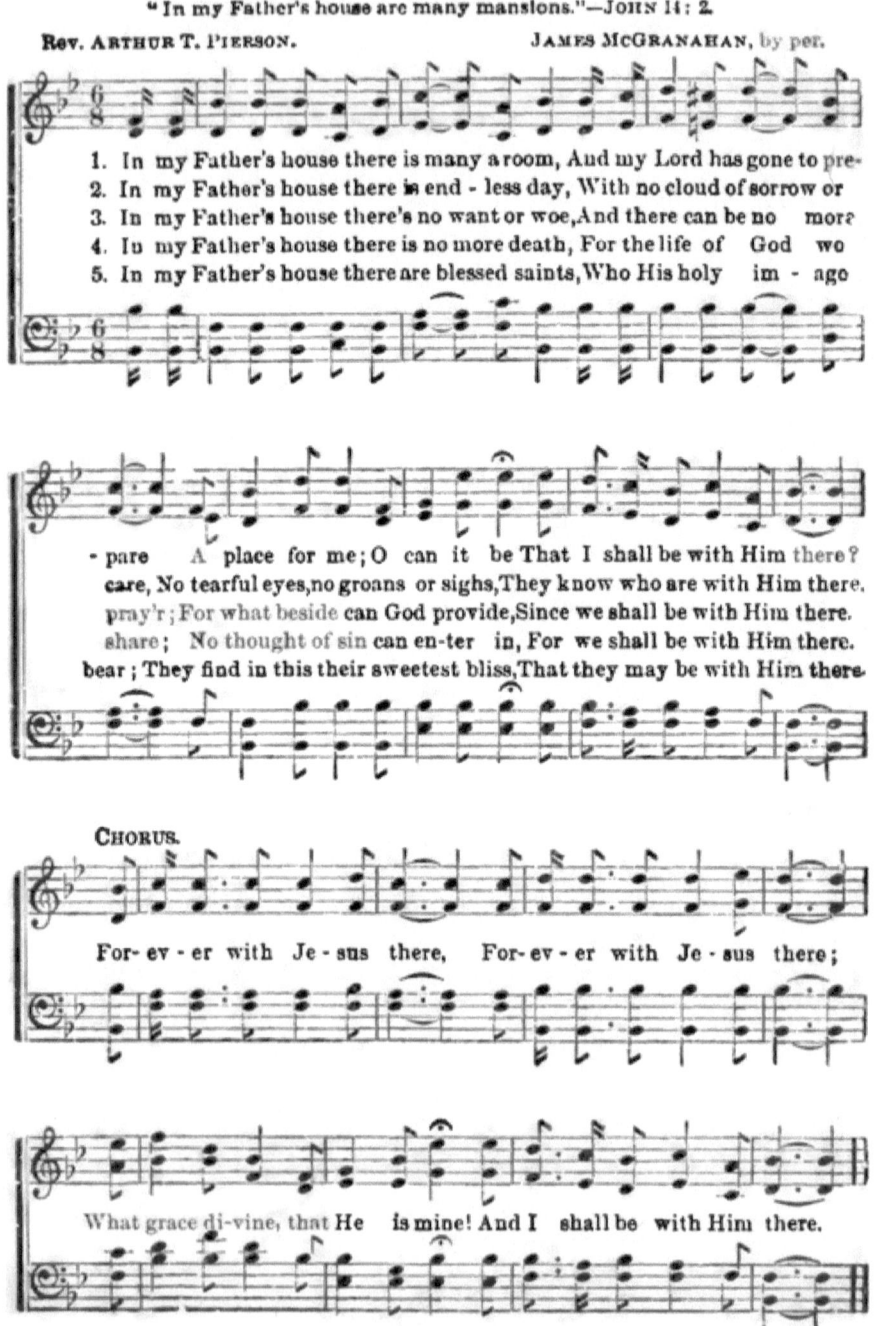

No. 275. **Ten Thousand Times.**

"The number of them was ten thousand times ten thousand."—Rev. 5:11.

Henry Alford, D.D.   Ira D. Sankey, by per.

1. Ten thousand times ten thou-sand, In sparkling rai-ment bright,
2. What rush of hal-le-lu-jahs Fill all the earth and sky!
3. O, then what rap-tured greet-ings On Canaan's hap-py shore!

The ar-mies of the ran-som'd saints Throng up the steeps of light;
What ring-ing of a thou-sand harps Bespeaks the tri-umphs nigh
What knitting sev-ered friendships up, Where partings are no more!

'Tis fin-ished, all is fin-ished, Their fight with death and sin;
O day, for which cre-a-tion And all its tribes were made!
Then eyes with joy shall spark-le, That brimm'd with tears of late;

Fling o-pen wide the gold-en gates, And let the vic-tors in.
O joy, for all its form-er woes A thou-sand-fold re-paid
Or-phans no lon-ger fa-ther-less, Nor wid-ows des-o-late.

REFRAIN.

Hal-le-lu-jah! Hal-le-lu-jah to the Lamb who once was

Ten Thousand Times.—Concluded.

slain! Hal-le-lu-jah! Hal-le-lu-jah to Him who lives a-gain!

Copyright, 1878, by Biglow & Main

No. 276. **Singing all the Time.**

"Then was our mouth filled with singing."—Ps. 126: 2.

Rev. E. P. HAMMOND.   GEO. C. STEBBINS, by per.

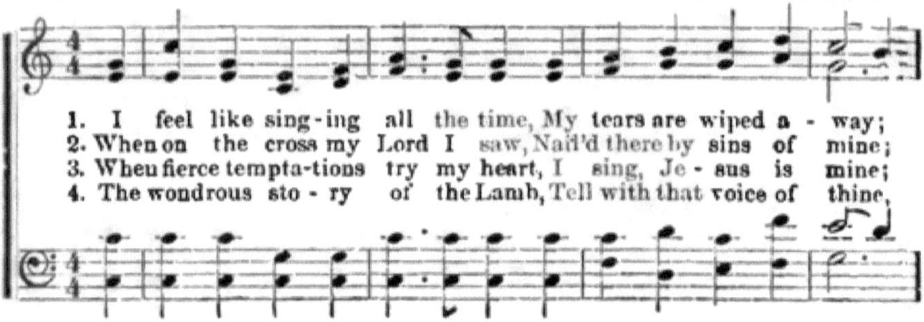

1. I feel like sing-ing all the time, My tears are wiped a-way;
2. When on the cross my Lord I saw, Nail'd there by sins of mine;
3. When fierce tempta-tions try my heart, I sing, Je-sus is mine;
4. The wondrous sto-ry of the Lamb, Tell with that voice of thine,

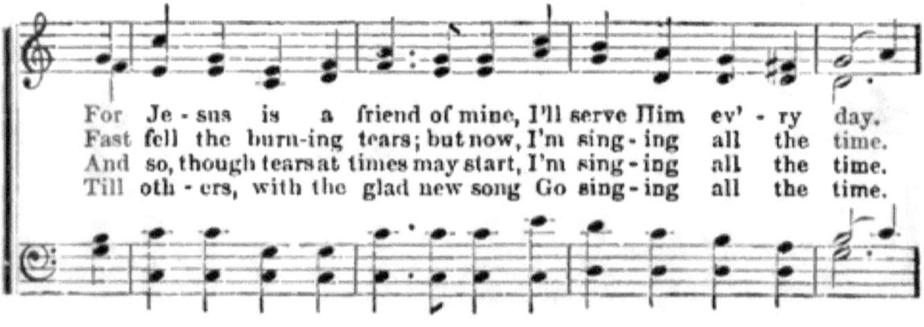

For Je-sus is a friend of mine, I'll serve Him ev'-ry day.
Fast fell the burn-ing tears; but now, I'm sing-ing all the time.
And so, though tears at times may start, I'm sing-ing all the time.
Till oth-ers, with the glad new song Go sing-ing all the time.

CHORUS.

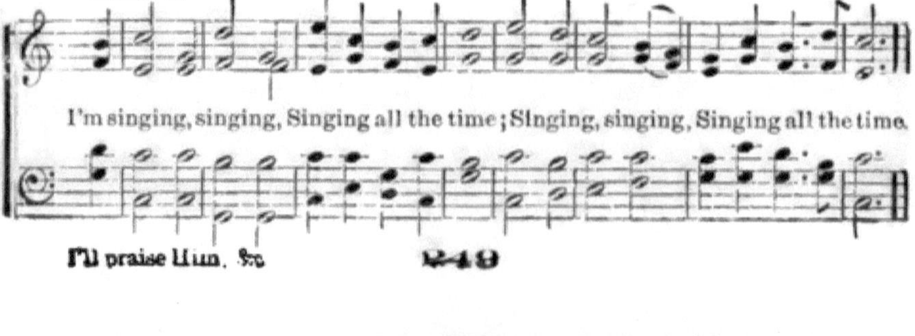

I'm singing, singing, Singing all the time; Singing, singing, Singing all the time.

I'll praise Him, &c.

No. 277. **Mine!**

"And all mine are thine, and thine are mine."—JOHN 17: 10.

E. L. B. *Alt.* JAMES McGRANAHAN, by per.

1. Mine! what rays of glory bright Now upon the promise shine!
I have found the Lord my light; I am His, and He is mine.

2. Mine! the promise often read, Now in living truth impress'd,
Once acknowledg'd in the head, Now a fire within the breast.

3. Mine! the promise cannot change, Mine! tho' oft my eyes are dim;
Naught can from His love estrange, Those who place their trust in Him.

4. Mine! tho' oft my hand may fail, *He* is strong and holds me fast;
By His blood I shall prevail, He shall lead me home at last.

5. Mine! when death the bars shall break,'Mid those glories all divine
"Satisfied" I shall awake, Clasp His feet, and call Him *mine*.

CHORUS.

Mine, oh, mine, Mine, oh, mine, Jesus Christ, my Lord and Saviour, I am His and He is mine!

No. 278. "Sing and Pray!"

Last words of a faithful minister of Christ, who recently died in the hope of the gospel.

MARY S. WHEELER.   P. P. BLISS, by per.

1. E-ter-ni-ty dawns on my vis-ion to-day, Gath-er round me my loved ones to sing and to pray;
The shadows are past, and the veil is withdrawn, Brightly now does the morn of e-ter-ni-ty dawn.

2. E-ter-ni-ty dawns! Oh, the glo-ries that rise, How they burst on my soul in its bliss-ful surprise;
With rap-ture the gleam of the cit-y I see, Where the crown and the man-sion are wait-ing for me.

CHORUS.
Hal-le-lu-jah! Hal-le-lu-jah! Hal-le-lu-jah, we sing! Je-sus conquered the grave, robbing death of its sting; Ho-san-na! a-gain let the glad anthem ring, "Sing and pray! Eter-ni-ty dawns!"

3 "Eternity dawns!" There will be no more night,
I am nearing the gates of the city of light;
The shadows of time are passing away,
Tarry not, O my Saviour, come quickly, I pray.

4 "Eternity dawns!" Earth recedes from my view;
Weeping friends, now farewell, I must bid you adieu;
I'm resting in Jesus, His merits I plead,
Fear ye not, "for my God shall supply all your need."

5 "Eternity dawns!" 'Tis a source of content,
That in preaching salvation my life has been spent;
'Tis "Jesus my All," and the Saviour of men,
May His grace be upon you forever. Amen.

Where is my Boy to-night?—Concluded.

heart o'erflows, for I love him, he knows; O where is my boy to-night?

No. 280. Only for Thee.

"To me to live is Christ."—PHIL. 1 : 21.

ELIZA ANN WALKER, 1884.   JAS. MCGRANAHAN, by per.

1. { Pre-cious Saviour, may I live, On - ly for Thee! Spend the powers Thou dost give On - ly for Thee!
   { Be my spir-it's deep de-sire On - ly for Thee! May my in-tel-lect as-pire On - ly for Thee!
2. { In my joys may I re - joice, On - ly for Thee! In my choic-es make my choice On - ly for Thee!
   { Meek-ly may I suf-fer grief, On - ly for Thee! Grateful-ly ac-cept re-lief, On - ly for Thee!
3. { Be my smiles and be my tears, On - ly for Thee! Be my young and ri-per years, On - ly for Thee!
   { Be my peace and be my strife On - ly for Thee! Be my love and be my life, On - ly for Thee!

CHORUS.

On - ly Christ who died for me Paid the price and made me free, Now, and thro' eterni-ty, On - ly for Thee!

No. 282. Wonderful Words of Life.

"The words that I speak unto you, they are spirit, and they are life."—JOHN 6: 61.

P. P. B.
P. P. BLISS, by per.

1. Sing them o-ver a-gain to me, Won-der-ful words of Life; Let me more of their beau-ty see, Won-der-ful words of Life. Words of life and beau-ty, Teach me faith and du-ty;
2. Christ, the bless-ed One, gives to all Won-der-ful words of Life; Sin-ner, list to the lov-ing call, Won-der-ful words of Life. All so free-ly giv-en, Woo-ing us to heav-en.
3. Sweet-ly ech-o the gos-pel call, Won-der-ful words of Life; Of-fer par-don and peace to all, Won-der-ful words of Life. Je-sus, on-ly Sav-iour, Sanc-ti-fy for-ev-er

Beau-ti-ful words, wonderful words, Wonderful words of Life, Life.

No. 283. What must it be to be There?

"There shall be no more death, neither sorrow, nor crying."—Rev. 21:4

Mrs. Elizabeth Mills.   Geo. C. Stebbins, by per.

DUET.

1. We speak of the land of the blest, A coun-try so bright and so fair, And oft are its glo-ries con-fest, But what must it be to be there?
2. We speak of its path-ways of gold, Its walls deck'd with jew-els so rare, Its won-ders and pleas-ures un-told, But what must it be to be there?
3. We speak of its peace and its love, The robes which the glo-ri-fied wear, The songs of the bless-ed a-bove, But what must it be to be there?
4. We speak of its free-dom from sin, From sor-row, temp-ta-tion and care, From tri-als with-out and with-in, But what must it be to be there?
5. Do Thou, Lord, midst pleas-ure or woe, For heav-en our spir-its pre-pare, Then short-ly we al-so shall know, And *feel* what it is to be there!

REFRAIN.

To be there, to be there, Oh, what must it be to be there?
To be there, to be there, to be there?
To be there, to be there, Oh, what must it be to be there?
To be there, to be there, to be there

No. 285. There's a Work for each of Us.

"For the Son of man is as a man taking a far journey, who left his home, and gave authority to his servants, and to every man his work."—MARK 13: 34.

A. A. A.
JAMES McGRANAHAN, by per.

1. Our Master has taken His jour-ney To a country that's far a - way,
2. In this "little while," doth it matter, As we work, and we watch, and we wait,
3. There's only one thing should concern us, To find just the task that is ours;
4. Our Master is coming most sure - ly, To reckon with ev'-ry one;

And has left us the care of the vineyard, To work for Him day by day.
If we're filling the place He assigns us, Be its ser - vice small or great.
And then, having found it, to *do* it With all our God-given pow'rs.
Shall we *then*, count our toil or our sorrow, If His sentence be, "Well done."

CHORUS.

There's a work for me and a work for you, Something for each of us now to do,

Yes, a work for me and a work for you, Something for each of us now to do.

No. 289. Triumph By and By.

"I press toward the mark."—PHIL. 3: 14.

Dr. C. R. BLACKALL. H. R. PALMER, by per.

1. The prize is set be-fore us, To win, His words implore us, The eye of God is o'er us From on high, from on high; His lov-ing tones are call-ing While sin is dark, ap-pall-ing, 'Tis Je-sus gen-tly call-ing, He is nigh, He is nigh.

2. We'll fol-low where He lead-eth, We'll pas-ture where He feed-eth, We'll yield to Him who plead-eth From on high, from on high; Then naught from Him shall sev-er, Our hope shall brighten ev-er, And faith shall fail us nev-er, He is nigh, He is nigh.

3. Our home is bright a-bove us, No tri-als dark to move us, But Je-sus dear to love us There on high, there on high; We'll give Him best en-deav-or, And praise His name for-ev-er, His pre-cious words can nev-er, Nev-er die, nev-er die.

CHORUS.

By and by we shall meet Him, By and by we shall greet Him, And with

Triumph By and By.—Concluded.

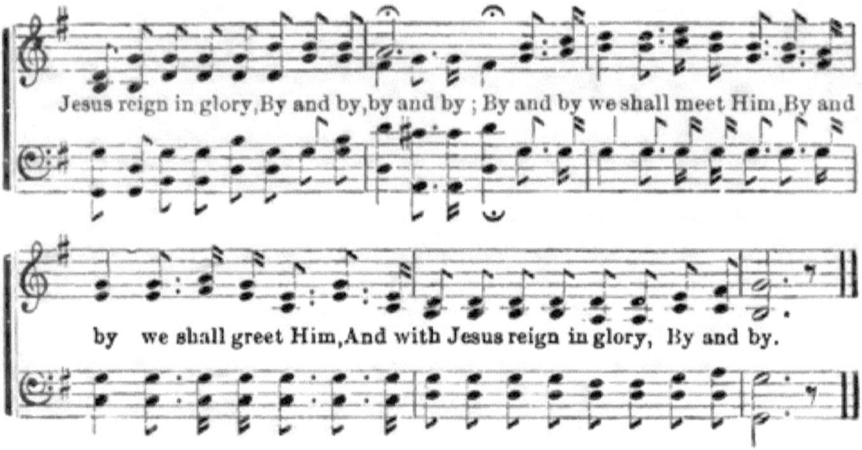

Jesus reign in glory, By and by, by and by; By and by we shall meet Him, By and by we shall greet Him, And with Jesus reign in glory, By and by.

No. 290. **I am Trusting Thee.**

"Trusting in the Lord."—Ps. 112:7.

Miss FRANCES R. HAVERGAL.   IRA D. SANKEY, by per.

1. I am trusting Thee, Lord Jesus, Trusting only Thee! Trusting Thee for full salvation, Great and free.
2. I am trusting Thee for pardon, At Thy feet I bow; For Thy grace and tender mercy Trusting now.
3. I am trusting Thee for cleansing In the crimson flood; Trusting Thee to make me holy By Thy blood.
4. I am trusting Thee to guide me, Thou alone shalt lead, Ev'ry day and hour supplying All my need.
5. I am trusting Thee for power; Thine can never fail; Words which Thou Thyself shalt give me Must prevail.
6. I am trusting Thee, Lord Jesus, Never let me fall! I am trusting Thee forever And for all!

Good News.—Concluded.

To guilt-y sin-ners thro' the blood Of the In-car-nate Son of God.

No. 292.   **Evening Prayer.**

"Bless me—O my Father."—GEN. 27 : 38.

J. EDMESTON.   GEO. C. STEBBINS, by per.

1. Sav - iour, breathe an eve - ning bless - ing, Ere re-
2. Tho' de - struc - tion walk a - round us, Tho' the
3. Tho' the night be dark and drear - y, Dark - ness
4. Should swift death this night o'er - take us, And our

- pose our spir - its seal: Sin and want we
ar - rows past us fly; An - gel - guards from
can - not hide from Thee; Thou art He who,
couch be - come our tomb, May the morn in

come con - fess - ing, Thou canst save and Thou canst heal.
Thee sur - round us, We are safe if Thou art nigh.
nev - er wea - ry, Watch - est where Thy peo - ple be.
heaven a - wake us, Clad in bright and death - less bloom.

Sound the High Praises.—Concluded.

Je - sus our King, He came and He conquer'd, His vic-to-ry sing.

No. 294.   **Pressing On.**

"There remaineth therefore a rest."—HEB. 4: 9.

HORATIUS BONAR, D. D.   GEO. C. STEBBINS, by per.

1. This is the day of toil Beneath earth's sultry noon, This is the day of service true, But resting cometh soon.
2. Spend and be spent would we, While lasteth time's brief day; No turning back in coward fear, No lingering by the way.
3. Onward we press in haste, Upward our journey still; Ours is the path the Master trod Thro' good report and ill.
4. The way may rougher grow, The weariness increase, We gird our loins and hasten on,—The end, the end is peace.

CHORUS.

Hal-le-lu-jah! Hal-le-lu-jah! There remains a rest for us. Hal-le-lu-jah! Hal-le-lu-jah! There remains a rest for us.

There is Joy.—Concluded.

wan-der'd, Comes with-in the Sav-iour's fold.
wander'd, long has wander'd,

No. 296. Over the Ocean Wave.

"I will give thee the heathen for thine inheritance."—Ps. 2: 8.

ANON. (MISSIONARY.) Wm. B. BRADBURY, by pr.

1. O - ver the o - cean wave, far, far a - way, There the poor
2. Here in this hap - py land we have the light Shin - ing from
3. Then, while the mis - sion ships glad tid - ings bring, List! as that

CHORUS.—Pit - y them, pit - y them, Christians at home, Haste with the

hea - then live, wait - ing for day; Grop - ing in ig - norance,
God's own word, free, pure, and bright; Shall we not send to them
hea - then band joy - ful - ly sing, "O - ver the o - cean wave,

bread of life, has - ten and come.

D. C. CHORUS.

dark as the night, No bless - ed Bi - ble to give them the light.
Bi - bles to read, Teachers, and preachers, and all that they need?
oh, see them come, Bring-ing the bread of life, guid - ing us home."

Memories of Earth.—Concluded.

own; For the love so strong and ten-der, That redeem'd and bro't us home.

No. 298. Must I Go and Empty Handed?

After a month only of Christian life, nearly all of it upon a sick bed, a young man of nearly 30 years lay dying. Suddenly a look of sadness crossed his face, and to the query of a friend he exclaimed: "No, I am not afraid, Jesus saves me now; but oh, must I go and empty handed?"

C. C. LUTHER. (DAN. 12: 3.) GEO. C. STEBBINS, by per.

DUET.

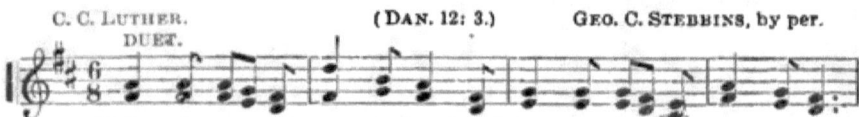

1. "Must I go and emp-ty hand-ed," Thus my dear Re-deem-er meet?
2. Not at death I shrink nor fal-ter, For my Sav-iour saves me now;
3. Oh, the years of sin-ning wast-ed, Could I but re-call them now,
4. Oh, ye saints, a-rouse, be earn-est, Up and work while yet 'tis day,

Not one day of ser-vice give Him, Lay no tro-phy at His feet.
But to meet Him emp-ty hand-ed, Tho't of that now clouds my brow.
I would give them to my Sav-iour, To His will I'd glad-ly bow.
Ere the night of death o'er-takes thee, Strive for souls while still you may.

CHORUS.

"Must I go and emp-ty hand-ed," Must I meet my Sav-iour so?

Not one soul with which to great Him, Must I emp-ty hand-ed go?

No. 299. **My Faith still Clings.**

"Watch, stand fast in the faith."—Rom. 14:1.

Rev. H. F. Colby.   W. H. Doane, by per.

1. My sin is great, my strength is weak, My path be-set with snares:
2. The world is dark with-out Thee, Lord, I turn me from its strife
3. Temp-ta-tions lure and fears as-sail My frail, in-con-stant heart
4. Un-fold Thy pre-cepts to my mind, And cleanse my blind-ed eyes;

But Thou, O Christ, hast died for me, And Thou wilt hear my prayers.
To find Thy love a sweet re-lief; Thou art the light of life.
But pre-cious are Thy prom-is-es, And they new strength impart.
Grant me to work for Thee on earth, Then praise Thee in the skies.

REFRAIN.

To Thee, to Thee, the Cru-ci-fied, The sin-ner's on-ly plea,

Re-ly-ing on Thy promised grace, My faith still clings to Thee.

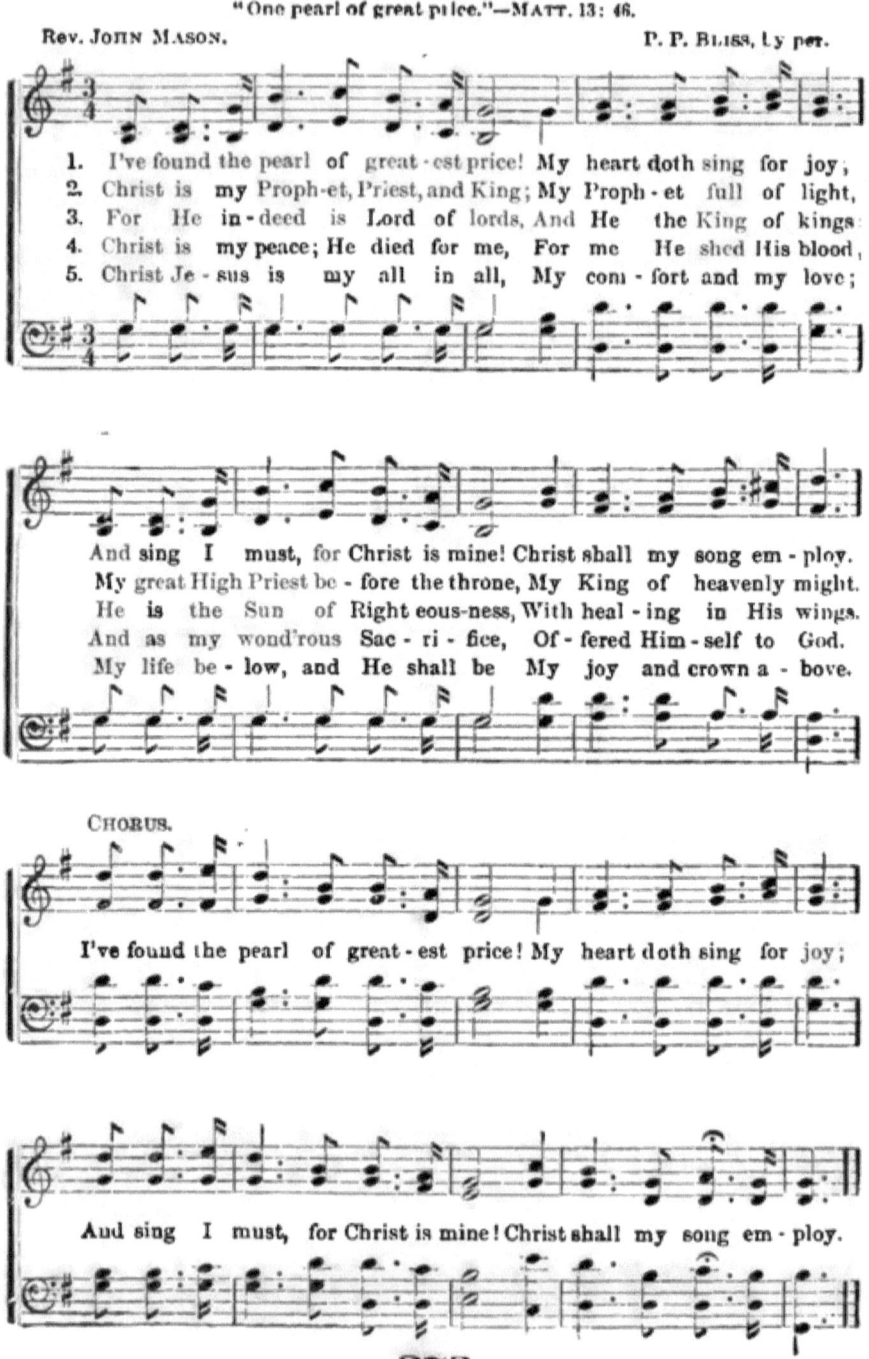

No. 305. **Beulah Land.**

"Sorrow and sighing shall flee away."—ISA. 35: 10

Rev. EDGAR PAGE STITES. JNO. R. SWENEY, by per.

1. I've reach'd the land of corn and wine, And all its rich-es free-ly mine;
2. The Saviour comes and walks with me, And sweet communion here have we;
3. A sweet perfume up-on the breeze Is borne from ev-er ver-nal trees,
4. The zephyrs seem to float to me, Sweet sounds of heaven's mel-o-dy,

Here shines undimm'd one bliss-ful day, For all my night has pass'd a-way.
He gen-tly leads me with His hand, For this is heaven's bor-der-land.
And flow'rs that nev-er fad-ing grow Where streams of life for-ev-er flow.
As angels, with the white-robed throng, Join in the sweet redemption song.

CHORUS.

O Beu-lah land, sweet Beu-lah land, As on thy high-est mount I stand,

I look a-way a-cross the sea, Where mansions are prepared for me.

Beulah Land.—Concluded.

No. 306.   I'm a Pilgrim.

Mrs. MARY S. B. DANA SHINDLER.   ITALIAN AIR.

2 Of that city, to which I journey;
  My Redeemer, my Redeemer is the light;
  There is no sorrow, nor any sighing,
  Nor any tears there, nor any dying :—*Cho.*

3 There the sunbeams are ever shining,
  Oh, my longing heart, my longing heart is there;
  Here in this country, so dark and dreary,
  I long have wandered forlorn and weary :—*Cho.*

He Knows.—Concluded.

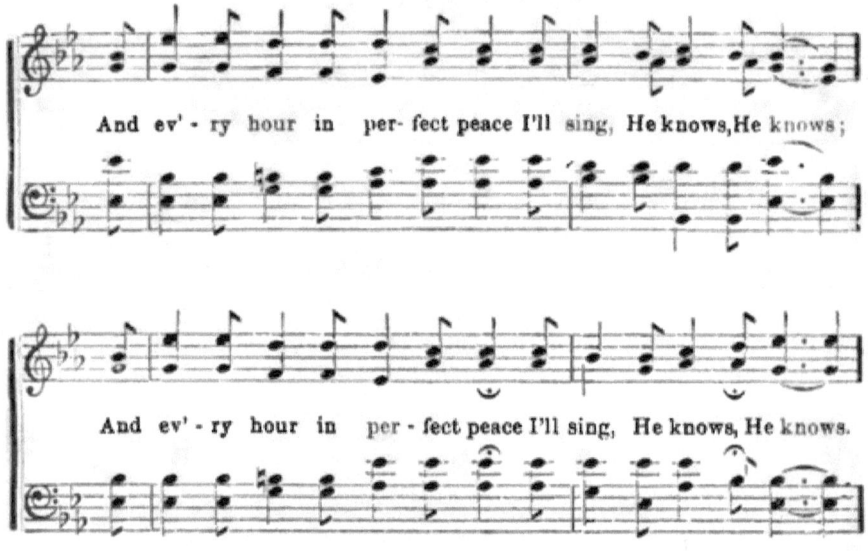

After last verse only.

3 O blissful lack of wisdom,
   'Tis blessed not to know;
He holds me with His own right hand,
   And will not let me go,
   And lulls my troubled soul to rest
   In Him who loves me so.

4 So on I go not knowing,
   I would not if I might;
I'd rathed walk in the dark with **God**
   Than go alone in the light;
   I'd rather walk by faith with Him
   Than go alone by sight.

"Come."—Concluded.

Are you coming Home?—Concluded.

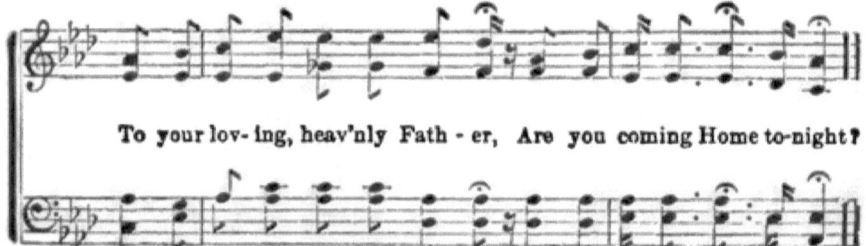

No. 312. Where is Thy Refuge?

"What is a man profited, if he shall gain the whole world, and lose his own soul."—MATT. 16 : 26.

FANNY J. CROSBY.   SILAS J. VAIL, by per.

1. Say, where is thy refuge, poor sinner, And what is thy prospect to-day?
2. The Mas-ter is calling thee, sinner, In tones of compassion and love,
3. As summer is waning, poor sinner, Repent, ere the season is past;

Why toil for the wealth that will perish, The treasures that rust and decay?
To feel that sweet rapture of pardon, And lay up thy treasure a-bove:
God's goodness to thee is extend-ed, As long as the day-beam shall last;

Oh! think of thy soul, that forev-er Must live on e-ter-ni-ty's shore,
Oh! kneel at the cross where He suffered, To ransom thy soul from the grave;
Then slight not the warning repeated With all the bright moments that roll,

When thou, in the dust art forgot-ten, When pleasure can charm thee no more.
The arm of His mercy will hold thee, The arm that is mighty to save.
Nor say, when the harvest is end-ed, That no one hath cared for thy soul.

CHORUS.

'Twill prof-it thee nothing, but fearful the cost, To gain the whole world if thy soul should be lost! To gain the whole world if thy soul should be lost.

No. 313. Brightly Gleams our Banner.

"Lift ye up a banner upon the high mountains."—ISA. 13: 2

Rev. THOMAS J. POTTER. Sir ARTHUR S. SULLIVAN.

1. Brightly gleams our ban - ner, Point-ing to the sky, Wav-ing wand'rers on - ward,
2. Je - sus, Lord and Mas - ter, At Thy sa - cred feet, Here with hearts re-joic - ing,
3. All our days di - rect us, In the way we go, Lead us on vic - to - rious
4. Then with Saints and An - gels May we join a - bove, Off'-ring end-less prais - es

To their home on high; Journeying o'er the des - ert, Glad - ly thus we pray,
See Thy chil - dren meet; Oft - en have we left Thee, Oft - en gone a - stray,
O - ver ev' - ry foe; Bid Thine an - gels shield us, When the storm-clouds lower,
At Thy throne of love; When the toil is o - ver, Then comes rest and peace,—

CHORUS.

And with hearts u - nit - ed, Take our heav'nward way. Brightly gleams our
Keep us, might-y Sav - iour, In the nar - row way.
Par - don Thou and save us In the last dread hour.
Je - sus, in His beau - ty;— Songs that nev - er cease.

ban - ner, Pointing to the sky, Waving wand'rers onward To their home on high.

No. 316. Father, Take my Hand.

"For thy name's sake lead me, and guide me."—Ps. 31: 3

Rev. H. N. Cobb. S. J. Vail, 1862, by per.

1. The way is dark, my Father! Cloud upon cloud Is gathering thickly o'er my head, and loud The thunders roar above me. Yet see, I stand like one bewildered! Father, take my hand, And thro' the gloom lead safely home, safely home, Safely home, Lead safely home Thy child!

2 The day declines, my Father! and the night
Is drawing darkly down. My faithless sight
Sees | ghostly | visions. Fears like a spectral band
Encompass me. O Father, | take my | hand,
    And from the night lead **up** to light,
        Up to light, up to light,
    Lead up to light Thy child!

3 The way is long, my Father! and my soul
Longs for the rest and quite | of the | goal;
While yet I journey through this weary land,
Keep me from wandering. Father, | take my | **hand**
    And in the way to endless day,
        Endless day, endless day,
    Lead safely on Thy child!

4 The path is rough, my Father! **Many a thorn**
Has pierced me! and my feet, all torn
And bleeding, | mark the | way. Yet Thy command
Bids me press forward. Father, | take my | hand;
    Then safe and blest, O lead to **rest**,
        Lead to rest, lead to rest,
    O lead to rest Thy child!

5 The throng is great, my Father! Many a doubt
And fear of danger compass me about;
And foes op- | press me | sore. I cannot stand
Or go, alone. O Father! | take my | hand;
    And through the throng, lead **safe along**.
        Safe along, safe along,
    Lead safe along Thy child.

6 The cross is heavy, Father! **I have borne**
It long, and | still do | bear it. Let my worn
And fainting spirit, rise to that bright land
Where crowns are given. Father, | take my | hand.
    And, reaching down, lead to the **crown**,
        To the crown, to the crown,
    Lead to the crown Thy child.

No. 318. **Mercy's Free.**

"Without money and without price."—ISA. 55: 1.

R. JUKES. From D. F. E. AUBER.

1. By faith I view my Saviour dying, On the tree, On the tree;
   To ev'ry nation He is crying, Look to me, Look to me;
   He bids the guilty now draw near, Repent, believe, dismiss their fear:
   Hark, hark, what precious words I hear, Mercy's free, Mercy's free.

2 Did Christ, when I was sin pursuing,
    Pity me, Pity me?
  And did He snatch my soul from sin?
    Can it be, Can it be?
  Oh, yes! He did salvation bring;
  He is my Prophet, Priest, and King;
  And now my happy soul can sing,
    Mercy's free, Mercy's free.

3 Jesus my weary soul refreshes:
    Mercy's free, Mercy's free,
  And every moment Christ is precious
    Unto me, Unto me;
  None can describe the bliss I prove,
  While through this wilderness I rove,
  All may enjoy the Saviour's love,
    Mercy's free, Mercy's free.

4 Long as I live, I'll still be crying,
    Mercy's free, Mercy's free,
  And this shall be my theme when dying,
    Mercy's free, Mercy's free,
  And when the vale of death I've passed,
  When lodged above the stormy blast,
  I'll sing, while endless ages last,
    Mercy's free, Mercy's free.

No. 319. Tune—MEAR. C. M. Key F.

1 Spirit of truth, oh, let me know
    The love of Christ to me;
  Its conqu'ring, quick'ning pow'r bestow
    To set me wholly free.

2 I long to know its depth and height
    To scan its breadth and length;
  Drink in its ocean of delight,
    And triumph in its strength.

3 It is Thine office to reveal
    My Saviour's wond'rous love;
  Oh, deepen on my heart Thy seal,
    And bless me from above.

4 Thy quick'ning pow'r to me impart
    And be my constant Guide;
  With richer gladness fill my heart.
    Be Jesus glorified.

ANON.

No. 320. **St. Thomas.** S. M.

Rev. WM. HAMMOND. Arr. by AARON WILLIAMS.

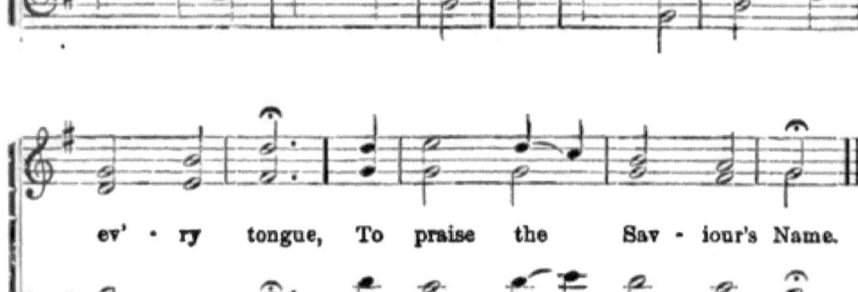

1. A-wake, and sing the song Of Moses and the Lamb; Wake, ev'-ry heart and ev'-ry tongue, To praise the Sav-iour's Name.

2 Sing of His dying love;
  Sing of His risen power;
  Sing how He intercedes above
  For those whose sins He bore.

3 Ye pilgrims, on the road
  To Zion's city, sing;
  Rejoice ye in the Lamb of God,—
  In Christ, th' eternal King.

4 There shall each raptured tongue
  His endless praise proclaim;
  And sweeter voices tune the song
  Of Moses and the Lamb.

No. 321. Tune—DUKE STREET. L. M.

1 From all that dwell below the skies,
  Let the Creator's praise arise;
  Let the Redeemer's Name be sung,
  Through every land, by every tongue.

2 Eternal are Thy mercies, Lord;
  Eternal truth attends Thy word:
  Thy praise shall sound from shore to shore,
  Till suns shall rise and set no more.

ISAAC WATTS.

No. 322. Tune—WARD. L. M.

1 Jesus, and shall it ever be,
   A mortal man ashamed of Thee?
   Ashamed of Thee, whom angels praise,
   Whose glories shine thro' endless days?

2 Ashamed of Jesus! sooner far
   Let evening blush to own a star;
   He sheds the beams of light divine
   O'er this benighted soul of mine.

3 Ashamed of Jesus, that dear friend
   On whom my hopes of heaven depend!
   No, when I blush, be this my shame,
   That I no more revere His Name.

4 Ashamed of Jesus! yes, I may,
   When I've no guilt to wash away,
   No tear to wipe, no good to crave,
   No fear to quell, no soul to save.

5 Till then, nor is my boasting vain,
   Till then I boast a Saviour slain;
   And O, may this my glory be,
   That Christ is not ashamed of me.
                              JOSEPH GRIGG.

No. 323. Tune—WINDHAM. L. M.

1 Stay, Thou insulted Spirit, stay,
   Tho' I have done Thee such despite,
   Cast not the sinner quite away,
   Nor take Thine everlasting flight.

2 Though I have most unfaithful been
   Of all who e'er Thy grace received;
   Ten thousand times Thy goodness seen,
   Ten thousand times Thy goodness grieved.

3 Yet O, the chief of sinners spare,
   In honor of my great High Priest,
   Nor in Thy righteous anger swear
   I shall not see Thy people's rest.

4 O Lord, my weary soul release,
   Upraise me by Thy gracious hand;
   Guide me into Thy perfect peace,
   And bring me to the promised land.
                              CHARLES WESLEY.

No. 324. Tune—ST. THOMAS. S. M.

1 O Holy Spirit, come,
   And Jesus' love declare;
   Oh, tell us of our heavenly home,
   And guide us safely there.

2 Our unbelief remove
   By Thine almighty breath;
   Oh, work the wondrous work of love,
   The mighty work of faith.

3 Come with resistless power,
   Come with almighty grace,
   Come with the long-expected shower,
   And fall upon this place.
                              OSWALD ALLEN.

No. 325. Tune—NO. 1, NO. 113.

1 Come, every joyful heart,
   That loves the Saviour's name!
   Your noblest powers exert
   To celebrate His fame;
   Tell all above, and all below,
   The debt of love to Him we owe.

2 He left His starry crown,
   And laid His robes aside;
   On wings of love came down,
   And wept, and bled, and died;
   What He endured, no tongue can tell,
   To save our souls from death and hell

3 From the dark grave He rose—
   The mansion of the dead;
   And thence His mighty foes
   In glorious triumph led;
   Up thro' the sky the Conqueror rode,
   And reigns on high the Saviour God.

4 From thence He'll quickly come—
   His chariot will not stay—
   And bear our spirits home
   To realms of endless day;
   There shall we see His lovely face,
   And ever be in His embrace.
                              SAMUEL STENNET.

No. 326. LOOKING HOME.
Tune—BRADBURY TRIO, p. 160.

1 Ah, this heart is void and chill,
   'Mid earth's noisy thronging;
   For my Father's mansion, still
   Earnestly, I'm longing.

CHO.—Looking home, looking home,
   T'wards the heavenly mansion,
   Jesus hath prepared for me,
   In His Father's kingdom.

2 Soon the glorious day will dawn,
   Heavenly pleasures bringing;
   Night will be exchanged for morn,
   Sighs give place to singing.

3 Oh, to be at home, and gain
   All for which we're sighing;
   From all earthly want and pain
   To be swiftly flying.

4 Blessed home! oh, blessed home!
   There no more to sever;
   Soon we'll meet around the throne
   Praising God forever.
                              C. J. ? SMITH.

Tell it Out.—Concluded.

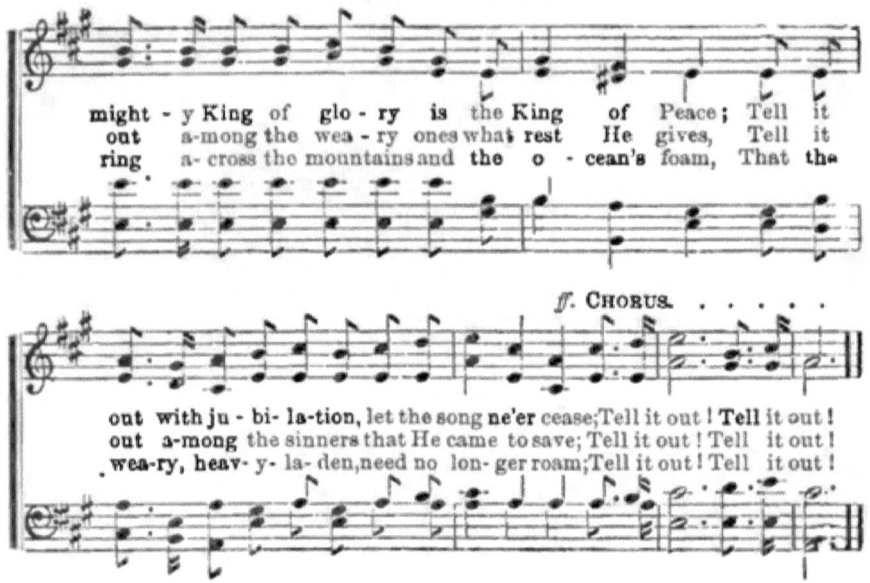

might-y King of glo-ry is the King of Peace; Tell it
out a-mong the wea-ry ones what rest He gives, Tell it
ring a-cross the mountains and the o-cean's foam, That the

f. CHORUS.

out with ju-bi-la-tion, let the song ne'er cease;Tell it out! Tell it out!
out a-mong the sinners that He came to save; Tell it out! Tell it out!
wea-ry, heav-y-la-den, need no lon-ger roam;Tell it out! Tell it out!

No. 330. **Light after Darkness.**

"Sorrow and sighing shall flee away."—ISA. 85: 10.

FRANCES R. HAVERGAL.   IRA D. SANKEY.

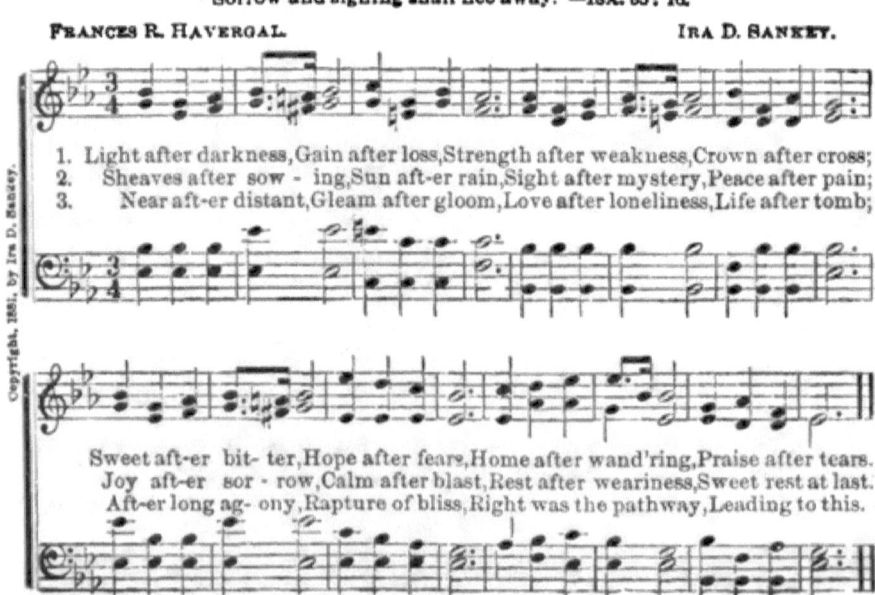

1. Light after darkness, Gain after loss, Strength after weakness, Crown after cross;
2. Sheaves after sow-ing, Sun aft-er rain, Sight after mystery, Peace after pain;
3. Near aft-er distant, Gleam after gloom, Love after loneliness, Life after tomb;

Sweet aft-er bit-ter, Hope after fears, Home after wand'ring, Praise after tears.
Joy aft-er sor-row, Calm after blast, Rest after weariness, Sweet rest at last.
Aft-er long ag-ony, Rapture of bliss, Right was the pathway, Leading to this.

Copyright, 1881, by Ira D. Sankey.

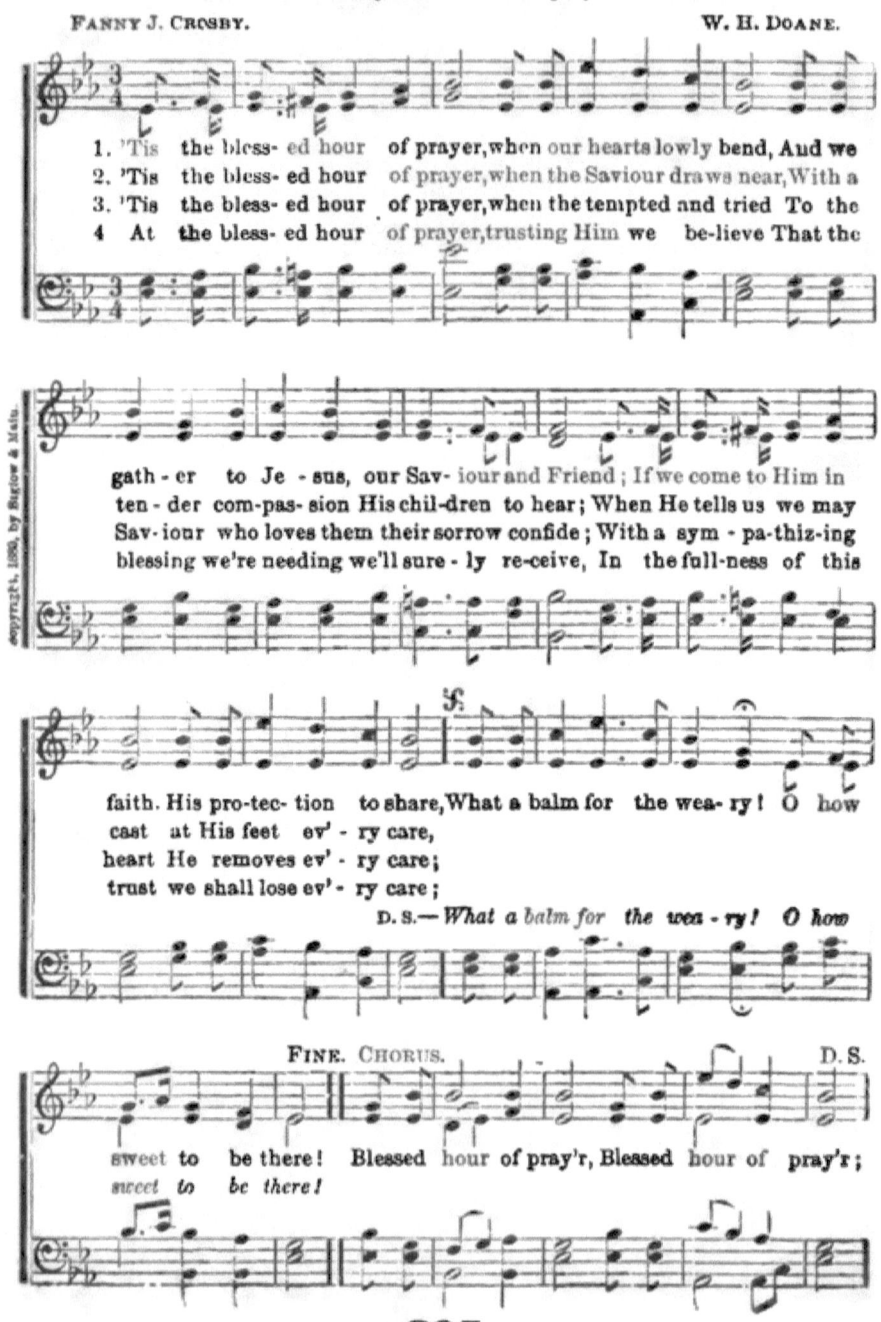

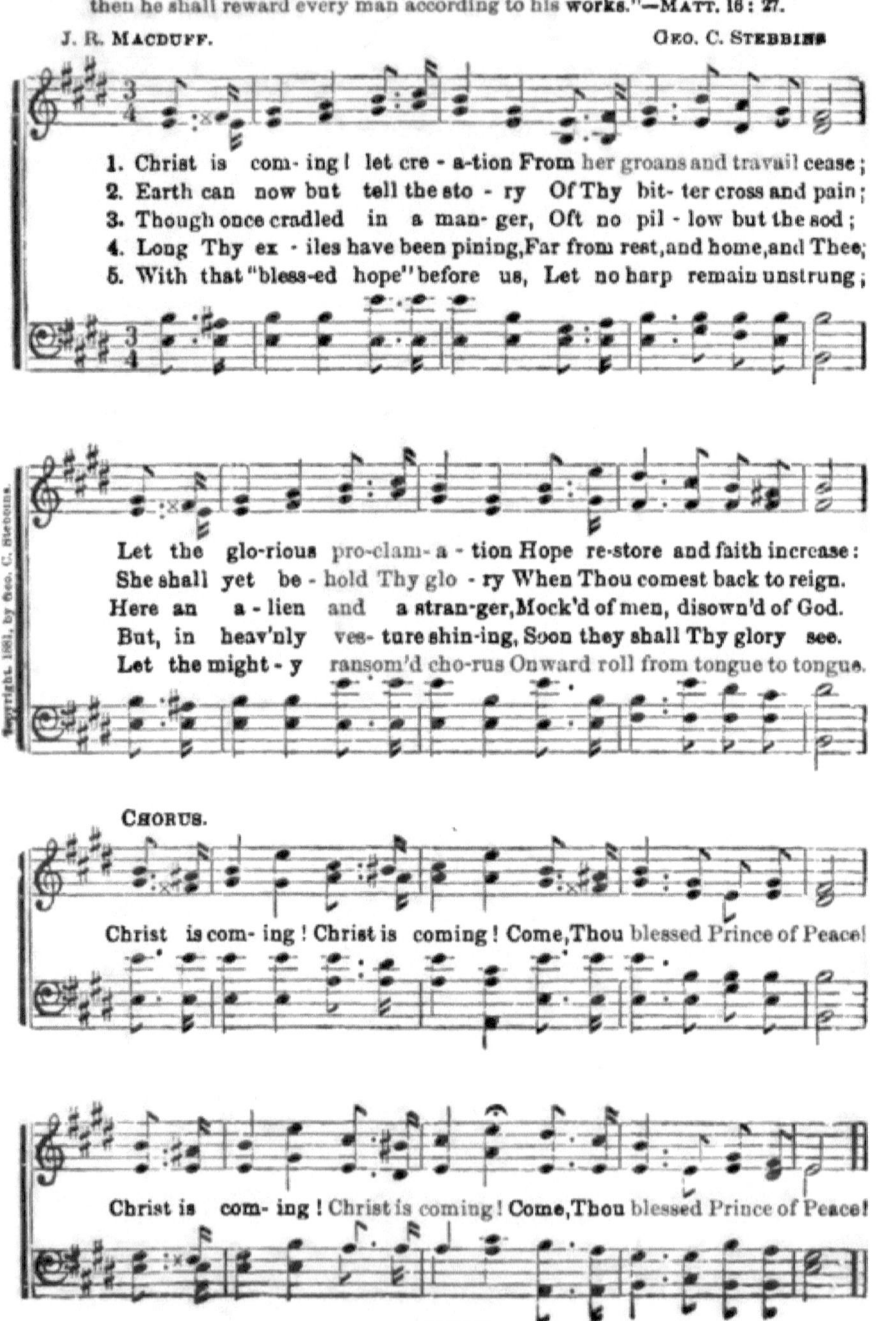

No 339. Rise Up and Hasten.

"Rise up, my love, my fair one, and come away."—Song of Sol. 2: 13.

J. Denham Smith, Arr. Arr. by James McGranahan.

1. Rise up, and hast-en! my soul, haste a- long! And speed on thy jour-ney with hope and with song;
   Home, home is near-ing, 'tis coming in- to view, A lit-tle more of toil-ing and then to earth a-dieu.
2. Why should we lin-ger when heaven lies be-fore! While earth's fast re-ced-ing, and soon will be no more;
   Pleas-ures and treasures which once here we knew, No more can they charm us with such a goal in view.

CHORUS.

Come then, come, and raise the joy-ful song! Ye chil-dren of the wil-der-ness, our time can-not be long. Home, home, home, oh, why should we de-lay? The morn of heav'n is dawn-ing, we're near the break of day.

Rise Up and Hasten.—Concluded.

3 Loved ones in Jesus they've passed on before,
Now resting in glory, they weary are no more;
Toils all are ended, and nothing now but joy,
And praises, ascending their ever glad employ.
    Come then, come, &c.

4 No condemnation! how blessed is the word,
And no separation! forever with the Lord;
He will be with us who loved us long before,
And Jesus, our Jesus, is ours for evermore.
    Come then, come, &c.

No. 340. The Sweet Story of Old.

"And he took them up in his arms, put his hands upon them, and blessed them."—MARK 10: 16.

Mrs. JEMIMA LUKE.   J. C. ENGLEBRECHT.

1. I think when I read that sweet sto-ry of old, When Je-sus was here
2. I wish that His hands had been placed on my head, His arms had been thrown
3. Yet still to His foot-stool in prayer I may go, And ask for a share
4. In that beauti-ful place He is gone to pre-pare, For all that are washed

a-mong men, How He called lit-tle chil-dren as lambs to His fold, I should
a-round me, And that I might have seen His kind look when He said, "Let the
in His love; And if I now earn-est-ly seek Him be-low, I shall
and for-given; And ma-ny dear chil-dren are gath-r-ing there, "For of

FINE. REFRAIN.   D. S.

like to have been with them then. I should like to have been with them then.
lit-tle ones come un-to Me." "Let the lit-tle ones come un-to Me."
see Him and hear Him a-bove, I shall see Him and hear Him a-bove.
such is the king-dom of heaven." "For of such is the king-dom of heaven."

Over Jordan.—Concluded.

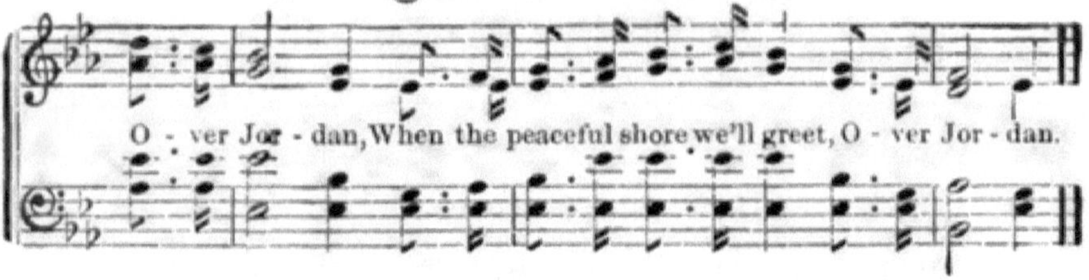

O - ver Jor - dan, When the peaceful shore we'll greet, O - ver Jor - dan.

No. 344.   ## Praise Ye the Lord.

*"It is good to sing praises unto our God; He healeth the broken in heart * * He telleth the number of the stars."—Ps. 147: 1, 3, 4.*

Rous' Version, 1619.   C. E. POLLOCK, by per.

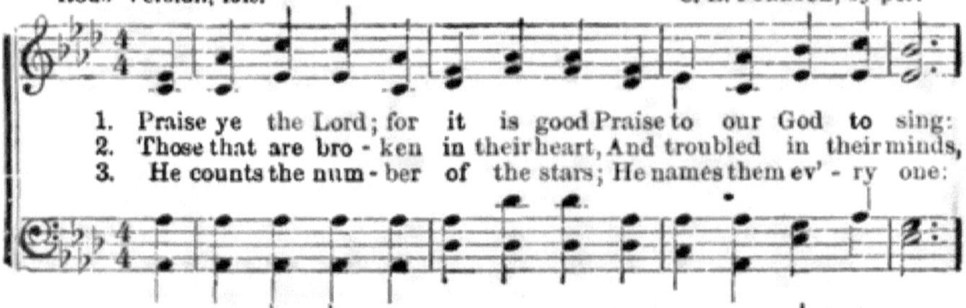

1. Praise ye the Lord; for it is good Praise to our God to sing:
2. Those that are bro - ken in their heart, And troubled in their minds,
3. He counts the num - ber of the stars; He names them ev' - ry one:

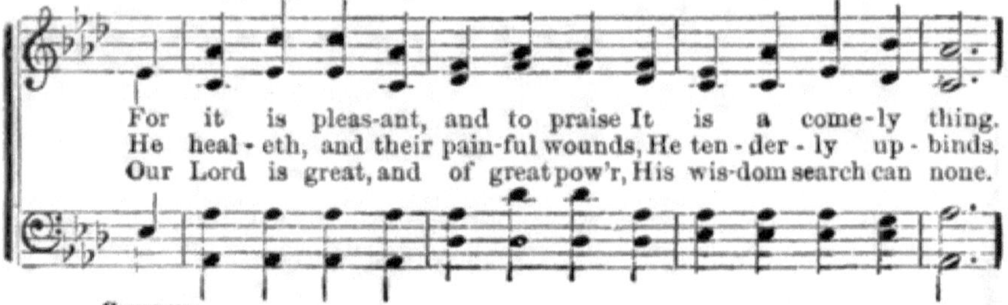

For it is pleas-ant, and to praise It is a come-ly thing.
He heal - eth, and their pain-ful wounds, He ten - der - ly up - binds.
Our Lord is great, and of great pow'r, His wis-dom search can none.

CHORUS.

Praise the Lord, it is good Praise to our God to sing:
Praise ye the Lord, for it is good, Praise to sing,

For it is pleasant, and to praise It is a come-ly thing.

I Left it all with Jesus.—Concluded.

From my wea-ry heart the burden roll'd a-way; Hap-py day! hap-py day!
Then with all my weakness leaning on His might, All is light! all is light!
Love es-teems it joy of heav-en to a-bide, At His side! at His side!
Yes, His ten-der loving mercy makes thee room, Oh, come home! Oh, come home!

No. 346. **Depth of Mercy.**

"God is Love."—1 John, 4: 8.

CHARLES WESLEY. From Stevenson.

1. { Depth of mer-cy! can there be Mer-cy still re-served for me?
   { Can my God His wrath for-bear? Me, the chief of sin-ners, spare? }

CHORUS.

God is love! I know, I feel; Je-sus lives, and loves me still;
Je - - sus lives, He lives, and loves me still.

2 I have long withstood His grace
Long provoked Him to His face;
Would not hearken to His calls;
Grieved Him by a thousand falls.

3 Now incline me to repent;
Let me now my sins lament;
Now my foul revolt deplore,
Weep, believe, and sin no more.

No. 348. Is my Name written There?

"Rejoice because your names are written in heaven."—LUKE 10. 20.

Mrs. MARY A. KIDDER. FRANK M. DAVIS, by per.

1. Lord, I care not for riches, Neither silver nor gold; I would make sure of heaven, I would enter the fold. In the book of Thy kingdom, With its pages so fair, Tell me, Jesus, my Saviour, Is my name written there?

2. Lord, my sins they are many, Like the sands of the sea, But Thy blood, oh, my Saviour! Is sufficient for me; For Thy promise is written, In bright letters that glow, "Tho' your sins be as scarlet, I will make them like snow."

3. Oh! that beautiful city, With its mansions of light, With its glorified beings, In pure garments of white; Where no evil thing cometh, To despoil what is fair; Where the angels are watching, Yes, my name's written there.

CHORUS.

Is my name written there, On the page white and fair?
Chorus for 2d & 3d Verses. Yes, my name's, &c.
In the book of Thy kingdom, Is my name written there?
2d & 3d V.—Yes, my name's, &c.

My Soul will Overcome.—Concluded.

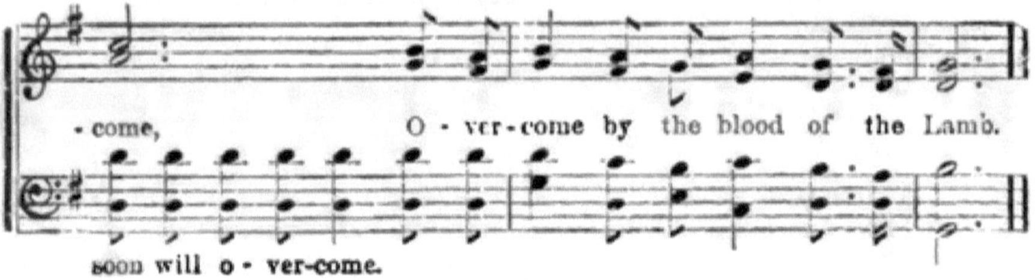

come, O-ver-come by the blood of the Lamb.
soon will o-ver-come.

No. 350. ## We Worship Thee.

"Whom having not seen, ye love."—1 Pet. 1: 8.

FRANCES R. HAVERGAL.   JAMES McGRANAHAN.

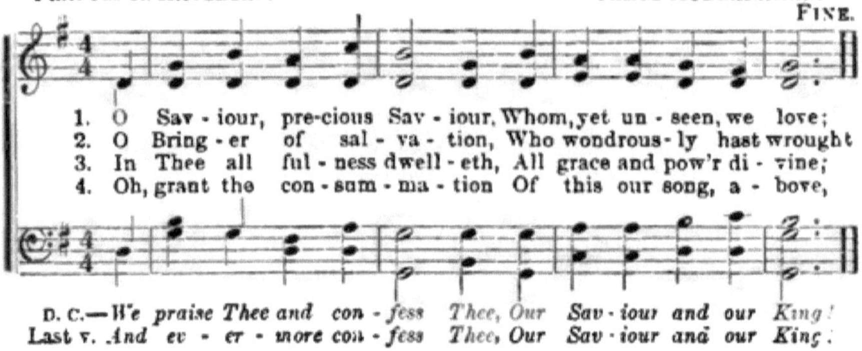

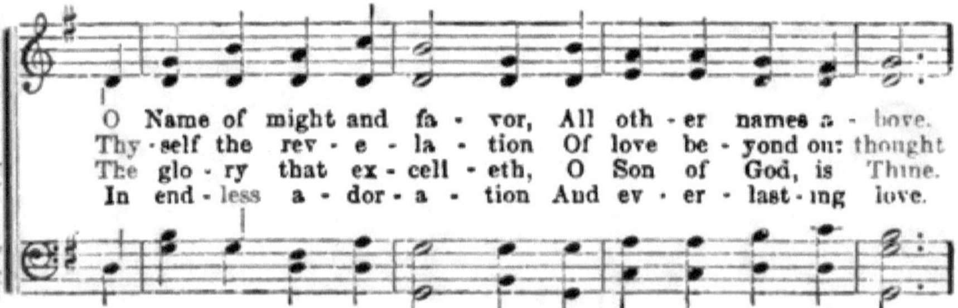

1. O Saviour, precious Saviour, Whom, yet un-seen, we love;
2. O Bring-er of sal-va-tion, Who wondrous-ly hast wrought;
3. In Thee all ful-ness dwell-eth, All grace and pow'r di-vine;
4. Oh, grant the con-sum-ma-tion Of this our song, a-bove,

D. C.—We praise Thee and con-fess Thee, Our Sav-iour and our King!
Last v. And ev-er-more con-fess Thee, Our Sav-iour and our King!

O Name of might and fa-vor, All oth-er names a-bove,
Thy-self the rev-e-la-tion Of love be-yond our thought
The glo-ry that ex-cell-eth, O Son of God, is Thine.
In end-less a-dor-a-tion And ev-er-last-ing love.

CHORUS.   D. C.

We wor-ship Thee! we bless Thee! To Thee a-lone we sing!
Last v. Then shall we praise and bless Thee! Where per-fect prais-es ring!

Copyright, 1879, by James McGranahan.

No. 352.

Trust On!

"Trust in the Lord with all thine heart."—Prov. 3: 5.

ANON.
GEO. C. STEBBINS.

1. Trust on! trust on believ-er! Tho' long the con-flict be
Thou yet shalt prove vic-to-rious; Thy God shall fight for thee

2. Trust on! trust on; thy fail-ings May bow thee to the dust,
But in thy deep-est sor-row, O give not up thy trust.

3. Trust on! the dan-ger press-es; Temp-ta-tion strong is near,
Yet o'er life's dangerous rap-ids, He shall thy pas-sage steer.

4. O Christ is strong to save us, He is a faith-ful Friend,
Trust on! trust on! be-liev-er, O trust Him to the end.

CHORUS.

Trust on! (trust on!) Trust on! (trust on!) Tho' dark the night and drear;

Trust on! (trust on!) trust on! (trust on!) The morn-ing dawn is near.

Gathering Home.—Concluded.

Lord shall pre-pare For all who the glo-ry with Him shall share.
fierce-ly and wild Yet they reach the home of the un-de-filed.
banks o-ver-flow, Some-times in rip-ples and small waves go.
deep-est midnight, Now guide us, and send us the staff and light.

REFRAIN.
Gath'ring home! gath'ring home! Fording the riv-er one by one!

Gath'-ring home! gath'-ring home, yes, one by one!

No. 362. **Only a Little While.**

"Weeping may endure for a night, but joy cometh in the morning."—Ps. 30: 5.

Mrs. M. P. A. CROZIER.　　　　　　　　　　　　　　　Geo. C. STEBBINS.

1. On-ly a lit-tle while Of walking with wea-ry feet,
2. Suf-fer if God shall will, And work for Him while we may, From
3. On-ly a lit-tle while, For toil-ing a few short days, And

Pa-tient-ly o-ver the thorn-y way That leads to the gold-en street.
Cal-va-ry's cross to Zi-on's crown, Is on-ly a lit-tle way.
then comes the rest, the qui-et rest, E-ter-ni-ty's end-less praise.

No. 363. **Behold, what Love!**

"Behold, what manner of love the Father hath bestowed upon us, that we should be called the sons of God."—JOHN 3:1.

M. S. S.   JAMES McGRANAHAN.

1. Be-hold, what love, what boundless love, The Fa-ther hath bestowed
2. No long-er far from Him, but now By "precious blood" made nigh;
3. What we in glo-ry soon shall be, It doth not yet ap-pear;
4. With such a bless-ed hope in view, We would more ho-ly be,

On sin-ners lost, that we should be Now called the sons of God!
Ac-cept-ed in the "Well-be-loved," Near to God's heart we lie.
But when our pre-cious Lord we see, We shall His im-age bear.
More like our ris-en, glo-rious Lord, Whose face we soon shall see.

CHORUS.

Be-hold, what manner of love!............ What manner of
    What manner of love,
love the Fa-ther hath be-stowed up-on us, That we...... that
we should be call'd, ... Should be call'd the sons of God.
    the sons of God.

Copyright, 1879, by James McGranahan.

No. 364. I hear the Words of Jesus.

"Christ is all, and in all."—Col. 3: 2.

Geo. C. Needham.
C. C. Case.

1. I hear the words of Je - sus, They speak of peace with God: I see the Lamb, Christ Je-sus, Who bore my heav-y load, I trust the blood of Je - sus, From sin it sets me free, I love the name of Je - sus, Who gave Him-self for me.

2. His word di - vine - ly bless - ed, It shows me what I am; His cross it brings sal - va - tion, The vic - tim was the Lamb His blood pro - cur - eth par - don, And jus - ti - fies the soul, His name, how sweet and pre - cious, It makes the sin - ner whole.

3. Oh! hear the words of Je - sus, The tid - ings are for thee; Oh! clasp the cross of Je - sus, And there for ref - uge flee; Oh! trust the blood of Je - sus, Be saved this ver - y hour, Oh! love the name of Je - sus, Blest name of wondrous pow'r.

Copyright, 1881, by C. C. Case.

No. 367. 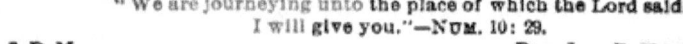 Deliverance will Come.

"We are journeying unto the place of which the Lord said,
I will give you."—Num. 10: 29.

J. B. M.   Rev. Jno. B. Matthias, 1836.

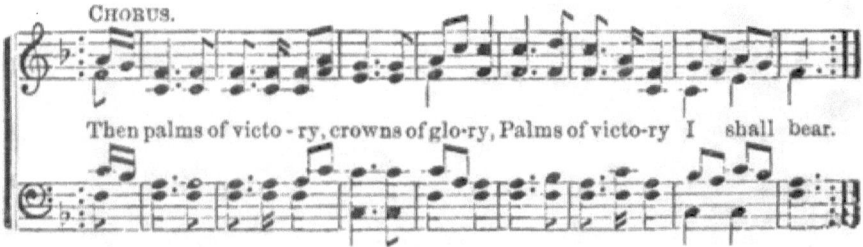

1. I saw a way-worn trav'-ler In tat-ter'd garments clad,
   His back was la-den heav-y, His strength was al-most gone,
2. The sum-mer sun was shin-ing, The sweat was on his brow,
   But he kept press-ing on-ward, For he was wend-ing home;
3. The song-sters in the ar-bor, That stood be-side the way,
   His watchword be-ing "On-ward!" He stopped his ears and ran,

And struggling up the moun-tain, It seem'd that he was sad;
Yet he shout-ed as he journeyed, De-liv-er-ance will come.
His gar-ments worn and dust-y, His step seem'd ver-y slow:
Still shout-ing as he journeyed, De-liv-er-ance will come
At-tract-ed his at-ten-tion, In-vit-ing his de-lay:
Still shout-ing as he journeyed, De-liv-er-ance will come.

CHORUS.

Then palms of victo-ry, crowns of glo-ry, Palms of victo-ry I shall bear.

4 I saw him in the evening,
    The sun was bending low,
    He'd overtopped the mountain,
    And reached the vale below:
He saw the golden city,—
    His everlasting home,—
And shouted loud, Hosanna,
    Deliverance will come!

5 While gazing on that city,
    Just o'er the narrow flood,
A band of holy angels
    Came from the throne of God:

They bore him on their pinions
    Safe o'er the dashing foam;
And joined him in his triumph,
    Deliverance had come!

6 I heard the song of triumph
    They sang upon that shore,
Saying, Jesus has redeemed us
    To suffer nevermore:
Then, casting his eyes backward
    On the race which he had run,
He shouted loud, Hosanna,
    Deliverance has come!

No. 372. We Praise Thee and Bless Thee.

"Oh ye servants of the Lord, praise the name of the Lord."—Ps. 113: 1.

EL. NATHAN.   JAMES MCGRANAHAN.

1. We praise Thee and bless Thee, Our Father in heaven,
For the joy of salvation Thy gospel hath given.

2. We praise Thee and bless Thee: Once sinful and sad,
By the word thou hast given, To Christ we were led.

3. We praise Thee and bless Thee: The Spirit hath come
To dwell with, and teach us, And guide us safe home.

CHORUS.
Hallelujah! we praise Thee Thro' Jesus our Lord;
Hallelujah! we bless Thee For the gift of Thy word!

4 We praise Thee and bless Thee,
  For food by the way;
The manna from heaven
  Provided each day.

5 We praise Thee and bless Thee:
  Thy word hath gone forth,
That Christ shall be King and
  Reign over the earth.

6 We praise Thee and bless Thee,
  And wait His return
To fulfil every promise
  He made to His own.

7 We praise Thee and bless Thee
  We'll reign with Him then,
To praise Thee and bless Thee
  For ever. Amen.

Only Waiting.—Concluded.

From my Saviour on the other shore.

No. 376. Oh, Revive Us by Thy Word.

"I will cause the shower to come down in his season. There shall be showers of blessing."—Ezek. 34: 26.

El. Nathan.   James McGranahan.

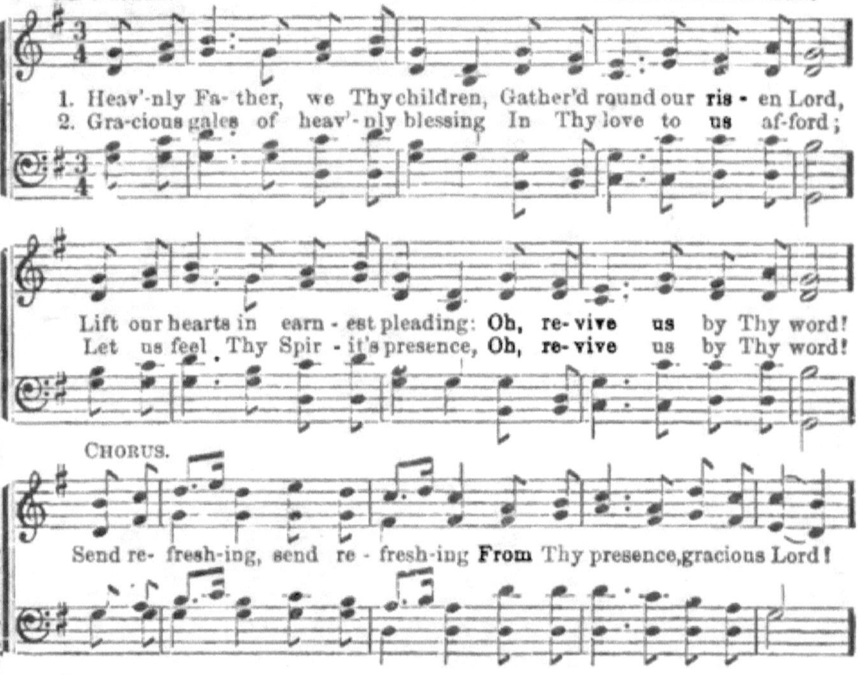

1. Heav'nly Father, we Thy children, Gather'd round our ris-en Lord,
2. Gracious gales of heav'nly blessing In Thy love to us afford;

Lift our hearts in earnest pleading: Oh, revive us by Thy word!
Let us feel Thy Spirit's presence, Oh, revive us by Thy word!

CHORUS.

Send refreshing, send refreshing From Thy presence, gracious Lord!

Send refreshing, send refreshing, And revive us by Thy word!

3. Weak and weary in the conflict,
"Wrestling not with flesh and blood,"
Help us, Lord, as faint we falter;
Oh, revive us by Thy word!

4. With Thy strength, O Master, gird us;
Be our Guide and be our Guard:
Fill us with Thy holy Spirit,
Oh, revive us by Thy word!

No. 377. I Never Knew You.

"I never knew you: depart from Me."—MATT. 7:23.

Mrs. G. C. NEEDHAM.   C. C. CASE.

1. When the King in His beau-ty shall come to His throne, And a-round Him are gather'd His lov'd ones, His own; There be some who will knock at His fair pal-ace door, To be an-swer'd with-in "There is mer-cy no more."
2. They had known whence He came, and the grace which He brought; In their pres-ence He heal'd, in their streets He had taught; They had mention'd His name and their friend-ship pro-fess'd; But they nev-er be-lieved, for of them He con-fess'd
3. Now the right-eous are reign-ing with A-bra-ham there; But for these is ap-point-ed an end-less de-spair; It is vain that they call: He once knock'd at their gate, But they wel-come'd Him not; so now this is their fate:
4. O sin-ner, give heed to this sto-ry of gloom, For the hour is fast near-ing that fix-es your doom; Will you still re-ject mer-cy? still hard-en your heart? Oh, then, what will you do as the King cries?—"Depart!"

CHORUS

"I have nev-er known you," "I have nev-er known you," "I have nev-er, I have nev-er, I have nev-er known you."

No. 378. Beyond the Smiling and the Weeping.

"And God shall wipe away all tears from their eyes; and there shall be no more death, neither sorrow, nor crying, neither shall there be any more pain."—Rev. 21: 4.

HORATIUS BONAR, D. D.   GEO. C. STEBBINS.

1. Be-yond the smiling and the weeping, I shall be soon, I shall be soon; Be-yond the waking and the sleeping, Be-yond the sowing and the reaping, I shall be soon, I shall be soon.

2. Be-yond the blooming and the fading, I shall be soon, I shall be soon; Be-yond the shining and the shading, Be-yond the hoping and the dreading, I shall be soon, I shall be soon.

3. Be-yond the parting and the meeting, I shall be soon, I shall be soon; Be-yond the farewell and the greeting, Be-yond the pulse's fever beating, I shall be soon, I shall be soon.

4. Be-yond the frost-chain and the fever, I shall be soon, I shall be soon; Be-yond the rock-waste and the river, Be-yond the ever and the never, I shall be soon, I shall be soon.

REFRAIN.

Love, rest, and home! Sweet, sweet home! Lord, tarry not, Lord, tarry not, but come.

Who is on the Lord's Side.—Concluded.

No. 382. Lead me on.

"For Thy name's sake lead me and guide me."—Ps. 31 : 3.

C. C. Converse, by per.

4 Through the water, through the fire,
  Never let me fall or tire,
  Every step brings Canaan nigher :
    Lead me on !

5 Bid me stand on Nebo's height,
  Gaze upon the land of light,
  Then transported with the sight,
    Lead me on !

6 When I stand on Jordan's brink,
  Never let me fear or shrink ;
  Hold me, Father, lest I sink
    Lead me on !

7 When the victory is won,
  And eternal life begun,
  Up to glory lead me on !
    Lead me on, lead me on

He Came to Bethany.—Concluded.

His love is ever the same! Open wide the door,
is ever the same!
let Him enter now! for His love is ever the same!
is ever the same!

No. 386. Child of Sin and Sorrow.

"Come, for all things are now ready."—LUKE 14: 17.

TH. HASTINGS.   THOMAS HASTINGS.

1. { Child of sin and sor-row, Fill'd with dis-may, }
   { Wait not for to-mor-row, Yield thee to-day: } Heav'n bids thee [come,
2. { Child of sin and sor-row, Why wilt thou die? }
   { Come while thou canst borrow Help from on high; } Grieve not that love

While yet there's room; Child of sin and sor-row, Hear and o-bey.
Which from a-bove, Child of sin and sor-row, Would bring thee nigh.

357

No. 388. Not what these Hands have Done.

"Having made peace through the blood of His cross."—COL. 1: 20.

HORATIUS BONAR, D. D.   JAMES McGRANAHAN.

1. Not what these hands have done, Can save this guilt-y soul;
2. Not what I feel or do, Can give me peace with God;
3. Thy love to me, O God, Not mine, O Lord, to Thee,
4. No oth-er work save Thine, No mean-er blood, will do;
5. I praise the God of grace, I trust His love and might;

Not what this toil-ing flesh has borne, Can make my spir-it whole.
Not all my pray'rs, or sigh, or tears, Can ease my aw-ful load.
Can rid me of this dark un-rest, And set my spir-it free.
No strength, save that which is di-vine, Can bear me safe-ly through
He calls me His, I call Him mine; My God, my joy, my light

REFRAIN.

Thy work a-lone, my Sav-iour, Can ease this weight of sin;

Thy blood a-lone, O Lamb of God, Can give me peace with-in.

We'll gather there in Glory.—Concluded.

No. 396. To Him be Glory evermore.

"Thou hast redeemed us to God by Thy blood."—Rev. 5: 9.

EL. NATHAN.   JAMES McGRANAHAN.

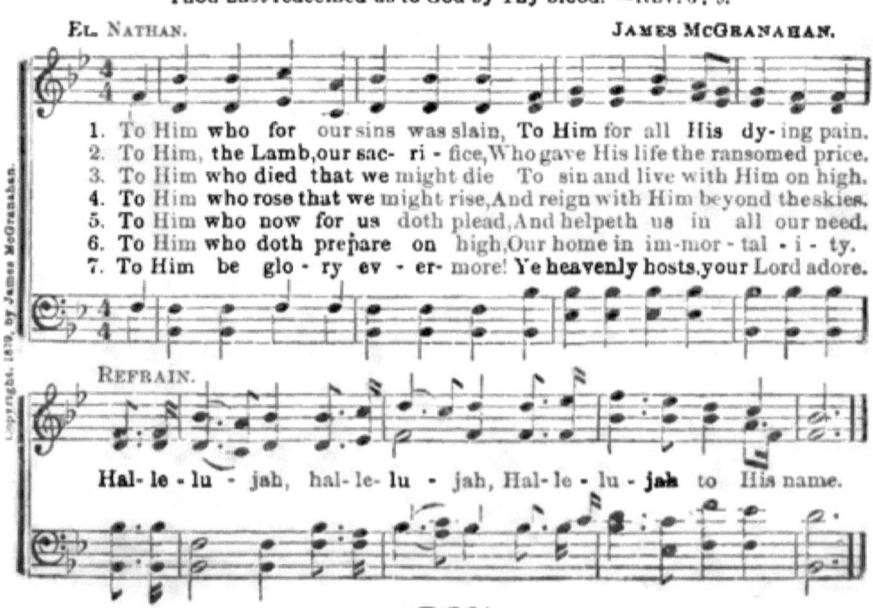

1. To Him who for our sins was slain, To Him for all His dy-ing pain.
2. To Him, the Lamb, our sac-ri-fice, Who gave His life the ransomed price.
3. To Him who died that we might die To sin and live with Him on high.
4. To Him who rose that we might rise, And reign with Him beyond the skies.
5. To Him who now for us doth plead, And helpeth us in all our need.
6. To Him who doth prepare on high, Our home in im-mor-tal-i-ty.
7. To Him be glo-ry ev-er-more! Ye heavenly hosts, your Lord adore.

REFRAIN.

Hal-le-lu-jah, hal-le-lu-jah, Hal-le-lu-jah to His name.

No. 397.   **The Sands of Time.**

"Thine eyes shall behold the land that is very far off."—ISA. XXXIII. 17.

Mrs. A. R. COUSIN. IRA D. SANKEY.
Moderato.

1. The sands of time are sink-ing, The dawn of heav-en breaks,
2. I've wres-tled on t'ward heav-en,'Gainst storm and wind and tide,
3. Deep wa-ters crossed life's pathway, The hedge of thorns was sharp;

The sum-mer morn I've sighed for—The fair, sweet morn a-wakes:
Now, like a wea-ry trav'-ler That lean-eth on his guide,
Now these lie all be-hind me—O! for a well turned harp!

Dark, dark hath been the mid-night, But day-spring is at hand,
A-mid the shades of ev'-ning, While sinks life's ling'ring sand,
O, to join the hal-le-lu-jah With yon tri-umphant band!

And glo-ry, glo-ry dwell-eth In Im-man-uel's land.
I hail the glo-ry dawn-ing From Im-man-uel's land.
Who sing where glo-ry dwell-eth In Im-man-uel's land.

No. 398. I know that my Redeemer Lives.

"I know that my Redeemer lives."—Job 19: 25.

Rev. Sam. Medley.   James McGranahan.

1. I know that my Re-deem-er lives! What comfort this sweet message gives!
2. He lives, to bless me with His love; He lives, to plead for me a-bove,
3. He lives, triumphant from the grave; He lives, e-ter-nal-ly to save;
4. He lives, my mansions to pre-pare; He lives to bring me safe-ly there;

He lives, who once was dead; He lives, all glorious in the sky;
My hun-gry soul to feed; He lives, to grant me rich sup-ply;
And while He lives I'll sing: He lives, my ev-er faithful Friend;
My Je-sus still the same: What joy this blest as-surance gives!—

He lives, ex-alt-ed there on high, My ev-er-last-ing Head.
He lives, to guide me with His eye, To help in time of need.
He lives, and loves me to the end, My Pro-phet, Priest, and King!
"I know that my Re-deem-er lives:" All glo-ry to His name!

Copyright, by 1879, by James McGranahan.

CHORUS.

He lives! He lives! I know that my Re-deemer lives!
     He lives!   He lives!

He lives! He lives! I know that my Re-deemer lives.
     He lives!   He lives!

A Little While.—Concluded.

Come take Thy long-ing chil-dren home, And end earth's wea-ry night!

No. 400. Hamburg.

ISAAC WATTS. Ad. by LOWELL MASON.

1. When I survey the wondrous cross On which the Prince of Glory died,
My richest gain I count but loss. And pour contempt on all my pride.

2. Forbid it, Lord, that I should boast, Save in the death of Christ my God
All the vain things that charm me most, I sac-ri-fice them to His blood.

3 See! from His head, His hands, His feet,
Sorrow and love flow mingled down!
Did e'er such love and sorrow meet,
Or thorns compose so rich a crown?

4 Were the whole realm of nature mine,
That were an offering far too small:
Love so amazing, so divine,
Demands my soul, my life, my all.

2 Oh, loving attitude! He stands
With melting heart and laden hands;
Oh, matchless kindness! and He shows
This matchless kindness to His foes.

3 But will He prove a friend indeed?
He will, the very friend you need—
The Friend of sinners; yes, 'tis He
With garments dyed on Calvary

4 Rise, touched with gratitude divine.
Turn out His enemy and thine;
That soul-destroying monster, sin;
And let the heavenly Stranger in.

No. 401.

1 Behold a Stranger at the door:
He gently knocks, has knocked before;
Has waited long, is waiting still
You treat no other friend so ill.

J. GRIO

No. 402. Waiting.

"Waiting for the coming of our Lord Jesus Christ."—1 Cor. 1:7

Mrs. FRANCES L. MACE.
IRA D. SANKEY.

1. On - ly wait-ing till the shadows Are a lit - tle lon - ger grown;
2. On - ly wait-ing till the reap-ers Have the last sheaf gather'd home;
3. On - ly wait-ing till the an-gels O - pen wide the pearl-y gate,
4. Wait-ing for a brighter dwelling Than I ev - er yet have seen,

On - ly wait- ing till the glimmer Of the day's last beam is flown;
For the sum-mer - time has fad - ed And the au-tumn winds have come.
At whose por-tals long I've lingered, Wea-ry, poor, and des - o - late:
Where the tree of life is bloom-ing, And the fields are ev - er green:

Till the night of death has fad-ed From the heart once full of day;
Quickly, reapers! gath- er quickly, All the ripe hours of my heart;
E - ven now I hear their footsteps, And their voi-ces far a - way;
Waiting for my full re-demp-tion, When my Saviour shall re-store

Till the stars of heav'n are breaking Thro' the twilight soft and gray.
For the bloom of life is withered, And I has - ten to de - part.
If they call me, I am wait-ing, On - ly wait-ing to o - bey.
All that sin has caused to with-er; Age and sor- row come no more.

The Palace o' the King.—Concluded.

We like the gild-ed sim-mer, wi' its mer-ry, mer-ry tread
It's here we hae oor tri-als, an' it's here that He pre-pares
The time for saw-in' seed, it is a wear-in', wear-in' dune;
It's iv-'ry halls are bon-nie up-on which the rain-bows shine,
We see oor freen's a-wait us ower yon-ner at His gate;

An' we sigh when hoar-y win-ter lays its beau-ties wi' the dead;
His cho-sen for the rai-ment which the ransomed sin-ner wears.
An' the time for win-nin' souls will be o-wer ver-ra sune.
An' its E-den bow'rs are trellised wi' a nev-er fad-in' Vine;
Then lat us a' be read-y, for ye ken it's get-tin' late;

For tho' bon-nie are the snawflakes, an' the doon on Win-ter's wing,
An' its here that He wad hear us 'mid oor trib-u-la-tions sing,
Then lat us a' be ac-tive, if a fruit-fu' sheaf we'd bring
An' the pearl-y gates o' Heav-en do a glo-rious radiance fling,
Let oor lamps be bricht-ly burn-in'; let us raise oor voice and sing,

It's fine to ken it daur-na touch the pal-ace o' the King.
"We'll trust oor God wha' reigneth i' the pal-ace o' the King.
To a-dorn the Roy-al ta-ble i' the pal-ace o' the King.
On the star-ry floor that shimmers i' the pal-ace o' the King.
For sune we'll meet, to pairt nae mair, i' the pal-ace o' the King.

No. 405.

Redeemed.

"Let the redeemed of the Lord say so."—Ps. 107:2

El. Nathan.
James McGranahan.

1. "Redeemed!" "redeemed!" Oh, sing the joyful strain!
2. What grace! what grace! That He who calmed the wave,
3. "Redeemed!" "redeemed!" The word has brought repose,
4. "Redeemed!" "redeemed?" O joy, that I should be

"Redeemed!" "redeemed!"
What grace! what grace!

Give praise; give praise and glory to His name;
Should stoop, my soul, my guilty soul to save!
And joy, and joy that each redeemed one knows,
In Christ, in Christ, from sin forever free!

Give praise! give praise!
Should stoop, my soul,

Who gave His blood our souls to save, And purchased freedom
That He the curse should bear for me, A sinful wretch, His
Who sees his sins on Jesus laid, And knows His blood the
Forever free to praise His name, Who bore for me the

for the slave! And purchased freedom for the slave
enemy! A sinful wretch His enemy!
ransom paid, And knows His blood the ransom paid.
guilt and shame, Who bore for me the guilt and shame!

And purchased freedom, purchased freedom for the slave!
A sinful wretch, His enemy, His ene-
And knows His blood the ransom paid, the ransom
Who bore for me the guilt and shame, the guilt and

Copyright, 1879, by James McGranahan.

Redeemed.—Concluded.

CHORUS.

"Redeemed!" "redeemed" from sin and all its woe! "Redeemed!" "redeemed" e-ter-nal life to know! "Re-deemed!" "Re-deemed" by Je-sus' blood, "Redeemed!" "Re-deemed!" Oh, praise the Lord!

* The CHORUS may be omitted if desired.

No. 406.   Grace before Meals.

"The eyes of all wait upon Thee, and Thou givest them their meat in due season."—Ps. 145: 15.

P. P. BLISS.

God is great, and God is good, And we thank Him for this food: By His hand must all be fed, Give us, Lord, our dai-ly bread.

No. 407. **Peace! Be Still!**

"*Jesus rebuked the wind, and said unto the sea, Peace! be still!*"—MARK 1. 39.

Miss M. A. BAKER.   H. R. PALMER.

1. Mas-ter, the tempest is rag-ing! The bil-lows are toss-ing high!
2. Mas-ter, with anguish of spir-it I bow in my grief to-day;
3. Mas-ter, the ter-ror is o-ver, The el-e-ments sweetly rest;

The sky is o'ershadowed with blackness, No shel-ter or help is nigh;
The depths of my sad heart are troubled; Oh, wak-en and save, I pray!
Earth's sun in the calm lake is mirrored, And heaven's with-in my breast;

"Car-est Thou not that we per-ish?"—How canst Thou lie a-sleep,
Torrents of sin and of anguish Sweep o'er my sink-ing soul;
Lin-ger, O bless-ed Re-deemer, Leave me a-lone no more;

When each moment so mad-ly is threat'ning A grave in the an-gry deep?
And I per-ish! I per-ish! dear Mas-ter; Oh! has-ten, and take con-trol.
And with joy I shall make the blest harbor, And rest on the bliss-ful shore.

Copyright, 1874, by John Church & Co.

Peace! Be Still!—Concluded.

I am the Door.—Concluded.

by Me if a-ny man en-ter in, He shall be sav'd, he shall be sav'd.

No. 409. Rathbun.

By JOHN NEWTON. ITHAMAR CONKEY.

1. Sav-iour! vis-it Thy plan-ta-tion; Grant us, Lord! a gra-cious rain:
2. Keep no long-er at a distance;—Shine up-on us from on high,

All will come to des-o-la-tion, Un-less Thou re-turn a-gain.
Lest for want of Thine as-sist-ance, Ev'-ry plant should droop and die.

3 Let our mutual love be fervent,
   Make us prevalent in prayers;
Let each one, esteemed Thy servant,
   Shun the world's enticing snares.

 Break the tempter's fatal power;
   Turn the stony heart to flesh;
And begin from this good hour,
   To revive Thy work afresh.

No. 410.

Jesus hail! enthroned in glory,
   There for ever to abide;
All the heavenly hosts adore Thee,
   Seated at Thy Father's side.

2 There for sinners Thou art pleading,
   There Thou dost our place prepare
Ever for us interceding,
   Till in glory we appear.

3 Worship, honor, power and blessing
   Thou art worthy to receive:
Loudest praises, without ceasing,
   Meet it is for us to give.

4 Help, ye bright angelic spirits!
   Bring your sweetest, noblest lays;
Help to bring our Saviour's merits,—
   Help to chant Immanuel's praise.

By JOHN BAKEWELL.

Along the River of Time.—Concluded.

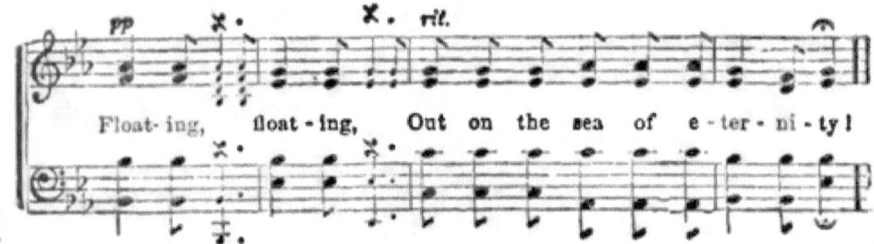

Floating, floating, Out on the sea of eternity!

No. 412. Belmont.

Rev. SAMUEL STENNETT. From MOZART.

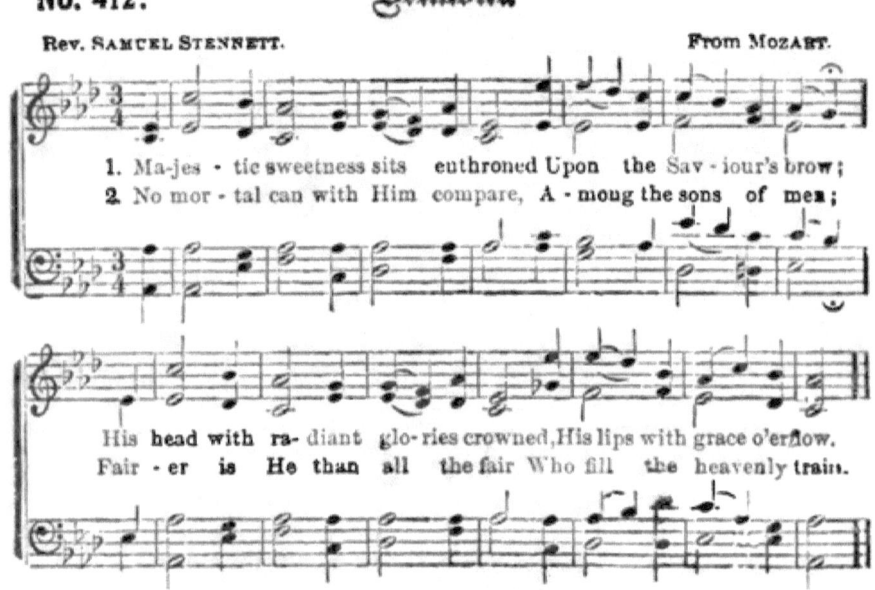

1. Majestic sweetness sits enthroned Upon the Saviour's brow;
His head with radiant glories crowned, His lips with grace o'erflow.

2. No mortal can with Him compare, Among the sons of men;
Fairer is He than all the fair Who fill the heavenly train.

3 He saw me plunged in deep distress,
  And flew to my relief;
For me He bore the shameful cross,
  And carried all my grief.

4 To heaven, the place of His abode,
  He brings my weary feet;
Shows me the glories of my God,
  And makes my joys complete.

5 Since from Thy bounty I receive
  Such proofs of love divine,
Had I a thousand hearts to give,
  Lord! they should all be Thine.

No. 413. Tune—BRADBURY TRIO, p. 194. Key E♭.

1 Jesus loves me! this I know,
For the Bible tells me so:
Little ones to Him belong;
They are weak, but He is strong.

CHO.—Yes, Jesus loves me! Yes, Jesus
  loves me!
Yes, Jesus loves me! The Bible
  tells me so!

2 Jesus from His throne on high
Came into this world to die;
That I might from sin be free,
Bled and died upon the tree.

3 Jesus loves me!—He who died
Heaven's gate to open wide!
He will wash away my sin,
Let His little child come in.

4 Jesus, take this heart of mine;
Make it pure and wholly Thine:
Thou hast bled and died for me,
I will henceforth live for Thee.

ADNA WARNER.

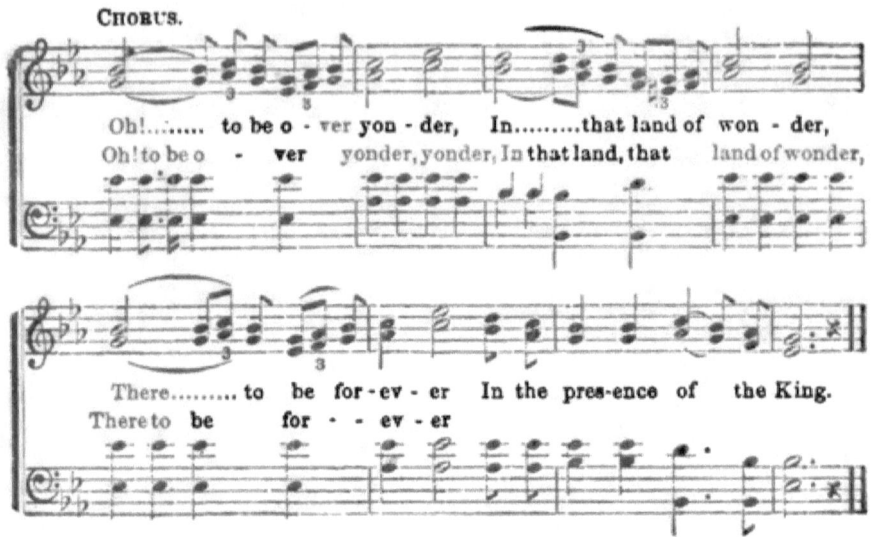

The Crowning Day.—Concluded.

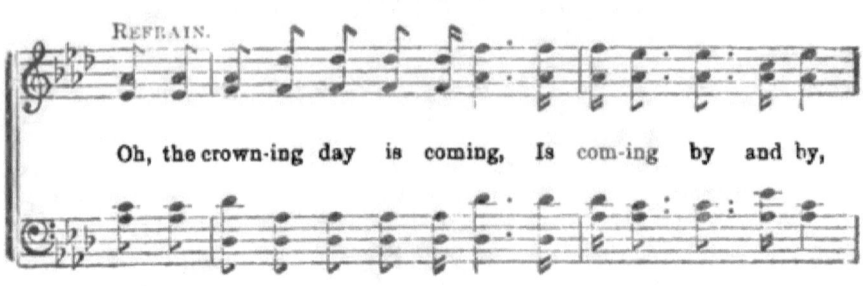
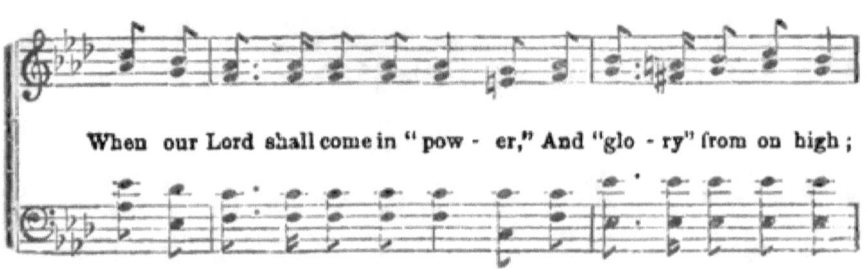

2 I've His gude word o' promise that some gladsome day; the King
To His ain royal palace His banished hame will bring;
Wi' een an' wi' hert rinnin' ower we shall see
The King in His beauty, in oor ain countrie.
My sins hae been mony, an' my sorrows hae been sair,
But there they'll never vex me, nor be remembered mair;
For His bluid has made me white, an' His han' shall dry my e'e,
When He brings me hame at last, to mine ain countrie.

3 Sae little noo I ken, o' yon blessèd bonnie place,
I only ken its Hame, whaur we shall see His face;
It wad surely be eneuch for ever mair to be
In the glory o' His presence in oor ain countrie.
Like a bairn to his mither, a wee birdie to its nest,
I wad fain be gangin' noo, unto my Saviour's breast,
For He gathers in His bosom witless, worthless lambs like me,
An' carries them Himsel', to His ain countrie.

4 He's faithfu' that hath promised, an' He'll surely come again,
He'll keep His tryst wi' me, at what hour I dinna ken;
But He bids me still to wait, an' ready aye to be,
To gang at ony moment to my ain countrie.
Sae I'm watching aye, an' singin' o' my hame as I wait,
For the soun'ing o' His footfa' this side the gowden gate,
God gie His grace to ilka ane wha' listens noo to me,
That we a' may gang in gladness to oor ain countrie.

No. 418. **Italian Hymn.**

Rev. JAMES ALLEN. F. GIARDINI, 1768.

1. Glory to God on high! Let heav'n and earth reply, "Praise ye His name!" His love and grace adore, Who all our sorrows bore; Sing loud for-ev-er-more, "Worthy the Lamb!"

2 While they around the throne
  Cheerfully join in one,
    Praising His name,—
  Ye who have felt His blood
  Sealing your peace with God,
  Sound His dear name abroad,
    "Worthy the Lamb!"

3 Join, all ye ransomed race,
  Our Lord and God to bless:
    Praise ye His name!
  In Him we will rejoice,
  And make a joyful noise,
  Shouting with heart and voice,
    "Worthy the Lamb!"

4 Soon must we change our place,
  Yet will we never cease
    Praising His name:
  To Him our songs we bring;
  Hail Him our gracious King;
  And, through all ages sing,
    "Worthy the Lamb!"

—o—

No. 419.

1 Come, Thou almighty King,
  Help us Thy name to sing,
    Help us to praise:
  Father! all-glorious,
  O'er all victorious,
  Come, and reign over us,
    Ancient of Days!

2 Come, Thou incarnate Word,
  Gird on Thy mighty sword;
    Our prayer attend;
  Come, and Thy people bless,
  And give Thy word success:
  Spirit of holiness!
    On us descend.

3 Come, holy Comforter!
  Thy sacred witness bear,
    In this glad hour:
  Thou, who almighty art,
  Now rule in every heart,
  And ne'er from us depart,
    Spirit of power!

4 To the great One-in-Three,
  The highest praises be,
    Hence evermore!
  His sovereign majesty
  May we in glory see,
  And to eternity
    Love and adore.

CHARLES WESLEY.

No. 420. Autumn.

HENRY F. LYTE. Spanish.

1. Jesus, I my cross have taken, All to leave and follow Thee,
Naked, poor, despised, forsaken, Thou from hence my all shalt be,
Perish ev'ry fond ambition, All I've sought, or hoped, or known,
D.S. Yet how rich is my condition, God and heav'n are still my own.

2 Let the world despise and leave me,
  They have left my Saviour, too;
Human hearts and looks deceive me—
  Thou ar' not, like them, untrue;
Oh! while thou dost smile upon me,
  God of wisdom, love, and might,
Foes may hate, and friends disown me,
  Show Thy face, and all is bright.

3 Haste thee on from grace to glory,
  Armed by faith, and wing'd by pray'r!
Heaven's eternal day's before thee;
  God's own hand shall guide thee there:
Soon shall close thy earthly mission,
  Soon shall pass thy pilgrim days,
Hope shall change to glad fruition,
  Faith to sight, and prayer to praise.

—o—

No. 421.

1 Jesus wept! those tears are over
  But His heart is still the same,
Kinsman, Friend, and Elder Brother,
  Is His everlasting name.

‖: Saviour, who can love like Thee,
  Gracious One of Bethany. :‖

2 When the pangs of trial seize us,
  When the waves of sorrow roll,
I will lay my head on Jesus,
  Pillow of the troubled soul.
‖: Surely, none can feel like Thee,
  Weeping One of Bethany :‖

3 Jesus wept! and still in glory,
  He can mark each mourner's tear
Living to retrace the story
  Of the hearts He solaced here
‖: Lord, when I am called to die
  Let me think of Bethany :‖

4 Jesus wept! those tears of sorrow
  Are a legacy of love;
Yesterday, to-day, to-morrow,
  He the same doth ever prove,
‖: Thou art all in all to me,
  Living One of Bethany!

Sir EDWARD DENNY.

No. 422. **Wilmot.**

Sir JOHN BOWRING.   C. M. VON WEBER.

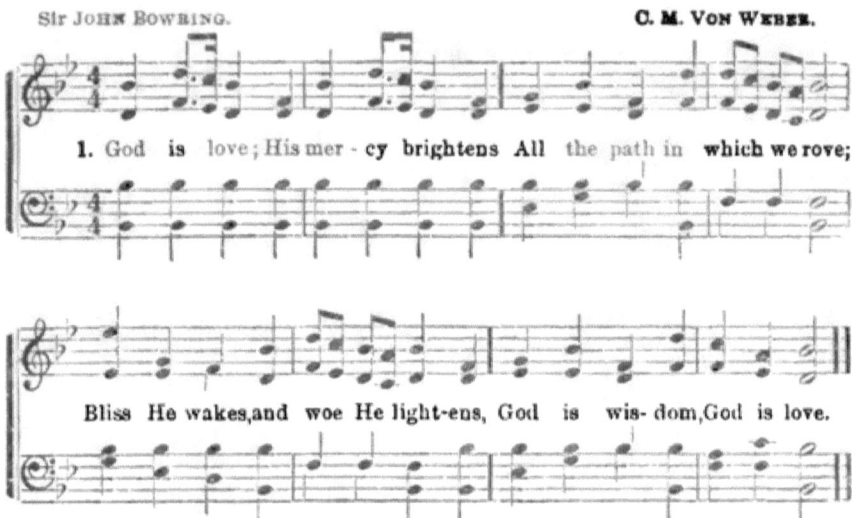

1. God is love; His mercy brightens All the path in which we rove; Bliss He wakes, and woe He lightens, God is wisdom, God is love.

2 Time and change are busy ever;
   Man decays, and ages move;
But His mercy waneth never;
   God is wisdom, God is love.

3 E'en the hour that darkest seemeth
   Will His changeless goodness prove;
From the gloom His brightness streameth,
   God is wisdom, God is love.

4 He with earthly cares entwineth
   Hope and comfort from above;
Everywhere His glory shineth;
   God is wisdom, God is love.

No. 423.

1 Jesus only, when the morning
   Beams upon the path I tread;
Jesus only when the darkness
   Gathers round my weary head.

2 Jesus only, when the billows
   Cold and sullen o'er me roll;
Jesus only, when the trumpet
   Rends the tomb and wakes the soul.

3 Jesus only, when in judgment
   Boding fears my heart appall;
Jesus only, when the wretched
   On the rocks and mountains call.

4 Jesus only, when, adoring,
   Saints their crowns before Him bring;
Jesus only, I will, joyous,
   Through eternal ages sing.
               Rev. ELIAS NASON.

No. 424.

1 Come, ye sinners, poor and needy,
   Weak and wounded sick and sore,
Jesus ready stands to save you
   Full of pity, love, and power.

2 Now, ye needy, come and welcome,
   God's free bounty glorify;
True belief and true repentance,
   Every grace that brings you nigh.

3 Let not conscience make you linger,
   Nor of fitness fondly dream,
All the fitness He requireth,
   Is to feel your need of Him.

4 Come, ye weary, heavy laden,
   Bruised and mangled by the fall,
If you tarry till you're better,
   You will never come at all.

5 Agonizing in the garden,
   Lo! your Maker prostrate lies!
On the bloody tree behold Him—
   Hear Him cry before He dies.
               Rev. JOSEPH HART.

No. 425. **Hendon.**

Rev. J. S. B. MONSELL.   C. H. A. MALAN.

1. Ask ye what great thing I know That delights and stirs me so? What the high reward I win? Whose the name I glory in? Jesus Christ, the Crucified.

2 What is faith's foundation strong?
What awakes my lips to song?
He who bore my sinful load,
Purchased for me peace with God,
   Jesus Christ, the Crucified.

3 Who defeats my fiercest foes?
Who consoles my saddest woes?
Who revives my fainting heart,
Healing all its hidden smart?
   Jesus Christ, the Crucified.

4 Who is life in life to me?
Who the death of death will be?
Who will place me on His right
With the countless hosts of light?
   Jesus Christ, the Crucified.

5 This is that great thing I know;
This delights and stirs me so;
Faith in Him who died to save,
Him who triumphed o'er the grave,
   Jesus Christ, the Crucified.

No. 426.

1 Wait, my soul, upon the Lord,
  To His gracious promise flee,
Laying hold upon His word
‖:"As thy days thy strength shall be.":‖

2 If the sorrows of thy case,
  Seem peculiar still to thee,
God has promised needful grace
‖:"As thy days thy strength shall be.":‖

3 Days of trial, days of grief
  In succession thou may'st see,
This is still thy sweet relief
‖:"As thy days thy strength shall be.":‖

4 Rock of Ages, I'm secure,
  With Thy promise full and free,
Faithful, positive, and sure—
‖:"As thy days thy strength shall be.":‖

WM. F. LLOYD

INDEX.

Titles in Small Caps.—First Lines in Roman.

A

	No.
AH MY HEART	34
Ah, this heart is void and chill	326
Alas! and did my Saviour	111, 167
A LIGHT UPON THE SHORE	233
A LITTLE WHILE	161, 399
"A little while," and He shall	399
ALL FOR ME	146
All glory to Jesus be given	201
All hail the power of Jesus' name	101
All my doubts I give to Jesus	139
All people that on earth do dwell	1
All-seeing, gracious Lord	356
ALL THE WAY MY SAVIOUR LEADS	60
ALL TO CHRIST I OWE	35
ALMOST PERSUADED	75
ALONG THE RIVER OF TIME	411
A long time I wandered	66
Amazing grace! how sweet	213
Am I a soldier of the Cross	115
ARE YOU COMING HOME TO-NIGHT?	311
ARISE AND SHINE	198
Arise my soul, arise!	119
ARLINGTON. C. M.	115
A SINNER FORGIVEN	64
Ask ye what great thing I know	425
ART THOU WEARY	195
A ruler once came to Jesus	237
AT THE FEET OF JESUS	160
AUTUMN	420
Awake, and sing the song	320

B

BEAUTIFUL MORNING!	392
BEAUTIFUL VALLEY OF EDEN	252
Behold a Stranger at the door	401
BEHOLD THE BRIDEGROOM	168
BEHOLD, WHAT LOVE!	363
BELMONT. C. M.	412
Beneath the cross of Jesus	43
Be our joyful song to-day	286
Beside the well at noon-time	302
BEULAH LAND	305
BEYOND THE SMILING AND THE	378
BLESSED HOME-LAND	260
BLESSED HOPE	245
Blessed hope that in Jesus is given	245
BLESSED RIVER	170
BLESS ME NOW	82
Blest be the tie that binds	114
BOYLSTON S. M.	113
Brightly beams our Father's mercy	65
BRIGHTLY GLEAMS OUR BANNER	313
BRINGING IN THE SHEAVES	370
Brother, art thou worn and weary	359
By faith I view my Saviour dying	318

C

CALLING NOW	9
CALL THEM IN	153
CAN IT BE RIGHT?	269
CHILD OF SIN AND SORROW	386
CHRIST FOR ME	258
CHRIST IS COMING!	338
CHRIST RETURNETH	239
CLOSE TO THEE	176
"COME"	309
COME BELIEVING!	390
Come every soul, by sin oppressed	94
Come, every joyful heart	325
COME, FOR THE FEAST IS SPREAD	191
Come, Holy Spirit, heavenly Dove	128
Come home, come home!	38
Come, my soul, thy suit prepare	217

	No.
COME NEAR ME	231
Come near me, O my Saviour	231
COME NOW, SAITH THE LORD	255
COME, PRODIGAL, COME	335
Come, sing, my soul, and praise	337
Come, sing the Gospel's joyful	134
Come souls that are longing for	255
Come, Thou Almighty King	419
Come Thou Fount of every	116
COME, THOU WEARY	415
Come to Jesus, come to Jesus!	132
COME TO THE SAVIOUR	62
COME UNTO ME, AND REST	359
Come ye sinners, poor and	127–424
Come, we that love the Lord	250
COME YE DISCONSOLATE	197
CONSECRATION	234
CORONATION. C. M	101
CROSS AND CROWN. C. M	206
CROSS OF JESUS	43
CROWN HIM	262
CUT IT DOWN	238

D

DARE TO BE A DANIEL	158
DARK IS THE NIGHT	148
DELIVERANCE WILL COME	367
DENNIS. S. M	114
DEPTH OF MERCY	99–346
Did Christ o'er sinners weep	131
DOERS OF THE WORD	369
Down life's dark vale we wander	52
Do you see the Hebrew Captive	143
DRAW ME NEARER	138
DUNDEE. C. M	111

E

ETERNITY	203
Eternity dawns on my vision	278
ETERNITY IS DRAWING NIGH	357
EVAN. C. M	107
EVEN ME	87
EVENING PRAYER	292
EVERY DAY AND HOUR	48
EXPOSTULATION	205

F

Fade, fade each earthly joy	179
FAINT, YET PURSUING	301

	No.
Faith is a living power from	215
FATHER, TAKE MY HAND	316
Fierce and wild the storm is	253
FIX YOUR EYES UPON JESUS	263
FOREVER WITH JESUS THERE	274
Free from the law, oh happy	16
Fresh from the throne of glory	170
From all that dwell below	321
From the riven rock there floweth	270
From every stormy wind that blows	105
FULLY PERSUADED	76
FULLY TRUSTING	139

G

GATE AJAR	15
GATHERING HOME	361
GIVE ME THE WINGS OF FAITH	186
Gliding o'er life's fitful waters	260
GLORIA PATRI	328
GLORY BE TO JESUS' NAME	331
Glory be to the Father	328
Glory, glory be to Jesus	331
Glory to God on high	418
GO BURY THY SORROW	61
God loved the world of sinners lost	30
GOOD NEWS	291
God is great and God is good	406
God is Love; His mercy brightens	422
GOSPEL BELLS	235
GOSPEL TRUMPET'S SOUNDING	266
GO WORK IN MY VINEYARD	98
GRACE BEFORE MEALS	406
Grace 'tis a charming sound	49
GREAT PHYSICIAN	56
Guide me, O thou great Jehovah	88

H

HALLELUJAH! HE IS RISEN	180
HALLELUJAH, 'TIS DONE!	2
HALLELUJAH! WHAT A SAVIOUR	140
HAMBURG. L. M	400
Hasten, sinner, to be wise	214
Hark! the voice of Jesus, crying	120
HAVE YOU ANY ROOM FOR JESUS?	284
Have you on the Lord believed?	31
HEAR THE CALL	149
HEAR THOU MY PRAYER	356
Hear ye the glad Good News from	315

	No.
HEAVENLY CANAAN	264
Heavenly Father, bless me now	32
Heavenly Father, we beseech Thee	317
Heavenly Father, we thy children	376
HEBRON. L. M.	212
HE CAME TO BETHANY	385
HE LEADETH ME.	51
Helpless I come to Jesus' blood	349
HE KNOWS	307
HENDON. 7s.	425
HE THAT BELIEVETH	315
HE WILL HIDE ME	225
HIDE THOU ME	374
HIDING IN THEE	233
HIS WORD A TOWER	182
HO, EVERY ONE THAT THIRSTETH.	302
HOLD FAST TILL I COME	173
HOLD THE FORT	14
HOLY, HOLY, HOLY! LORD GOD..	222
HOLY SPIRIT, FAITHFUL GUIDE..	40
HOME AT LAST	189
HOME OF THE SOUL	20
HOME OVER THERE	92
Ho! my comrades, see the signal.	14
HO! REAPERS OF LIFE'S HARVEST	150
HOW CAN I KEEP FROM SINGING?.	389
HOW HAPPY ARE WE	244
How solemn are the words	70
How sweet the name of Jesus	71
How sweet the word of Christ	287

I

	No.
I AM COMING.	366
I AM COMING TO THE CROSS	59
I am far frae my hame	417
I am now a child of God	178
I AM PRAYING FOR YOU	11
I am so glad that our Father in	23
I AM SWEEPING THROUGH THE	178
I AM THE DOOR	408
I am Thine, O Lord, I have heard.	138
I am trusting, Lord, in Thee	59
I AM TRUSTING THEE	290
I am waiting for the morning	375
I BRING MY SINS TO THEE	156
I CANNOT TELL HOW PRECIOUS	251
I feel like singing all the time	276
If never the gaze of the sun	243

	No.
I gave My life for thee	17
I have a Saviour, He's pleading in.	1
I have entered the Valley of blessing	196
I have heard of a land far away	261
I have heard of a Saviour's love	157
I have read of a beautiful city	310
I heard the voice of Jesus say	123
I hear the Saviour say	35
I HEAR THE WORDS OF JESUS	364
I HEAR THY WELCOME VOICE..	62
I know not the hour, when my Lord	13
I know not what awaits me	307
I KNOW THAT MY REDEEMER LIVES	398
I LEFT IT ALL WITH JESUS	90–345
I'LL STAND BY YOU TILL THE MORN	253
I LOVE TO TELL THE STORY	39
I love to think of the heavenly land	152
I love thy Kingdom, Lord	211
I'M A PILGRIM	306
I'M GOING HOME	256
IMMANUEL'S LAND	147
I NEED THEE EVERY HOUR	3
I NEVER KNEW YOU	377
In my Father's house there is	274
In some way or other, the Lord	5
In the Christian's home in glory	130
In the cross of Christ I glory	68
IN THE PRESENCE OF THE KING	58
IN THE SILENT MIDNIGHT WATCH.	183
In Thy cleft, O Rock of Ages	374
In Zion's Rock abiding	171
I saw a way-worn traveler	367
I SHALL BE SATISFIED	351
IS JESUS ABLE TO REDEEM?	241
IS MY NAME WRITTEN THERE?..	348
I STOOD OUTSIDE THE GATE	172
IS YOUR LAMP BURNING?	403
ITALIAN HYMN	418
I think when I read that sweet	340
It's a bonnie, bonnie warl'	404
IT IS FINISHED	281
IT IS WELL WITH MY SOUL	206
It may be at morn, when the day.	239
IT PASSETH KNOWLEDGE	73
I'VE FOUND A FRIEND	224
I've found a joy in sorrow	151
I've found the Pearl of greatest	300
I've reached the land of corn and.	305
I'VE PASSED THE CROSS	382

	No.
I waited for the Lord, my God ...	125
I will sing of my Redeemer......	229
I will sing you a song of that.....	20

J

Jesus, and shall it ever be.......	322
JESUS CALLS THEE................	228
JESUS CHRIST IS PASSING BY.....	230
Jesus, gracious one, calleth now..	228
Jesus hail! enthroned in glory...	410
Jesus, I my cross have taken.....	420
JESUS IS COMING................	379
JESUS IS MIGHTY TO SAVE.......	201
JESUS IS MINE..................	179
JESUS IS MY SAVIOUR............	365
JESUS, I WILL TRUST THEE......	341
Jesus, keep me near the cross.....	45
JESUS LOVES EVEN ME...........	23
Jesus loves me, this I know......	413
JESUS, LOVER OF MY SOUL......	85-193
Jesus, my Lord, to Thee I cry....	368
JESUS OF NAZARETH PASSETH BY.	8
JESUS ONLY.....................	257
Jesus only, when the morning....	423
JESUS, ONLY JESUS..............	286
JESUS SHALL REIGN	141
Jesus wept! those tears are over..	421
JEWELS........................	97
JOY IN SORROW	151
JOY TO THE WORLD..............	230
Joy to the world, the Lord is come	110
JUST AS I AM..................	54
JUST A WORD FOR JESUS.........	163

K

KNOCKING, KNOCKING, WHO.....	17

L

LABAN. S. M..................	112
LAND OF BEULAH................	187
LEAD ME ON...................	382
LENOX. 6s & 8s................	119
Let us gather up the sunbeams...	174
LET THE LOWER LIGHTS..........	65
LIFE FOR A LOOK...............	80
LIGHT AFTER DARKNESS..........	330
Light in the darkness, sailor......	83
Lift up, lift up thy voice with....	198

	No.
Long in darkness we have........	227
LOOK AWAY TO JESUS...........	164
Look unto Me, and be ye saved...	383
Lord dismiss us with Thy blessing	159
Lord, I care not for riches........	348
Lord, I hear of showers of blessing	87
Lord Jesus, I long to be perfectly.	169
Lord, my trust I repose in Thee..	387
Lo! the day of God is breaking....	149
Look, ye saints, the sight is......	262

M

Majestic sweetness sits enthroned.	413
"Man of Sorrows," what a name..	140
MARCHING TO ZION..............	250
Master, the tempest is raging.....	407
MEMORIES OF EARTH............	297
MERCY'S FREE..................	318
MINE !.........................	277
Mine! what rays of glory bright..	277
More holiness give me...........	93
MORE LOVE TO THEE, O CHRIST..	136
MORE THAN TONGUE CAN TELL...	355
MORE TO FOLLOW...............	31
MUST I GO, AND EMPTY HANDED...	298
Must Jesus bear the cross alone...	206
MY AIN COUNTREE..............	417
My days are gliding swiftly by....	219
My faith looks up to Thee........	117
MY FAITH STILL CLINGS..........	299
My God and Father while I stray.	373
My God, I have found...........	221
My heart that was heavy and sad.	100
My heavenly home is bright and..	256
MY HIGH TOWER................	171
My hope is built on nothing less..	162
My latest sun is sinking fast......	187
My life flows on in endless song..	389
MY JESUS, I LOVE THEE..........	314
MY PRAYER.....................	93
MY REDEEMER..................	229
My sin is great, my strength......	298
MY SONG SHALL BE OF JESUS......	142
My soul, be on thy guard.........	112
My soul is happy all day long....	365
MY SOUL WILL OVERCOME.....	349

N

Nearer, my God, to Thee........	118

	No.
Near the Cross	45
Nettleton. 8s & 7s	116
New Haven. 6s & 4s	117
New Song	44
Ninety and Nine	6
None but Christ can satisfy	333
None of Self and all of Thee	268
No other Name	73
Not all the blood of beasts	113
Not half has Ever been told	310
Nothing but Leaves	96
Nothing but the Blood of Jesus	332
Nothing either great or small	281
Not my Own	342
Not now my Child	47
Not what these Hands have	388
Now just a word for Jesus	163
No works of law have we to boast	384

O

O Christ, in Thee my soul hath	333
O Christ, what burdens bowed	57
O Crown of Rejoicing	181
O for a faith that will not shrink	108
O for a thousand tongues to sing	102
O happy day, that fixed my choice	133
O Holy Spirit, come	324
O land of rest, for thee I sigh	304
Once again the Gospel message	390
Once more we come, God's word	369
Only a little While	362
Only Waiting	375
Only waiting till the shadows	402
O safe to the Rock that is higher	232
O Saviour, precious Saviour	350
O soul in the far-away country	335
O what a Saviour, that He died	242
O! what shall I do to be saved	202
Oh, bliss of the purified	46
Oh, come to the Saviour, believe	95
Oh, do not let the Word depart	246
Oh, for the peace that floweth as a	161
Oh, how happy are we	244
Oh, how He Loves	36
Oh, I am so happy in Jesus	265
Oh, I left all with Jesus	345
Oh, revive us by Thy Word	376
Oh, sing of His Mighty Love	46
Oh, Spirit, o'erwhelmed by thy	173

	No.
Oh, tender and sweet was the	247
Oh, the bitter pain and sorrow	268
Oh, the clanging bells of time	203
Oh, think of the home over there	92
Oh, to be Nothing	74
Oh, to be over yonder	58-414
Oh, turn ye, oh, turn ye	205
Oh, what are you going to do	194
Oh, where are the Reapers	155
Oh, word of words the sweetest	303
Old Hundred. L. M	1
Old, Old Story	37
Olive's Brow. L. M	216
Once for all	16
Once I was dead in sin	129
One more Day's Work for Jesus	28
One offer of salvation	78
One sweetly solemn thought	192
One there is above all others	36
On Jordan's stormy banks	303
Only an Armor Bearer	82
Only a step to Jesus	144
Only for Thee	280
Only Trust Him	94
Only trusting in my Saviour	272
Onward, Christian Soldiers	175
Onward Go	354
Onward! Upward!	135
Our lamps are trimmed and burn	168
Our Lord is now rejected	416
Our Master has taken His journey	285
Our way is often rugged	358
Out of Darkness into Light	227
Out of the Ark	209
Over Jordan	343
Over the Line	247
Over the Ocean Wave	296
O what shall I do to be saved?	408

P

Palace of the King	208
Paradise	287
Parting Hymn	317
Pass me Not	27
Peace, be Still	407
Pleyel's Hymn. 7s	214
Praise God, from whom all blessings	1
Praise Ye the Lord	344

	No.
Pray, brethren, pray	357
PRECIOUS BLOOD	347
PRECIOUS NAME	72
PRECIOUS PROMISE	50
Precious Saviour, may I live	280
PRESSING ON	294
PRODIGAL CHILD	38
PULL FOR THE SHORE	83

R

RATHBUN. 8s & 7s.	409
REDEEMED	405
REDEMPTION GROUND	337
REFUGE. 7s D	193
REJOICE AND BE GLAD	24
REJOICE WITH ME	288
REMEMBER ME	167
Repeat the story o'er and o'er	154
RESCUE THE PERISHING	18
REVIVE THY WORK	223
REVIVE US AGAIN	25
RING THE BELLS OF HEAVEN	19
RISE UP, AND HASTEN	339
ROCKINGHAM. L. M.	103
ROCK OF AGES	86
ROOM FOR THEE	188

S

Sad and weary, lone and dreary	366
SAFE IN THE ARMS OF JESUS	4
SALVATION	134
Salvation! O the joyful sound	109
SAVED BY THE BLOOD	254
SAVE, JESUS, SAVE!	248
Saviour, breathe an evening	292
Saviour, like a Shepherd lead us	126
Saviour, more than life to me	48
Saviour, Thy dying love	26
Saviour, visit Thy plantation	409
SAY, ARE YOU READY?	353
Say, is your lamp burning, my	403
Say, where is thy refuge, poor	312
SCATTER SEEDS OF KINDNESS	174
SEEKING TO SAVE	177
SESSIONS. L. M	215
SEYMOUR. 7s	99
Shall we gather at the river?	124
SHALL WE MEET BEYOND THE	199
She only touched the hem	267

	No.
SHIRLAND. S. M	211
Should the death-angel knock at	353
Simply trusting every day	165
SING AND PRAY!	278
SINGING ALL THE TIME	276
SINGING AS WE JOURNEY	380
Sing them over again to me	282
SING OF HIS MIGHTY LOVE	46
Sinners, turn, why will ye die?	106
SOLID ROCK (THE)	162
So let our lips and lives express	104
SOMETHING FOR JESUS	26
SONG OF SALVATION	157
Soon shall we see the glorious	371
Soul of mine, in earthly temple	351
SOUND THE ALARM!	391
SOUND THE HIGH PRAISES	293
Sowing in the morning	370
Sowing the seed by the daylight fair	79
Spirit of truth, oh, let me know	319
Standing by a purpose true	158
Stand up, stand up for Jesus	121
Stay, Thou insulted Spirit, stay	323
ST. THOMAS. S. M	320
SUBSTITUTION	57
Suffering Saviour, with thorn	146
SUN OF MY SOUL	84
SWEET BY-AND-BY	204
SWEET HOUR OF PRAYER	77

T

TAKE ME AS I AM	368
Take my life and let it be	234
Take the name of Jesus with you	72
TELL IT OUT	329
TELL ME MORE ABOUT JESUS	394
TELL ME THE OLD, OLD STORY	37
TEMPTED AND TRIED	249
Tenderly the Shepherd	177
TEN THOUSAND TIMES	275
THAT WILL BE HEAVEN FOR ME	13
The blood has always precious been	347
THE CROSS OF JESUS	43
THE CROWNING DAY	416
THE GATE AJAR FOR ME	15
THE GLORIOUS MORNING	371
THE GOSPEL BELLS	235
THE GOSPEL OF THY GRACE	327

	No.
The Gospel Trumpet's Sound	266
The Great Physician	56
The Half was never Told	154
The Heavenly Canaan	264
The Heavenly Land	152
The Hem of His Garment	267
The Holy Spirit	42
The Home over There	92
The Lamb is the Light thereof	243
The Land of Beulah	187
The Light of the World	41
The Lord's my Shepherd, I'll not	107
The Lord will Provide	5
The love that Jesus had for me	355
The Mistakes of my Life	190
The New Song	44
The Ninety and Nine	6
The Palace of the King...208,	404
The Pearl of Greatest Price	300
The Precious Name	72
The prize is set before us	289
The Prodigal Child	38
There are lonely hearts to cherish	360
There is a Fountain	91
There is a gate that stands ajar	15
There is a Green Hill far away	273
There is a land of pure delight.67,	264
There is Joy among the Angels	295
There is Life for a Look	80
There is love, true love	385
There's a beautiful land on high	218
There's a land that is fairer	204
There's a Light in the Valley	207
There's a Work for each of Us	285
There were ninety and nine that	6
The Smitten Rock	270
The Spirit, oh, sinner	42
The Sands of Time are...147–	397
The Solid Rock	162
The Sweet Story of Old	340
The Valley of Blessing	196
The way is dark, my Father	316
The whole world was lost in the	41
The Wondrous Gift	49
The word of God is given	395
They dreamed not of danger	209
They're gathering homeward	361
Think Jesus, Thine	226

	No.
Thine, most gracious Lord	137
This I Know	387
This is the day of toil	294
This loving Saviour stands patiently	9
Thou art coming	271
Thou didst leave Thy Throne	188
Thou my everlasting portion	176
Through the valley of the shadow	207
Thy will be done	373
Till He Come	69
'Tis a goodly pleasant land	208
'Tis known on earth, and heaven	394
'Tis midnight, and on Olive's brow	216
'Tis the Blessed Hour	334
'Tis the promise of God, full	2
To be There	261
To Day	55
To-day the Saviour calls	55
To Him be Glory Evermore	396
To Him who for our sins was slain	396
To the hall of the feast came the	64
To the Work	145
Traveling to the better land	382
Triumph by and by	289
Trusting in the Lord thy God	354
Trusting Jesus, that is all	165
Trust On	352
'Twill not be Long	393

V

	No.
Valley of Blessing (The)	196
Varina. C. M. D.	67
Verily, Verily	242

W

	No.
Waiting	402
Waiting and watching for me	210
Wait, my soul, upon the Lord	420
Wandering afar from the dwellings	12
Warwick. C. M.	213
Watchman, tell me	185
We are children of a King	380
We are Going Home	358
We are waiting by the river	220
Weary gleaner whence comest thou	83
We'll Gather there in Glory	395
We'll work till Jesus Comes	304
We Praise Thee and Bless Thee	372
We praise Thee, O God	25

	No.
WE'RE GOING HOME TO-MORROW!	22
We're going Home, no more to roam	22
We're marching to Canaan	166
WE'RE MARCHING TO ZION	250
We're saved by the blood	254
We shall meet beyond the river	7
WE SHALL MEET BY AND BY	7
WE SHALL REIGN	336
WE SHALL SLEEP, BUT NOT FOR	184
We speak of the land of the blest	283
WE TAKE THE GUILTY SINNER'S	384
We've journeyed many a day	233
WE WORSHIP THEE	350
WHAT A FRIEND WE HAVE	29
What can wash away my stain?	332
WHAT HAST THOU DONE FOR ME?	21
What, "lay my sins on Jesus?"	53
What means this eager, anxious	8
WHAT MUST IT BE TO BE THERE	283
WHAT SHALL I DO TO BE SAVED	202
WHAT SHALL THE HARVEST BE?	79
What though clouds are hovering	257
What various hindrances we meet	103
When He cometh, when He cometh	97
When I survey the wondrous cross	400
WHEN JESUS COMES	52
When Jesus comes to reward	259
When my final farewell to the	210
When peace like a river	200
WHEN THE COMFORTER CAME	100
When the King in His beauty shall	377
When the Lord from heaven	336
When the storms of life are	225
WHEN WE GET HOME	308
When we reach our Father's	297

	No.
WHERE ARE THE NINE?	12
WHERE HAST THOU GLEANED?	33
WHERE IS MY BOY TO-NIGHT?	279
Where is my wandering boy	279
WHERE IS THY REFUGE	312
While foes are strong and danger	182
While life prolongs its precious	212
WHILE THE DAYS ARE GOING BY	360
WHITE AS SNOW	53
WHITER THAN SNOW	169
Whom have I, Lord, in heaven	258
"Whosoever heareth," shout,	10
WHOSOEVER WILL	10
WHO IS ON THE LORD'S SIDE	381
WHO'S ON THE LORD'S SIDE	166
WHOLLY THINE	137
WHY DO YOU WAIT?	240
WHY NOT TO-NIGHT?	246
WILL JESUS FIND US WATCHING?	259
WILMOT. 8s & 7s	423
WINDOWS OPEN TOWARD	143
WISHING, HOPING, KNOWING	66
With harps and with viols, there	44
With His dear and loving care	343
WONDERFUL WORDS OF LIFE	282
WONDROUS GIFT	49
WONDROUS LOVE	30
Work, for the night is coming	122
Would you lose your load of sin?	263

Y

	No.
YE MUST BE BORN AGAIN	237
YES, THERE IS PARDON FOR YOU	95
YET THERE IS ROOM	81
YIELD NOT TO TEMPTATION	92

TOPICAL INDEX.

Titles in SMALL CAPS. First Lines in Roman.

ADOPTION.

	NO.		NO.		NO.
Arise, my soul, arise!	119	COME, PRODIGAL, COME!	335	Ring the bells of Heaven	19
Behold, what love!	363	I am now a child of God	178	SINGING AS WE JOURNEY	380

ASSURANCE.

	NO.		NO.		NO.
Ask ye what great thing	425	Lord, I care not for riches	348	THAT WILL BE HEAVEN	13
CHRIST FOR ME!	258	Mine!	277	THE PEARL OF GREATEST	300
Fully persuaded	76	My God, I have found	231	THIS I KNOW	387
HE KNOWS	307	My hope is built on	162	'T is the promise of God	2
I know that my Redeemer	398	My Jesus, I love Thee	314	VERILY, VERILY	242
JESUS IS MINE	179	O happy day!	133	When peace, like a river	200
Look unto Me	383	Safe in the arms of Jesus	4	WISHING, HOPING, KNOWING	65

THE BLOOD OF JESUS.

	NO.		NO.		NO.
Alas! and did my?	111, 167	Just as I am	64	PRECIOUS BLOOD	347
Arise, my soul, arise!	119	JESUS IS MIGHTY TO SAVE	201	Rock of Ages	86
Come, every soul by sin	94	My hope is built on	162	SAVED BY THE BLOOD	254
EVERY DAY AND HOUR	48	MY SOUL WILL OVERCOME	349	There is a fountain	91
HALLELUJAH! 'T IS DONE	2	Not all the blood of beasts	113	WHAT HAST THOU DONE FOR?	21
I AM SWEEPING THRO' THE	178	NOTHING BUT THE BLOOD	332	WHITER THAN SNOW	169
I hear Thy welcome voice	63	O Christ, what burdens!	57	When I survey the wondrous	400

CHRIST SEEKING.

	NO.		NO.		NO.
Behold a Stranger	401	Jesus Christ is passing	230	NINETY AND NINE, THE	6
Come, thou weary!	415	JESUS OF NAZARETH	8	SEEKING TO SAVE	177
In the silent midnight	183	Knocking, knocking	17		

CHRIST SOUGHT BY THE SINNER.

	NO.		NO.		NO.
A SINNER FORGIVEN	64	I AM COMING!	366	Oh, tender and sweet!	247
BLESS ME NOW!	32	I bring my sins to Thee	156	Pass me not!	27
Come, my soul!	217	I hear Thy welcome voice	63	She only touched the hem	267
Fully persuaded	76	I stood outside the gate	172	TAKE ME AS I AM!	368
I am coming to the Cross	59	Just as I am	64	WHAT SHALL I DO?	202

CHRIST'S CROSS (THE CROSS OF CHRIST).

	NO.		NO.		NO.
Beneath the Cross	43	I'VE PASSED THE CROSS	383	PARADISE	287
BLESS ME NOW!	32	Must Jesus bear the Cross?	206	Rejoice and be glad!	24
I am coming to the Cross	59	NEAR THE CROSS	45	THE GATE AJAR	15
In the Cross of Christ	68	ONCE FOR ALL	16	When I survey	400

CHRIST'S SECOND COMING.

	NO.		NO.		NO.
A LITTLE WHILE	161, 399	CROWN HIM!	262	Till He come!	63
ARISE AND SHINE	198	How happy are we!	244	Watchman, tell me	185
BEHOLD, THE BRIDEGROOM	168	Jesus is coming	379	We shall reign	336
Christ is coming!	338	THE CROWNING DAY	416	WHEN JESUS COMES	52
CHRIST RETURNETH	239	Thou art coming!	271	WILL JESUS FIND US?	239

CHRIST THE SHEPHERD.

	NO.		NO.		NO.
Saviour, like a Shepherd	126	NINETY AND NINE, THE	6	The Lord's my Shepherd	107

CHILDREN.

	NO.		NO.		NO.
Come to the Saviour!	62	ONLY FOR THEE	280	THE LIGHT OF THE WORLD	41
DARE TO BE A DANIEL	158	Ring the bells of Heaven	19	THE SWEET STORY OF OLD	340
I cannot tell how precious	251	Safe in the arms	4	TRIUMPH BY-AND-BY	339
JESUS LOVES EVEN ME	23	SCATTER SEEDS OF KINDNESS	174	We are children of a King	380
Jesus loves me	413	SINGING ALL THE TIME	276	WE'RE MARCHING TO ZION	250
Oh, I am so happy!	365	Take the name of Jesus	72	When He cometh	97

TOPICAL INDEX.—Continued.

COMMUNION (or, THE LORD'S SUPPER).

	NO.		NO.		NO.
Alas! and did my?	111, 167	Not all the blood of beasts	113	'Tis midnight, and on Olive's	218
Come, for the feast is spread	191	Till He come!	69	When I survey the wondrous	400

CONFESSION.

	NO.		NO.		NO.
Am I a soldier?	115	Jesus, and shall it ever be?	322	THE HALF WAS NEVER TOLD	154
CHRIST FOR ME!	258	JUST A WORD FOR JESUS	163	The mistakes of my life	190
Depth of mercy!	99, 346	Mine!	277	THE PEARL OF GREATEST	306
I heard the voice of Jesus	123	Once I was dead in sin	129	We're marching to Canaan	166
I love to tell the story	39	So let our lips and lives	104	WE TAKE THE GUILTY	384
I need Thee every hour	3	TELL ME MORE ABOUT JESUS	394	WHERE ARE THE NINE?	12
I waited for the Lord	125	Tell me the old, old story	37	Who is on the Lord's side	381

CONSECRATION.

	NO.		NO.		NO.
All-seeing, Gracious God	356	Lord Jesus, I long to be	169	Saviour, more than life	48
CHRIST FOR ME!	258	More holiness give me	93	SOMETHING FOR JESUS	26
DRAW ME NEARER!	133	More love to Thee	136	TAKE ME AS I AM!	368
Fully persuaded	75	Nearer, my God	118	Take my life and let	234
I am coming to the Cross	59	NONE OF SELF	268	Thine, Jesus, Thine!	226
I bring my sins to Thee	156	Not my own	342	Thou, my everlasting	176
Jesus, I my Cross have	420	Oh, to be nothing!	74	WHAT HAST THOU DONE?	21
Just as I am	54	ONLY FOR THEE!	280	WHOLLY THINE	137

ETERNITY (See HEAVEN also).

	NO.		NO.		NO.
Along the river of Time	411	ETERNITY IS DRAWING	357	Oh, the clanging bells of time	203
Eternity dawns	278	HOME OF THE SOUL	20	The sands of time	147

FAITH.

	NO.		NO.		NO.
Can it be right?	259	My faith looks up	117	O spirit, o'erwhelmed	173
Faith is a living power	215	MY FAITH STILL CLINGS	299	THE HEM OF HIS GARMENT	267
I left it all with Jesus	90, 345	Oh for a faith!	108	'Tis the promise of God	2
I need Thee every hour	3	Oh, I left it all	345	VERILY, VERILY!	242

FELLOWSHIP WITH CHRIST.

	NO.		NO.		NO.
At the feet of Jesus	160	I've found a Friend!	224	Oh, I am so happy!	265
BEULAH LAND	305	JESUS IS MINE!	179	OH, SING OF HIS MIGHTY	45
CHRIST FOR ME!	258	JESUS ONLY	257, 423	Oh, word of words	309
CLOSE TO THEE!	176	JOY IN SORROW	151	ONLY FOR THEE!	280
Come near me!	231	Mine!	277	Safe in the arms	4
DRAW ME NEARER	133	More love to Thee	136	Sun of my soul	84
EVERY DAY AND HOUR	46	My Jesus, I love Thee	314	Take the name of Jesus	72
HE CAME TO BETHANY	385	NONE BUT CHRIST CAN	333	Thine, Jesus, Thine!	226
HEAR THOU MY PRAYER!	356	Oh happy day!	133	VALLEY OF BLESSING, THE	196
I need Thee every hour	3	OH, HOW HE LOVES!	36	What a Friend we have!	29

GUIDANCE.

	NO.		NO.		NO.
All the way my	60	Guide me, O Thou great	88	Precious promise	50
Brightly gleams our banner	313	HE KNOWS!	307	Saviour like a shepherd	126
Dark is the night	148	He leadeth me!	51	The Lord's my Shepherd	107
EVERY DAY AND HOUR	46	LEAD ME ON!	382	Thou, my everlasting	176
FATHER, TAKE MY HAND!	316	OVER JORDAN	343	Through the valley	207

FUNERAL AND BURIAL.

	NO.		NO.		NO.
Beyond the smiling and	378	Jesus, lover of my soul	85, 193	There's a land that is	204
Blessed hope	245	My heavenly home	256	There is a land of pure	264
GATHERING HOME	361	Oh, think of the home	92	WE SHALL MEET BY-AND-BY	7
Give me the wings	136	Shall we gather?	124	We shall sleep, but not	184
In the Christian's home	130	Shall we meet beyond?	199	When peace, like a river	200

HEAVEN. "ALMOST THERE."

	NO.		NO.		NO.
A LIGHT UPON THE SHORE	233	I'm a pilgrim	306	One sweetly solemn thought	192
A little while	399	LOOKING HOME	326	On Jordan's stormy banks	303
DELIVERANCE WILL COME	367	My days are gliding	219	The sands of time	147, 397
GATHERING HOME	361	My latest sun is sinking	187	'T will not be long	393
I am now a child of God	178	Oh, think of the home!	92	WAITING!	402
I am waiting	375	Oh to be over yonder!	56, 414	We are waiting by the	220

TOPICAL INDEX.—*Continued.*

HEAVEN.

	NO.		NO.		NO.
Beautiful valley of Eden	252	Not half has ever been	310	That will be Heaven for	13
Beyond the smiling and the	378	Over Jordan	343	'Tis a goodly pleasant land	208
BLESSED HOMELAND	260	Rise up and hasten	339	To be there!	261
For ever with Jesus	274	Shall we gather?	124	Waiting and watching	210
Give me the wings of	186	Shall we meet!	199	We are going home	358
Home at last!	159	Ten thousand times	275	We'll gather there in	595
Home of the soul	20	The Heavenly Land	152	We're going home to-morrow	22
In the Christian's home	130	The Lamb is the Light	243	We're marching to Zion	250
In the presence of the	58	The palace of the King	404	We shall meet	7
Is my name written there	345	There's a beautiful land	218	What must it be to be there	283
My ain countrie	417	There's a land that is	204	When we get home	308
My Heavenly home is bright	256	There is a land of pure	67, 264	When we reach our	297

THE HOLY SPIRIT.

Come, Holy Spirit	128	More to follow!	31	Stay, Thou insulted Spirit	328
Come, Thou Almighty	419	O Holy Spirit, come!	324	The Spirit, O sinner	42
Holy Spirit, Faithful	40	Spirit of Truth	319	When the Comforter	100

INVITATION.

Are you coming home?	311	Come, ye sinners, poor	127, 424	The Gospel trumpet's	266
Calling now	9	Expostulation	205	The prodigal child	38
Call them in!	153	Gospel bells	235	The valley of blessing	196
Child of sin and sorrow	386	Hasten, sinner, to be wise	214	There is life for a look	80
Come believing!	390	Have you any room for?	286	To-day!	55
Come, every soul!	94	Jesus calls thee!	223	Where is thy refuge?	312
Come, for the feast	191	Jesus Christ is passing	230	While life prolongs	212
"Come now!" saith	255	Oh, word of words!	198	Whosoever will	10
Come, prodigal, come!	335	Only a step to Jesus	144	Why do you wait?	240
Come to Jesus!	132	Out of the ark	209	Why not to-night?	246
Come to the Saviour!	62	Over the line	247	Yes, there is pardon	96
Come, ye disconsolate!	197	Sinners, turn!	106	Yet there is room!	81

JOY.

Christ for me!	258	My God, I have found	221	Rejoice with me!	288
Come sing, my soul	337	My life flows on	389	Ring the bells of heaven	19
Come, we that love	250	My soul is happy	365	Singing all the time	276
How happy are we!	244	O crown of rejoicing	181	Singing as we journey	380
I've found a joy!	151	O happy day!	133	The pearl of greatest	300
Joy to the world!	110, 236	Oh, I am so happy	265	There is joy among	295

LOVE FOR CHRIST.

Every day and hour	48	My Jesus, I love Thee	314	Something for Jesus!	26
More love to Thee	136	None but Christ can	333	The half was never told	154

LOVE OF CHRIST FOR US.

Behold, what love!	363	I've found a Friend!	224	Oh, sing of His mighty love	46
God is love!	422	Jesus loves me	413	Once I was dead in sin	129
God loved the world	30	Jesus loves even me	23	Safe in the arms	4
Have you on the Lord?	31	Jesus wept	421	Spirit of Truth	319
I have heard of a Saviour's	157	More than tongue can	355	Tell me the old, old story	37
I love to tell the story	39	My Redeemer		There is love	355
It passeth knowledge	73	Oh, how He loves!	36	What hast thou done for?	21

MISSIONARY.

Bringing in the sheaves	370	Jesus shall reign	141	Rescue the perishing	18
Go work in My vineyard	96	One more day's work	25	Something for Jesus!	26
Hear the Call!	149	Over the ocean wave	296	What shall the harvest be?	79

PEACE AND REST.

Ah, my heart!	34	I heard the voice of Jesus	123	Peace! be still!	407
Art thou weary?	195	It is well with my soul	200	Pressing on	294
Beautiful valley of Eden!	252	Near the Cross	45	Sad and weary	366
Come to Me!	359	Oh for the peace!	161	We'll work till Jesus	305

TOPICAL INDEX.—Continued.

PRAISE.

	NO.		NO.		NO.
All hail the power	101	GLORIA PATRI	328	Praise ye the Lord!	344
All people that on earth	1	GLORY BE TO JESUS' NAME!	331	Redeemed! redeemed!	406
Awake and sing	320	Glory to God on high!	413	REVIVE US AGAIN	25
Be our joyful song	286	Holy, holy, holy!	222	Sound the high praises	293
Come, sing the gospel's	134	How sweet the name!	71	Take the name of Jesus	72
Come, Thou Almighty King	419	Jesus, hail!	410	THE NEW SONG	44
Come, Thou Fount of every	116	Majestic sweetness	412	To Him who for our	396
Come, we that love	250	MY REDEEMER	229	We praise and bless Thee	372
CROWN HIM!	262	My song shall be of Jesus!	142	We worship Thee	354
From all that dwell	321	Oh for a thousand tongues!	102	Whom have I, Lord?	255

PRAYER.

	NO.		NO.		NO.
BLESS ME NOW	32	I need Thee every hour	3	Revive Thy work	223
Blest be the tie	114	Jesus, lover of my soul	85, 193	Rock of Ages	86
Come, Holy Spirit!	128	Lord, dismiss us!	159	Save, Jesus, save!	248
Come, my soul	217	My faith looks up	117	Saviour, breathe an evening	292
EVEN ME!	87	MY PRAYER	93	Saviour, visit Thy planta-	402
FATHER, TAKE MY HAND!	316	My sin is great	299	Sweet hour of prayer!	77
From every stormy wind	105	Nearer, my God	118	'Tis the blessed hour of	334
God is great	406	OH, REVIVE US BY THY WORD	376	What a Friend we have!	29
HEAR THOU MY PRAYER!	356	PARTING HYMN	317	What various hindrances!	103
I AM PRAYING FOR YOU	11	Pass me not	27	WINDOWS OPEN TOWARD	143

PRECIOUS PROMISES.

	NO.		NO.		NO.
COME!	309	Mine!	277	Wait, my soul!	426
HIS WORD A TOWER	182	Once more we come	369	WHOSOEVER WILL	10
JESUS LOVES EVEN ME	23	Precious promise	50	WONDERFUL WORDS OF LIFE	282

REFUGE.

	NO.		NO.		NO.
Dark is the night	148	HIDING IN THEE	232	Rock of Ages	86
From every stormy wind	105	HIS WORD A TOWER	182	Safe in the arms	4
HE WILL HIDE ME	225	Jesus, lover of my soul	85, 193	THE CROSS OF JESUS	43
HIDE THOU ME!	374	MY HIGH TOWER	171	THE SOLID ROCK	162

REPENTANCE.

	NO.		NO.		NO.
Alas! and did?	111	I bring my sins	156	TAKE ME AS I AM!	368
BLESS ME NOW!	32	I hear Thy welcome voice	63	The mistakes of my life	190
Depth of mercy!	99, 346	I stood outside the gate	172	There is joy among the	295
I am coming to the Cross	59	Just as I am	54	WE TAKE THE GUILTY	384
I AM THE DOOR	408	Stay, Thou insulted Spirit	323	WHAT SHALL I DO?	202

RESURRECTION.

	NO.		NO.		NO.
Beautiful morning!	392	Hallelujah, He is risen	180	THE GLORIOUS MORNING	271
Beyond the smiling and the	378	I SHALL BE SATISFIED	351	We shall sleep, but not	184

SALVATION.

	NO.		NO.		NO.
Amazing grace!	213	I hear the words	364	SAVED BY THE BLOOD	254
COME BELIEVING	390	Is Jesus able to redeem?	241	SONG OF SALVATION	157
Come, every soul!	94	IT IS FINISHED!	281	TAKE ME AS I AM	36,
Come, sing the gospel's	134	JESUS IS MIGHTY TO SAVE	201	THE GATE AJAR	15
DOERS OF THE WORD	369	Light after darkness	330	The gospel of Thy grace	327
Fierce and wild	253	Long in darkness	227	The Great Physician	56
FIX YOUR EYES UPON JESUS	263	MERCY'S FREE	318	The prize is set before us	289
Fresh from the throne	170	My hope is built on	162	The whole world	41
Good news	291	MY SOUL WILL OVERCOME	349	There is a fountain	31
Grace 'tis a charming sound	49	NO OTHER NAME	78	There is life for a look	80
HE THAT BELIEVETH	315	Not all the blood	113	'Tis the promise of God	2
HO, EVERY ONE THAT!	302	Not what these hands	386	WHAT SHALL I DO?	202
How solemn are the words!	70	NOTHING BUT THE BLOOD	332	WHITE AS SNOW	53
How sweet the word!	287	ONCE FOR ALL!	16	WISHING, HOPING, KNOWING	65
I AM THE DOOR	408	PULL FOR THE SHORE!	83	WHOSOEVER WILL	10
I hear the Saviour say	55	Salvation! oh, the joyful!	109	YE MUST BE BORN AGAIN	237

TOPICAL INDEX.—Continued.

SORROW.

	NO.		NO.		NO.
Ah, my heart!	34	Did Christ o'er sinners weep	131	Olive's brow	216
Art thou weary?	195	Go, bury thy sorrow!	61	Only a little while	362
Blessed hope!	245	Joy in sorrow	161	Only waiting	375
Come, ye disconsolate!	197	Not now, my child!	47	What shall I do?	203

SUFFERINGS OF CHRIST.

Alas! and did my?	111, 167	My Redeemer	229	There is a green hill	273
Did Christ o'er sinners?	131	O Christ, what burdens!	57	Thou didst leave Thy throne	138
I gave My life for thee	21	Olive's brow	216	To Him who for our sins	395
Man of sorrows!	140	Suffering Saviour	146	When I survey th.	400

TEMPTATION.

Come near me!	231	I need Thee	3	Tempted and tried	249
Faint, yet pursuing	301	My soul, be on thy guard!	112	Trust on!	352
Hiding in Thee	232	Singing all the time	276	What a Friend!	29
Hold fast till I come	173	Sweet hour of prayer	77	Yield not to temptation	89

TEMPERANCE.

Come, prodigal!	335	Long in darkness	227	The prodigal child	38
Dare to be a Daniel!	158	Rescue the perishing!	18	What shall the harvest?	79
I need Thee	3	Ring the bells of heaven	19	Where is my boy?	279
Let the lower lights	65	The mistakes of my life	190	Yield not to temptation	89

TRUST.

All the way	60	Jesus, I will trust Thee	341	The Lord will provide	6
Fully trusting	139	Look away to Jesus	164	Thy will be done	373
He knows	307	Only trusting in my	272	Trusting Jesus, that is	165
I am trusting Thee	290	Onward go!	354	Trust on!	352

WARNING.

Almost persuaded	75	I never knew you!	377	What shall the harvest?	79
Along the river of Time	411	Jesus of Nazareth!	8	Where is thy refuge?	312
Cut it down!	238	Nothing but leaves	96	While life prolongs	212
Eternity!	203	Out of the ark	209	Why do you wait?	240
Hasten, sinner, to be wise!	214	Say, are you ready?	353	Why not to-night?	246
Have you any room?	284	Sinners, turn! why will	106	Yet there is room!	81
In the silent midnight	183	Sound the alarm!	391	Yield not to temptation	89

WORK.

Am I a soldier?	115	Must I go and?	298	Scatter seeds of kind-	174
Brightly beams our	65	Nothing but leaves!	96	Stand up for Jesus!	121
Brightly gleams	313	Not now, my child!	47	The word of God is given	395
Bringing in the sheaves	370	Oh, what are you going?	194	Tell it out!	329
Dare to be a Daniel!	158	Oh, where are the reapers?	155	There's a work for each	285
Go, work in My vineyard	98	One more day's work	28	To the work!	145
Hark, the voice of Jesus!	120	Only an armour-bearer	82	We'll work till Jesus	304
Hold the fort!	14	Onward, Christian soldiers!	175	What shall the harvest?	79
Ho, reapers of life's	150	Onward go!	354	Where hast thou?	33
Is your lamp burning?	403	Onward, upward!	135	While the days are going	360
Lo! the day of God	149	Rescue the perishing!	18	Work, for the night	122

WORSHIP.

All hail the power	101	Come, ye disconsolate!	197	Salvation, oh, the joyful!	109
All people that on	1	Depth of mercy!	99, 346	Saviour, visit Thy planta-	409
Am I a soldier?	115	Even me!	87	Sweet hour of prayer!	77
Amazing grace!	213	How sweet the name	71	The Lord's my Shepherd	107
Arise and shine!	198	I love Thy kingdom	211	There is a fountain	91
Arise, my soul!	119	Nearer, my God	113	We worship Thee	350
Awake and sing	320	Oh, for a thousand tongues!	102	When I survey	400
Blest be the tie!	114	Olive's brow	216	Whiter than snow	169
Come, Thou Fount!	116	Rock of Ages	86	Wonderful words of life	262

PRICE LIST OF GOSPEL HYMNS.

☞ There are now so many editions and styles of binding of the Gospel Hymns Series that parties ordering cannot be too explicit in stating not only the number of the series wanted (i. e., 1, 2, 3 or 4, etc.) but also the style of binding and the price. If these points are observed, mistakes in filling orders can be avoided; otherwise they are liable to occur. Following are editions and prices:

WORDS ONLY EDITIONS.

		Abbreviations for Ordering.	Per copy by mail, postpaid.	Per 100 copies by express, not prepaid
Gospel Hymns No. 5, with Standard Selections. This is the latest of the series, but will not be combined with the other volumes.	80 pp., Paper	(No. 5, Nonp., Pa.)	.06	$ 5.00
	186 pp., Boards	(No. 5, Wds., Bds.)	.12	10.00
	186 pp., Limp Clo., Gilt Stamp	(No. 5, Wds , Clo.)	.17	15.00
No. 1, 2, 3, 4,	Paper Covers	(Wds., Paper, No. *)	.06	5.00
	Boards	(" Boards, ")	.11	10.00
	Limp Cloth	(" Cloth, ")	.11	10.00
†Combined,	Paper	(Comb., Wds., Pa.)	.12	10.00
"	Boards	(" " Bds.)	.17	15.00
"	Cloth	(" " Clo.)	.17	15.00
"	Cloth, large type	(" " Pica)	.55	50.00
¶Consolidated, 128 pp.,	Paper	(Cons., Nonp., Pa.)	.06	5.00
"	128 pp., Cloth	(" " Clo.)	.11	10.00
"	304 pp., Boards	(" Wds., Bds.)	.22	20.00
"	304 pp., Cloth	(" " Clo.)	.27	25.00
100 Select Gospel Hymns, Paper		(Select G. H.)	.05	3.00

There is no music edition of 100 Select Gospel Hymns, the Hymns are selected from Gospel Hymns Consolidated.

WORDS AND MUSIC EDITIONS.

			Per copy	Per 100
Gospel Hymns No. 5, with Standard Selections. This is the latest of the series, but will not be combined with the other volumes.	Boards	(No. 5, Music, Bds.)	.35	30.00
	Limp Cloth	(No. 5, " Clo.)	.55	50.00
No. 1, 2, 3, 4,	Paper	(Music, Pa., No. *)	.30	25.00
	Boards	(" Bds., ")	.35	30.00
	Flexible Cloth	(" Flex. Clo., ")	.60	50.00
	Stiff Cloth	(" Stiff " ")	.85	75.00
†Combined,	Paper	(Comb., Music, Pa.)	.58	50.00
"	Boards	(" " Bds.)	.70	60.00
"	Flexible Cloth	(" " Flex.Clo.)	.85	75.00
"	Stiff Cloth	(" " Stiff Clo.)	1.12	. . .
¶Consolidated,	Paper, Small Type	(Cons., Excel., Pa.)	.45	40.00
"	Boards, " "	(" " Bds.)	.50	45.00
"	Limp Cloth, " "	(" " Clo.)	.55	50.00
"	Boards	(" Music, Bds.)	.85	75.00
"	Limp Cloth	(" " Clo.)	1.10	. .
"	Cloth, Red Edge	(" " Red)	1.60	. .
"	Morocco, Stiff	(" " Morocco)	2.65	.
"	Full Levant	(" " Levant)	6.90	.
Gospel Hymns Consolidated in Aiken's 7-character music notes	Boards	(Cons., Bds., Pat.)	.85	75.00
	Cloth	(" Clo., ")	1.10	. . .

* Here insert No. 1, No. 2, No. 3 or No. 4, as may be desired.

FOR CORNET.

Gospel Hymns Consolidated. All the music in this book arranged in pleasing style for the Cornet. The hymns are not printed in this edition.	Paper	(G. H. Cornet, Pa.)	1.05	. . .
	Cloth	(" " Clo.)	1.55	. . .

† NOTE—GOSPEL HYMNS COMBINED contains everything found in Gospel Hymns No. 1, No. 2 and No. 3, all duplicates being omitted.
¶ GOSPEL HYMNS CONSOLIDATED contains everything in Gospel Hymns No. 1, No. 2, No. 3 and No. 4, all duplicates being omitted.
If you want Gospel Hymns "Consolidated" do not say "Combined." This is a common error, hence we call especial attention to it.

THE JOHN CHURCH CO.,
74 West Fourth St., Cincinnati, O.
19 East 16th St., New York.

BIGLOW & MAIN,
76 East Ninth St., New York.
81 Randolph St., Chicago.

www.ingramcontent.com/pod-product-compliance
Lightning Source LLC
Chambersburg PA
CBHW051742300426
44115CB00007B/670